CASTROISM AND
COMMUNISM IN
LATIN AMERICA, 1959-1976

AEI-Hoover
policy studies

The studies in this series are issued jointly
by the American Enterprise Institute
for Public Policy Research and the Hoover
Institution on War, Revolution and Peace.
They are designed to focus on
policy problems of current and future interest,
to set forth the factors underlying
these problems and to evaluate
courses of action available to policy makers.
The views expressed in these studies
are those of the authors and do not necessarily
reflect the views of the staff, officers
or members of the governing boards of
AEI or the Hoover Institution.

CASTROISM AND COMMUNISM IN LATIN AMERICA, 1959-1976,

The varieties of Marxist-Leninist experience

William E. Ratliff

American Enterprise Institute for Public Policy Research
Washington, D.C.

Hoover Institution on War, Revolution and Peace
Stanford University, Stanford, California

AEI-Hoover Policy Study 19, November 1976
(Hoover Institution Studies 56)

ISBN 0-8447-3220-6

Library of Congress Catalog Card No. 76-28554

Printed in the United States of America

Contents

Preface

The emergence of the Sino-Soviet dispute in the early 1960s ushered in an era of intense conflict and competition among leftist revolutionaries throughout the world. By the mid-1960s no vestige remained of the largely united international communist movement that had been fostered in earlier decades by the Communist International (Comintern, 1919–1943) and the Communist Information Bureau (Cominform, 1947–1956). Earlier challenges to the leadership position of the Communist Party of the Soviet Union (CPSU) by the exiled Leon Trotsky and by Tito's Yugoslavia paled in comparison to the opposition after 1960 from the Chinese Communist Party (CCP) and a variety of other Marxist-Leninist organizations.

Events and rival doctrines produced greater diversity among Marxist-Leninists in Latin America than in any other part of the world. This diversity owed much to the Sino-Soviet conflict, which raised substantive strategic and tactical issues, as well as (on a lower but sometimes equally important level) owing much to intra-party power struggles, which had their origins in personal conflicts and individual ideological and leadership rivalries. The diversity issued also from the activities and objectives of the revolutionary government established in Cuba in 1959, chiefly in the persons of Fidel Castro and Ernesto Che Guevara. To a significant number of Latin Americans, the Cubans, not their own local communist (or other) parties, seemed to understand the strategy and tactics for national independence and for political, economic, and social transformation.

The parties and organizations covered in this book are those that fall at least loosely within the two main lines of Marxism-Leninism in

Latin America—communism and castroism. The former present no problem. They are the parties that over the decades have consciously aligned themselves with the Communist Party of the Soviet Union, originally in the Comintern and subsequently in less formal but equally revealing ways, as, for example, attendance as a recognized delegation at the June 1969 International Meeting of Communist and Workers' Parties in Moscow. The pro-Chinese parties and organizations that emerged during the 1960s are so classified on their own testimony. In some cases the Chinese Communist Party granted what might be considered recognition to pro-Chinese (so-called "Marxist-Leninist") communist parties, and these are the main organizations examined as pro-Chinese in this volume. However, since the application of the words "pro-Chinese" or "Maoist" represents a judgment passed on the Latin American party, not on the Chinese, several groups are mentioned below that have professed adherence to the "invincible thought of Mao Tse-tung" without apparent recognition from Peking.

"Castroism" is a little more complicated. Castro calls himself a communist, but fully developed castroism as a road to the seizure of political power—which is the primary concern here—is not the road of either the pro-Soviet or pro-Chinese parties in their distinctive phases. The castroite road has its own distinguishing characteristics, not all of which were originated by Castro, Guevara, and Debray, the chief formulators of the castroite line in the 1960s. Indeed, after his endorsement of the Soviet bloc invasion of Czechoslovakia in 1968, Castro moved gradually away from the remaining castroites of Latin America. In June 1975 the Cuban prime minister was host at a meeting of twenty-four pro-Soviet communist parties and signed a declaration which (following upon his statements and policies of the early 1970s) placed him unequivocally in the pro-Soviet camp with marked and significant differences from the existing castroite and pro-Chinese lines. In an effort to break the one-to-one mental association between Castro the revolutionary leader and castroism, I have used a lower case "c" in castroism throughout this study.

The reader may wonder why, in that case, I have not lower-cased "Maoism" and "Marxism-Leninism" in these pages. The answer is that Mao and the Chinese communists have been and still are the guiding forces and dominant influences on most Maoist groups in Latin America, while my point is precisely that during many of the years covered in this study Castro and the Cuban communists did not occupy the same position with respect to the castroites in the area. Illustrating this is the fact that those identified as Maoists in most cases openly acknowledged the major role that Chinese strategy and tactics (embodied in the *Thought of Mao Tse-tung*) played in their analyses and policy formation. Most of those identified as castroites—particularly those operating in recent years—did not admit an equal indebtedness to Castro and the Cuban experience, and with good reason. On the practical level, it would have been foolish to dilute their nationalist image by playing up an international influence on their movement. What is more, to have done so would have been incorrect since (as is shown in the chapter on castroism) castroite revolutionary theory and practice developed an identity of its own quite apart from its namesake. Finally, although I think Marxism-Leninism is an even more abused term than castroism, proof of such an assertion is beyond the scope of this study, and thus I have retained the accepted capitalized form.

The study is devoted primarily to the strategy, tactics, and activities of communist and castroite parties and organizations seeking power or influence in Latin America during the period from 1959 to 1976, emphasizing the years of greatest diversity between 1964 and 1973. It begins with a very brief, descriptive (and necessarily generalized) introduction to the Latin American setting within which the Marxist-Leninist parties operated. Chapters 1 and 2 will deal with the three communist countries that have had a profound effect on Latin American Marxist-Leninists—the Soviet Union, the People's Republic of China, and Cuba—reviewing their attitudes and policies toward Latin America. These provide an essential background for the chapters on Latin American communists and castroites to follow. Chapters 3 and 4 are devoted to the avowedly pro-Soviet and pro-Chinese communist parties of Latin America during the period from 1959 to 1976. The pro-Soviet parties are treated first and in greater detail than the others, since in most countries they were far more important than their Maoist rivals. The chapters are intended to provide a general picture of communist parties in recent years, with information on size, activities among workers and intellectuals, and strategy and tactics of revolution. No effort is made to offer an exhaustive history of any single party, nor a partial history of every party. Rather, I have concentrated (1) on the most important parties during crucial periods in their histories, and (2) from time to time on less important parties that faced some unusual problem or that illustrate a general characteristic. The ultimate objective has been to offer a picture—at times by means of a documentary narrative—of the varieties of Latin American communist thought and experience during this turbulent period.

The discussions of castroite and castroite-influenced groups in Chapters 5 and 6 consider rural guerrilla warfare and urban guerrilla warfare, with background given in each case. Chapter 7 is devoted entirely to Chile and an examination of the conflicts there between the powerful Communist Party and assorted castroite groups, primarily the Movement of the Revolutionary Left, during the Popular Unity period (1970–1973). The four appendices that follow the main text are intended to provide additional information on the four important Marxist-Leninist conferences held during the period of this study.

The communists and the castroites were the most important self-professed Marxist-Leninists in Latin America over the 1959–1976 period. It is at least worth noting here, though it will not be belabored in the pages that follow, that many of these Marxist-Leninists, particularly the castroites, demonstrated little understanding of Lenin and less of Marx. Bertram D. Wolfe, one of the world's foremost students of Marxism, put the whole terminological mess into perspective when he wrote that Marx's original writings, thoughts, and deeds have been

> buried under successive layers of commentary and interpretation, popularization, oversimplification, and specious rationalization, to produce warring creeds, each evoking his name. There is Orthodox Marxism (with how many orthodoxies?); Revisionism (with what varied revisions!); Marxism-Leninism; Stalinism; Trotskyism; Khrushchevism; Titoism; Maoism; and such Marxisms of Asia, Africa and Latin America as Baathism, Nasserism, and Castroism, which, for intellectual purposes, we need not take too seriously yet whose influence on political acts and political passions may be serious indeed.[1]

But this is only the beginning of the terminological confusion. Many terms that once served a strict analytical purpose have become so encumbered with alternate meanings and so encrusted with value judgments as to be rendered useless if not deceptive in ordinary usage. Over the decades the word "bourgeois" has become less a term designating a class than an epithet of disdain or contempt. C. S. Lewis wrote that when he was called "bourgeois" in his youth, it usually implied

---

[1] Bertram Wolfe, *Marxism: 100 Years in the Life of a Doctrine* (New York: Dial Press, 1964), p. xv.

"not aristocratic, therefore vulgar," but when he was older it meant "not proletarian, therefore parasitic, reactionary." [2] Neither usage tells us much about the bourgeoisie, indisputably one of the most influential classes in modern history. "Fascism" and "communism" have also been applied with such abandon as pejorative epithets that their analytical value in ordinary discourse has been greatly diminished, if not indeed eliminated.

Among the most abused words, employed constantly by the organizations studied in this volume, are "revolutionary," "people," and "democracy." The self-professed "revolutionary" governments in Latin America range from Fidel Castro's to the right-wing military regime established in Brazil in 1964, and the various "revolutionary" parties and other organizations cover even a broader spectrum. On the surface, "the people" would seem to mean the people—the population of a country or region. But in Marxist-Leninist usage it generally means the vast majority of the population—the workers, peasants, petit-bourgeoisie, and others—who are expected to support the policies of the proletarian vanguard because of recognized class interests. At times, in a circular fashion, "the people" are those who support the parties and policies the Marxist-Leninists have decided represent the interests of the people, even when they do not constitute the majority of the population. After the March 1973 congressional election in Chile this latter usage was demonstrated when a paper controlled by the Communist Party of Chile headlined the outcome: "The People: 43 percent. The Mummies: 55 percent."

Finally, it may be asked, where is the common ground between the democracy of the Federal Republic of Germany (West Germany) and that of the German Democratic Republic (East Germany)? The Marxist-Leninist distinction is between "bourgeois" or "false" democracy in the former and "proletarian," "socialist," or "people's" democracy in the latter. Bourgeois democracy is considered a deceptive device whereby the minority exploits and oppresses the vast majority, without the latter's even realizing it, through the use of a fraudulent electoral system. People's democracy, by contrast, is described as a system whereby the vast majority of the people control their own affairs and exercise their will over the former exploiters, until the latter are eliminated completely.

---

[2] C. S. Lewis, *Studies in Words* (Cambridge: Cambridge University Press, 1967), p. 21.

In Western "bourgeois" democracies, the people generally express their opinions on political, social, and economic issues, and register their support for or opposition to political leaders, by means of public meetings, the press, and periodic elections. Serious or habitual assaults against the values and interests of substantial numbers of the population may lead to defeats in elections or even unscheduled shifts in local or national leadership, as occurred most dramatically in Chile in 1973 and the United States in 1974. Marx was the first Marxist to recognize that in countries with universal suffrage the proletarian revolution might come at the ballot box; in his later years, Engels was particularly taken with this possibility in Europe and the United States.[3] During the period covered in this study a number of communist parties emphasized this road (as, for example, those in Chile and Italy) while others, more in the spirit of Lenin's *State and Revolution,* laughed outright at those who thought "bourgeois" elections truly advanced the interests of the people. Among these was the leader of the Portuguese Communist Party in mid-1975.[4] It is apparent even to the most casual observer that in communist-dominated countries national political leaders are never elected by popular vote, since the popular vote is not considered the best method for measuring the popular will. If elections are held at all, they merely ratify decrees made by the ruling communist party, the self-proclaimed vanguard of the people, or choose between candidates approved by the party.

Having noted and commented on these terminological problems here, I have not thought it necessary to set off moralized or arguable terms with quotation marks in the pages that follow, so long as the context makes it clear that they express the views of the party or individual being discussed.

This book is in large part an outgrowth of my years as contributor to and Latin American editor of the *Yearbook on International Communist Affairs* and incorporates some passages from my own yearbook articles. The bulk of the research was carried out on trips to Latin America in 1958, 1970, and 1972, and in the rich collection of primary sources selected for the Hoover Institution Library by Latin American Curator Joseph W. Bingaman, for whom I have acted as occasional adviser over the past four years.

---

3 Wolfe, *Marxism,* Chapter 12.
4 See comments by Alvaro Cunhal to the Italian journalist Oriana Fallaci, published in the *New York Times Magazine,* 13 July 1975.

Among the sources used most frequently throughout this study are the *World Marxist Review,* the Toronto edition (unless otherwise specified) and its *Information Bulletin,* and *Granma,* organ of the Communist Party of Cuba (weekly English edition unless otherwise specified). All translations from Spanish and Chinese are my own, unless otherwise indicated.

Table of Acronyms

AD	Democratic Action (Acción Democrática) party, Venezuela
AFP	Agence France Presse
ALN	National Liberation Action (Acão Libertadora Nacional), Brazil
APAL	Latin American Press Agency (Agencia de Prensa América Latina)
API	Independent Popular Alliance (Alianza Popular Independiente), Chile
APR	Revolutionary People's Alliance (Alianza Popular Revolucionaria), Argentina
CCP	Chinese Communist Party
CGT	General Confederation of Labor (Confederación General del Trabajo), Argentina
CGTC	General Confederation of Costa Rican Workers (Confederación General de Trabajadores Costarricenses)
CGTP	General Confederation of Workers of Peru (Confederación General del Trabajadores del Peru)
CIA	Central Intelligence Agency, United States
CNT	National Convention of Workers (Convención Nacional de Trabajadores), Uruguay
COB	Bolivian Workers' Center (Central Obrera Boliviana)
COMECON	Council for Mutual Economic Assistance

COPEI	Social Christian Party (Partido Social Cristiano-COPEI), Venezuela
CPSU	Communist Party of the Soviet Union
CSTC	Trade Union Confederation of Workers of Colombia (Confederación Sindical de Trabajadores de Colombia)
CTAL	Confederation of Latin American Workers (Confederación de Trabajadores de América Latina)
CTC	Confederation of Workers of Colombia (Confederación de Trabajadores de Colombia)
CTE	Confederation of Ecuadorean Workers (Confederación de Trabajadores Ecuatorianos)
CTRP	Central Organization of Workers of the Peruvian Revolution (Central de Trabajadores de la Revolución Peruana)
CTU	Workers' Center of Uruguay (Central de Trabajadores del Uruguay)
CUFF	Unitary Command of the FLN-FALN (Comando Unico de FLN-FALN)
CUTCh	Single Center of Chilean Workers (Central Unica de Trabajadores de Chile)
CUTV	United Workers Confederation of Venezuela (Confederación Unitaria de Trabajadores de Venezuela)
DGI	General Directorate of Intelligence (Directorio General de Inteligencia), Cuba
ELN	National Liberation Army (Ejército de Liberación Nacional), Bolivia, Colombia, and Peru
EPL	People's Liberation Army (Ejército Popular de Liberación), Colombia
ERP	People's Revolutionary Army (Ejército Revolucionario del Pueblo), Argentina
FA	Broad Front (Frente Amplio), Uruguay
FALN	Armed Forces of National Liberation (Fuerzas Armadas de Liberación Nacional), Venezuela
FAR	Revolutionary Armed Forces (Fuerzas Armadas Revolucionarias), Cuba

FAR	Rebel Armed Forces (Fuerzas Armadas Rebeldes), Guatemala
FARC	Revolutionary Armed Forces of Colombia (Fuerzas Armadas Revolucionarias de Colombia)
FER	Revolutionary Students' Front (Frente Estudiantil Revolucionario), Chile
FEUU	Federation of University Students of Uruguay (Federación de Estudiantes Universitarios del Uruguay)
FGAJS	Antonio José de Sucre Guerrilla Front (Frente Guerrillero Antonio José de Sucre), Venezuela
FGEI	Edgar Ibarra Guerrilla Front (Frente Guerrillero Edgar Ibarra), Guatemala
FIDEL	Leftist Liberation Front (Frente Izquierda de Liberación), Uruguay
FJC	Communist Youth Federation (Federación Juvenil Comunista), Argentina
FLN–FALN	National Liberation Front–Armed Forces of National Liberation (Frente de Liberación Nacional–Fuerzas Armadas de Liberación Nacional), Venezuela
FRA	Anti-imperialist Revolutionary Front (Frente Revolucionaria Anti-imperialista), Bolivia
FRAP	Popular Action Front (Frente de Acción Popular), Chile
FSLN	Sandinist Front of National Liberation (Frente Sandinista de Liberación Nacional), Nicaragua
FSTMB	Mineworkers Federation of Bolivia (Federación Sindical de Trabajadores Mineros de Bolivia)
FTR	Revolutionary Workers' Front (Frente de Trabajadores Revolucionarios), Chile
GAWU	Guyanan Agricultural Workers' Union
IC	Christian Left (Izquierda Cristiana), Chile
INR	Bureau of Intelligence and Research, United States
ITT	International Telephone and Telegraph
JAP	Supply and Price Boards (Juntas de Abastecimientos y Precios), Chile

JCC	Communist Youth of Colombia (Juventud Comunista de Colombia)
JCCh	Communist Youth of Chile (Juventud Comunista de Chile)
JCR	Revolutionary Coordinating Committee (Junta de Coordinación Revolucionario)
JCV	Venezuelan Communist Youth (Juventud Comunista Venezolana)
LSR	Revolutionary Socialist League (Liga Socialista Revolucionaria), Peru
MAPU	Movement of United Popular Action (Movimiento de Acción Popular Unitaria), Chile
MAS	Movement toward Socialism (Movimiento al Socialismo), Venezuela
MCR	Revolutionary Peasant Movement (Movimiento Campesino Revolucionario), Chile
MIR	Movement of the Revolutionary Left (Movimiento de Izquierda Revolucionaria), Chile, Peru, Uruguay, and Venezuela
MLN	National Liberation Movement (Movimiento de Liberación Nacional), the Tupamaros, Uruguay
MPR	Movement of the Revolutionary Poor (Movimiento de Pobres Revolucionarios), Chile
MR-8	Revolutionary Movement-8 (Movimiento Revolucionario-8), Brazil
MR-13	13 November Revolutionary Movement (Movimiento Revolucionario 13 de Noviembre), Guatemala
MRLP	Liberal Revolutionary Movement of the People (Movimiento Revolucionario Liberal del Pueblo), Colombia
MUCS	Movement for Trade Union Unity (Movimiento por la Unidad y la Coordinación Sindical), Argentina
MUI	University Movement of the Left (Movimiento Universitario de Izquierda), Chile
OAS	Organization of American States

OLAS	Latin American Solidarity Organization (Organización Latinoamericano de Solidaridad)
PASO	Socialist Action Party (Partido de Acción Socialista), Costa Rica
PCA	Communist Party of Argentina (Partido Comunista de Argentina)
PCB	Communist Party of Bolivia (Partido Comunista de Bolivia)
PCB-ML	Communist Party of Bolivia, Marxist-Leninist (Partido Comunista de Bolivia, Marxista-Leninista)
PCC	Communist Party of Colombia (Partido Comunista de Colombia)
PCCh	Communist Party of Chile (Partido Comunista de Chile)
PCC-ML	Communist Party of Colombia, Marxist-Leninist (Partido Comunista de Colombia, Marxista-Leninista)
PCE	Communist Party of Ecuador (Partido Comunista del Ecuador)
PCES	Communist Party of El Salvador (Partido Comunista de El Salvador)
PCM	Mexican Communist Party (Partido Comunista Mexicano)
PCP	Paraguayan Communist Party (Partido Comunista Paraguayo)
PCP	Peruvian Communist Party (Partido Comunista Peruano)
PCRCh	Revolutionary Communist Party of Chile (Partido Comunista Revolucionario de Chile)
PCU	Communist Party of Uruguay (Partido Comunista del Uruguay)
PCV	Communist Party of Venezuela (Partido Comunista de Venezuela)
PDC	Christian Democratic Party (Partido Demócrata Cristiana), Chile
PGT	Guatemalan Party of Labor (Partido Guatemalteco del Trabajo)
PN	National Party (Partido Nacional), Chile

PNC	People's National Congress, Guyana
PPP	People's Progressive Party, Guyana
PR	Radical Party (Partido Radical), Chile
PRC	People's Republic of China
PRTB	Bolivian Workers' Revolutionary Party (Partido Revolucionario de los Trabajadores de Bolivia)
PSCh	Socialist Party of Chile (Partido Socialista de Chile)
PSD	Social Democratic Party (Partido Social Demócrata), Chile
PSN	Socialist Party of Nicaragua (Partido Socialista de Nicaragua)
PPS	Socialist People's Party (Partido Popular Socialista), Mexico
PSP	People's Socialist Party (Partido Socialista Popular), Cuba
PVP	People's Vanguard Party (Partido Vanguardia Popular), Costa Rica
UJC	Union of Communist Youth (Unión de la Juventud Comunista), Uruguay
UNO	National Opposition Union (Unión de Oposición Nacional), Colombia
UP	Popular Unity (Unidad Popular), Chile
VPR	Revolutionary People's Vanguard (Vanguarda Popular Revolucionaria), Brazil
UTC	Union of Workers of Colombia (Unión de Trabajadores de Colombia)
WFTU	World Federation of Trade Unions

Introduction

European political, economic, and social doctrines have profoundly influenced Latin America for almost 500 years. The first and in some respects still the most important influences were those of the Spanish and Portuguese colonial governments that exercised control over and dominated life in the area for as long as four centuries in some countries. Iberian domination over Latin America began to slip in the eighteenth century, particularly after the revolutions in the North American colonies and in France. Direct control was terminated altogether in all but a few countries during the early nineteenth century as one Latin American country after another won its independence. Yet most of the values and institutions of the colonial period remained intact long after independence was achieved; some survived the onslaught of the first half of the twentieth century and are under fire today from many reformers and all revolutionaries.

New forces came into play in Latin America during the nineteenth and twentieth centuries, setting the stage for many of the dramatic confrontations of recent decades. The industrial revolution and expanding market economy in Europe and North America brought extensive foreign investments in Latin America and increased the influence of European and later of U.S. interests throughout the area. The development of export economies and some domestic industrialization—and in some countries the influx of European immigrants—produced an urban working class and led to the emergence of a politically aggressive urban middle class or middle sector.

By 1960, a number of Latin American countries had passed through many years of rising nationalism and significant political, economic, and social change. Fidel Castro had begun to radicalize the Cuban revolution; apparently thoroughgoing revolutions had occurred in Mexico and Bolivia; and varying degrees of transformation had taken place in Argentina, Brazil, Chile, and several other countries. In some countries there had been rapid industrialization and an unprecedented movement of the population from rural to urban areas was under way. In general these changes tended to strengthen the middle— and to a lesser extent lower—sectors of society, with a corresponding decline in the political and economic power of the traditional ruling forces. In the mid- and late-1950s a series of military and political strongmen were overthrown, making prospects for further and greater change under moderate leftist political leadership seem uncommonly good.

But in many countries optimism over the prospects for peaceful and orderly political, economic, and social transformation—optimism reflected during the early 1960s in the Alliance for Progress—soon waned as the traditional structures and basic developmental problems proved remarkably stubborn. Reforms undertaken in good faith and with substantial national and international support were inadequate to provide complete, rapid, and lasting solutions to major problems. (In some countries, of course, few if any substantive reforms were even attempted.) In general, disparities in income and living conditions persisted among social classes and between urban and rural communities. Administrative inefficiency and corruption wasted precious resources. In most countries rural reform was hampered by low educational levels, poor communications, and outdated marketing and credit facilities. Some countries—most important among them Bolivia, Ecuador, Peru, and Guatemala—were faced by the challenge of integrating largely illiterate Indian populations into the national systems. Poverty and discontent in the countryside led to massive movement of rural workers out of the countryside, to the formation of shantytowns in most major cities, and to a rapidly increasing demand for social services, housing, and educational opportunities. Political demagogues often seized upon these problems with predictable results. Further complicating the other problems was the high birth rate—the highest sustained population growth in the world—resulting in an ever younger and often more dissatisfied population, with increasing demands for jobs on the one hand and rapid social transformation on the other. An increasing number of Latin Americans concluded that reforms led by

2

the middle sectors or national bourgeoisie were inadequate, and that revolution—led by themselves or their kindred spirits—was essential.

In this scene, the Marxist-Leninist parties and organizations, which operated with varying degrees of effectiveness in each country, formed one part of the political left. Even the more moderate Marxist-Leninist groups (in general the pro-Soviet communist parties) encountered opposition from the bulk of the Roman Catholic church and from segments of all social classes, from the workers and peasants on up. Above all they encountered opposition from the landholding and more conservative sectors of all nations. Military forces in most countries were hostile to Marxist-Leninist groups: although the military in several countries were willing to cooperate with communist parties (as in Peru after 1968), in only one country—Chile—did they join a Marxist-Leninist-dominated government at the highest levels and guarantee its survival during a time of great crisis. Foreign governments and business interests in Latin America generally did not look favorably upon the Marxist-Leninists. In some countries (for example Guyana under Forbes Burnham), the Marxist-Leninists were hard-pressed to offer programs significantly more "progressive" or revolutionary than those of their chief political opponents. At the same time, tradition, popular modes of thought, rising nationalism (sometimes simple chauvinism), and a number of other factors seemed to make the Marxist-Leninists of various tendencies more acceptable than they had been—and at times even desirable—to many Latin Americans.

First, the most important governments in Latin American history have been fundamentally authoritarian, incorporating varying degrees of central control over individual members of society. This was the case from the pre-Columbian empires of the Aztecs and Incas, throughout the Spanish and Portuguese colonial periods, to such contrasting contemporary regimes as those of Castro in Cuba and Stroessner in Paraguay. Even the Chilean democracy of the 1960s was marked by a high degree of state economic control. Thus some of the policies proposed by Marxist-Leninist groups were not so unusual, let alone abhorrent, for Latin Americans as they would have been for most residents of the United States.

Second, many Latin Americans of contrasting and even contradictory political beliefs tended to see domestic and international problems in what the popular jargon labels "Marxist" terms. Consequently, the political, economic, and social statements and policies of many

3

more moderate political parties, and of some military leaders, resembled those of the Marxist-Leninists, though in a less dogmatic form.

Third, in recent years the radically increased nationalistic temper in Latin America has been clear in official government attitudes toward the activities and interests of foreign governments and business enterprises. Political opportunism—hardly unique to Latin America—undoubtedly accounted for some of the exaggerated critiques presented by some of the area's more moderate leaders. The appeals of the Marxist-Leninists were part of a widespread atmosphere of criticism directed toward the status quo.

Fourth, from the implantation of the colonial system in the sixteenth century, through the American and French revolutions, to the present day, Latin Americans have been strongly influenced by foreign thought and events. Even that most Latin American of Marxist-Leninist ideologies, castroism, was theoretically underdeveloped until 1967 when it was systemized by a Frenchman.[1]

Among the doctrines that arrived in the nineteenth century was socialism, brought in large part by European immigrants who had been involved in (or exposed to) Marx's First International (1864–1874) and the Paris Commune (1871). These immigrants were responsible for the first Marxist thought in Latin America and for the formation of the earliest socialist parties at the turn of the century. The first communist parties were formed immediately after Lenin created the Communist International in 1919. Parties had been formed in six countries (Argentina, Mexico, Chile, Uruguay, Brazil, and Guatemala) before Lenin's death in January 1924; they existed in every South American country, and in many Central American and Caribbean countries, before the Comintern was dissolved in 1943.

During the four decades following the formation of the Comintern, the Latin American parties (notwithstanding the challenges of the Trotskyists and some internal dissension) remained loyal to the "fatherland" of world communism—the Soviet Union. Until the 1960s, Latin American communism was truly "monolithic." Of course, during the monolithic years Latin American communists imported their doctrines and most of their policies from the Soviet Union, and their for-

---

[1] On this general subject, see Rollie E. Poppino, *International Communism in Latin America: A History of the Movement, 1917-1963* (London: Free Press of Glencoe, 1964), especially Chapters 2 and 3, which are similar to my own analysis; and Robert J. Alexander, *Communism in Latin America* (New Brunswick, N.J.: Rutgers University Press, 1957), Chapter 1.

tunes were often determined more by Soviet strategists than by party leaders in their own countries. Throughout most of this period they sought above all to organize urban workers and intellectuals. Although on a few occasions they tried to seize power by means of an armed insurrection, they never attempted to carry out protracted rural or urban warfare. In 1935 the Seventh Congress of the Comintern ordered its member parties to abandon the isolationist positions they had followed since the Sixth Congress (1928) in favor of a "popular front" line. The new line, which brought the communists fully into the political life of many countries, was first introduced in Chile, where it proved crucial for the election of a Radical president, Pedro Aguirre Cerda, in 1937. Communist cooperation with all varieties of governments in the following years opened them up to the charges, made repeatedly during the 1960s, that they were mere opportunists or had become part of the "establishment."

Communist strength was greatest on the continent as a whole in the mid-1940s, before the beginning of the cold war, both in organized labor and in political representation. During this period the Confederation of Latin American Workers (CTAL), headed by Vicente Lombardo Toledano, an "independent Marxist" from Mexico whose international positions always coincided with those of the Soviet Union, exercised wide influence throughout Central and South America and the Caribbean.

Communists were elected to national legislative bodies in more than half the twenty republics, making their strongest showings in Brazil, Chile, Cuba, and Ecuador. Fulgencio Batista had communists in his cabinet in 1943 (Carlos Rafael Rodríguez, as minister without portfolio—a position he was given again by Fidel Castro in the 1960s) and 1944. A communist was on the three-man provisional junta that brought José María Velasco Ibarra to the presidency of Ecuador in 1944, and another served in Velasco's cabinet. For some months during 1946 and 1947, communists held three of nine seats in the cabinet of Chilean President Gabriel González Videla. But as Soviet-American relations worsened during the late 1940s communist strength began to wane in most Latin American countries.

Over the next decade, there was considerable communist influence in isolated instances, as in Venezuela immediately after the overthrow of Marcos Pérez Jiménez in 1958, but this influence was not a continent-wide phenomenon. Two countries where the influence was particularly important should, however, be noted. In Guatemala, communist influence increased markedly during the late 1940s and early 1950s; it was terminated with the overthrow of President Jacobo Arbenz in 1954. And in Cuba the communists, after remaining generally aloof from the anti-Batista struggle until 1958, asserted themselves in 1959. Though they never assumed the leading role in the new government, their importance increased and led to the first defections and the first imprisonments of members of Fidel Castro's 26th of July Movement, playing an important role in setting the tone and direction of Castro's future political line. As Fidel Castro settled in during 1959, there was little reason to think that Latin American Marxist-Leninists would be so active or disputatious as they turned out to be during the next fifteen years.

1

International Marxism-Leninism: The Soviet Union and The People's Republic of China

The contrasting (and often conflicting) policies and activities of castroites and communists in the various Latin American nations between 1959 and 1976 were the result of differing conditions within the countries and within the parties themselves, and of the influence of international powers and events—particularly the policies of the Soviet Union, the People's Republic of China, Cuba, and the United States. This chapter is devoted chiefly to the roles of the Soviet Union and China and, with the following chapter on Cuba, is intended to lay the foundations for the analyses of Latin American communists and castroites that follow.

The Soviet Union

For more than four decades after the October revolution in Russia, the Communist Party of the Soviet Union (CPSU) displayed only sporadic, though sometimes hopeful, interest in Latin America or the Latin American communists. Diplomatic relations were established (and broken) with a few countries between the 1920s and the victory of the Cuban Revolution in 1959, but no important diplomatic or economic presence was established. Through the Comintern the CPSU played a decisive role in setting the political lines of Latin American communist parties—notably in establishing the narrow and combative policies after 1928 and the Popular Front begun in 1935. However, it was in only a few instances (as in Brazil and Chile during the mid-1930s, and Guatemala in the early 1950s) that CPSU policy toward Latin American communists significantly influenced political affairs in any country as a whole.

Real CPSU interest in Latin America began in 1959. Soviet leaders were less impressed by Castro's triumph than by the speed with which he adopted the communist ideology. The Cuban success seemed to disprove the law of "geographic fatalism" and show that a national revolutionary struggle could be successful in the very shadow of "United States imperialism." They were further encouraged by the electoral victory of Jânio Quadros in Brazil (October 1960) and by what they regarded as a rapidly increasing anti-Americanism in the area. However, the installation of Soviet missiles in Cuba during 1962 turned moderate nationalist feelings in Latin America against the Soviet Union, while the withdrawal of the missiles struck the extreme left as capitulation to the United States; Soviet prestige in Latin America fell to its lowest point since the beginning of the cold war in the late 1940s.

Roads to Revolution. Throughout the period from 1959 to 1976, the Soviet Union held that no single road to national liberation could be advanced for all countries in Latin America. Soviet spokesmen (and Latin American communist leaders) repeatedly stated that local communist leaders were free to carry out armed or nonarmed ("peaceful") struggle, or a combination of the two, as they deemed appropriate to national conditions. In general the Soviet Union envisioned the nonarmed road in Latin America, emphasizing the need to increase party influence among organized workers and to create broad national fronts.

Any juxtaposition of this nonarmed road and an armed Sino-Cuban way, however, obscures an important degree of flexibility in Soviet policy. During the period from 1959 to 1976, the Soviet Union clearly acknowledged the need for armed struggle in Latin America under some conditions. This acknowledgment, which in some countries was a calculated response to the apparently more revolutionary proposals of the Cubans and the Chinese, was stated most openly in the mid-1960s. Several months after the military coup in Brazil that overthrew the leftist government of João Goulart, a Soviet theorist wrote in the journal *Kommunist* that an "analysis of recent events confirms the fact that, in the countries where dictators, puppets of the foreign monopolies, are in power, the development of a broad front in the struggle, including armed struggle, and the creation of partisan detachments combine to make a completely justified course." [1]

---

[1] A. M. Sivolobov, "The Peasant Movement in Latin America," *Kommunist,* August 1964, trans. in J. Gregory Oswald, *Soviet Image of Contemporary Latin America* (Austin: University of Texas Press, 1970), p. 176.

In December 1965 *Pravda* commented editorially on the "internationalist duty to give every kind of help and support to the national liberation and working-class movements in other countries." [2] This verbal support was continued at the Tricontinental Conference that met in Havana in January 1966. Sharaf R. Rashidov, leader of the forty-member Soviet delegation, said on 7 January 1966 that the "Soviet people has always supported people's wars, the armed struggle of the oppressed peoples and has been rendering them every possible support and assistance." He repeated the pledge of "fraternal solidarity with the armed struggle waged by the patriots of Venezuela, Peru, Colombia, and Guatemala for freedom against the puppets of imperialism." [3]

The reaction of Latin American governments to the Tricontinental Conference, and to the Soviet role in it, was immediate and unequivocal. On 2 February the Council of the Organization of American States condemned the Soviet Union, Communist China, and Cuba by name for pledging to "give financial, political, and military aid to communist subversive movements in this hemisphere." [4] Five days later the conference and its designs were denounced as a "flagrant violation of the principles and purposes of the United Nations charter" by eighteen permanent Latin American representatives in the United Nations in a letter to Secretary General U Thant. The letter condemned the objective of the conference, which was to "stimulate and promote violent change of governments and fundamental political institutions in different countries, striking against the sovereignty of States Members of the United Nations." It attacked the advocacy of forceful subversion, the establishment in Havana of permanent machinery for the purpose of coordinating this subversion, the attendance at the conference by certain unnamed states members of the United Nations, and in particular the section of the "General Declaration" proclaiming the "right and duty" of "progressive" governments to provide "material and moral support"

---

[2] *Information Bulletin* (Prague), no. 64 (1966), p. 7.

[3] *First Afro-Asian-Latin American People's Solidarity Conference and Its Projections* (Lavalle report) (Washington, D.C.: Organization of American States, 28 November 1966), English edition, vol. 2, pp. 66, 71. Rashidov was a candidate member of the CPSU Politburo and first secretary of the Uzbek Central Committee.

[4] Resolution adopted by the Council of the OAS on 2 February 1966, in ibid., pp. 275-77. Supported by Peru, Venezuela, Colombia, Bolivia, the Dominican Republic, the United States, Costa Rica, Haiti, El Salvador, Ecuador, Argentina, Panama, Nicaragua, Honduras, Paraguay, Guatemala, Brazil, Mexico, Uruguay, and Chile.

for subversive activities. The fact that the Soviet Union immediately made a formal reply to this letter indicated that few were uncertain as to who the unnamed states members were.[5]

This Latin American reaction to Soviet participation in the Tricontinental Conference came just as the Soviet Union was growing more interested in expanding economic and political relations with Latin American governments and as several pro-Soviet communist parties in Latin America were deciding to retreat from guerrilla warfare. It may have helped move the Soviet Union to adopt a moderate line toward Latin America. During the next few years the Soviet Union made a strong effort to improve diplomatic and trade relations with some of the countries (Colombia, for example) that it had only recently pledged to help subvert.

By 1968, under heavy attack (mostly indirect) from Cuba and the castroites around Latin America, the Soviet Union had adopted a strong stand against the "export of revolution." Victor Volsky commented at some length on this in his *Pravda* article of 19 March 1968:

> Cuba itself chose socialism, without any interference from outside. This is the best reply to those who shout about the "export of revolution." At the same time, this choice became possible thanks to the existence of the Soviet Union. The Soviet Union has given and is continuing to give Cuba comprehensive support and assistance; this has doomed to failure attempts at the military strangulation of the revolution and economic blockade. Both the friends and enemies of socialism in Latin America have had an opportunity to see for themselves that the U.S.S.R. does not interfere in the internal affairs of any country but always acts resolutely in defense of the right of peoples to self-determination.
>
> Every genuine revolution is, beyond question, the internal affair of the people concerned. Marxists are convinced that the implantation of revolution from outside will not produce the desired effect. A revolution can be victorious and its results lasting only if the ideas of the revolution ripen in the country itself and eventually come to be held by the majority of the people.
>
> But it is also perfectly obvious that no liberation movement and no genuine revolution, even though it has ripened on national soil, can or should be isolated or nationally exclusive.

[5] Latin American letter of 7 February 1966, in ibid., pp. 279-80; the same countries signed (see previous note), except the United States and Mexico. For the Soviet response of 19 February 1966 see ibid., pp. 289-90.

The very internationalism of revolutionary ideas emphatically poses the question of the solidarity of the peoples who are fighting for their freedom and of the necessity of consolidating all the international revolutionary forces fighting against the common enemy of imperialism and for the achievement of common ideals. The history of Latin America has many outstanding examples of solidarity—from the joint struggle of the newborn nations for independence to the present-day movement in defense of revolutionary Cuba.[6]

At the 34th Congress of the CPSU in April 1971, General Secretary Leonid Brezhnev said that "great changes" were taking place in a number of Latin American countries, referring in particular to Bolivia (under General Juan José Torres, overthrown in August 1971), Chile (under President Salvador Allende, overthrown in September 1973), and Peru (under General Juan Velasco Alvarado, overthrown in August 1975).[7] In late 1973 *Izvestia* produced theoretical justification for closer relations with Latin American military governments of a "new type" (such as those in Peru, Ecuador, and Panama) that tried to eliminate imperialism's "degrading domination and effect profound socioeconomic transformations." The article noted that the "ruling circles in many Latin American countries [were] demanding a fundamental reexamination of economic and political relations" with the United States.[8]

Attitudes toward China and Cuba. The Sino-Soviet split, as it emerged into the open in the early 1960s, was to some extent evident in Latin America as it was in other parts of the world. In view of the limited number of Soviet embassies and other contacts in the area during these years, the Soviet position against the Chinese was generally advanced by the pro-Soviet communist parties rather than by Soviet representa-

---

[6] Oswald, *The Soviet Union and Latin America,* pp. 67-68. Many Latin American governments have nonetheless charged Soviet officials with interfering in the affairs of their countries, before and after 1968. At least fifty-four Soviet official representatives were declared *personae non gratae* by Latin American governments between 1959 and 1973. The number expelled from various countries is: Chile (twenty), Colombia (five), Bolivia (two), Ecuador (three), Mexico (nine), Argentina (six), Uruguay (eight), Brazil (eleven); see James D. Theberge, *The Soviet Presence in Latin America* (New York: Crane-Russak & Co., 1974), pp. 28-29.

[7] *Information Bulletin,* nos. 7-8 (1971).

[8] Quoted from *Izvestia,* 5 December 1973, by Robert H. Donaldson, in *Yearbook on International Communist Affairs 1973* (Stanford: Hoover Institution Press, 1974), p. 95.

tives. Typical of the pro-Soviet critique, which did not vary significantly over the period of the dispute, is an article published in *El Siglo,* the daily organ of the Chilean Communist Party, on the nineteenth anniversary of the founding of the People's Republic of China. A commentator traced the establishment of communism in China and commented on that country's "painful recent history":

> Animated by a dangerous great-power chauvinism and by hegemonic urges incompatible with socialism, the Chinese leaders have embarked upon the dangerous task of dividing the international communist movement, and, above all, of entering into the most abusive provocations against the Soviet Union. Together with rejecting the general theoretical orientations derived at the Twentieth Congress of the CPSU, they have adopted, raising them to a much worse degree, the deformations of Stalinism, have restored a grotesque and distressing cult of Mao Tse-tung, and have promoted, for more than a year, the so-called proletarian cultural revolution which has only brought more disorder in the social and economic life [of the country] and has caused enormous damage to socialism itself.[9]

In several countries, such as Venezuela and Guatemala, where the communist parties did not split along Sino-Soviet lines, attacks on the Chinese were kept to a minimum or were nonexistent.

The problem of Soviet attitudes toward, and relations with, the Cuban government is much more complex than the problem of attitudes toward China. Though the Soviet Union and Cuba ran into some difficulties during the early 1960s, particularly in the withdrawal of Soviet missiles from Cuba in 1962, the difficulties were always patched over—at least on the surface—as they were at the November 1964 meeting of Latin American communist parties. By the mid-1960s, however, there had been a rise in tensions between the Cuban government, which was calling with increased determination for guerrilla wars around Latin America, and the Soviet Union, which was turning in the opposite direction. The dispute with Cuba was above all a dispute over the proper revolutionary road for Latin American countries, though a second issue was Cuban distress over Soviet efforts to increase Soviet political and economic ties in Latin America.

The Soviet-Cuban dispute, which reached its peak in 1967–1968, was less straightforward than the Soviet conflict with China. Attacks

---

[9] *El Siglo* (Santiago), 1 October 1968.

12

on Cuba came by way of comments on Cuba (themselves often indirect) by pro-Soviet communists in Latin America and Europe, sometimes with open Soviet endorsement, and through charges from the Soviet Union and its allies that guerrilla groups lavishly praised by Castro were "ultra-leftist," "petty bourgeois," or even "Maoist." Among the main points of contention were these: (1) Cuba's calls for immediate rural guerrilla warfare on the Cuban model in most Latin American countries; (2) Cuban attacks on the pro-Soviet communist parties, in particular the Communist Party of Venezuela, and charges that the pro-Soviet parties were not in the vanguard of the revolutionary struggle; (3) Soviet bloc contacts with what Castro termed the Latin American "oligarchs," which were intended to, and sometimes did, lead to diplomatic and economic relations; and (4) assorted Cuban domestic policies. These and other issues were involved in the trial and imprisonment of a leader of the pre-Castro communist party in Cuba, Aníbal Escalante, and his so-called pro-Soviet microfaction in January-February 1968.

A Soviet introduction to excerpts from Guevara's diary, published in a supplement to the Russian-language edition of *New Times*, stressed the fact that the guerrillas in Bolivia lacked any popular support and argued that Guevara himself had been pessimistic about his chances of success for many months before his death. The introduction concluded with Lenin's warning on revolutionary insurrection: "We do not need hysterical outbursts. We need the measured tread of iron battalions of the proletariat." [10]

A long article in *Pravda* the following month criticized those who denied the vanguard role of the communist parties merely because they would not all turn to a primary emphasis on guerrilla warfare at that time:

> Not a single communist party in Latin America denies the Marxist-Leninist propositions on the armed path of revolutionary struggle. But they do reject the thesis about the possibility of causing a revolution in a country artificially, and describe as a departure from Marxism the effort to regard Latin America as something uniform, without taking into account the national peculiarities and specific conditions of each country.[11]

[10] *New Times* (Moscow), 18 October 1968.
[11] *Pravda* (Moscow), 20 November 1968.

13

By the end of 1968, however, after Castro had given his support to the Soviet invasion of Czechoslovakia, Soviet-Cuban relations had begun to improve. Within two years they were so close that many former supporters of the Cuban revolution publicly expressed concern that Castro had "sold out" to the Russians.[12] Soviet-Cuban relations improved steadily during the early 1970s. The admission of Cuba into the Council for Mutual Economic Assistance (COMECON) as a full member in July 1972 demonstrated the incorporation of Cuba into the Soviet economic bloc. On 3 January 1973 it was announced that the Soviet Union had taken the initiative in offering the Cuban government a major five-point economic package, the agreements having been accepted by Castro. Relations between the two countries reached a new high between mid-1975 and early 1976 (on which see Chapter 2).

Attitudes toward Chile and the Aftermath. Soviet policy toward Latin America during the early 1970s was determined in large part by what happened in Chile. One Russian analyst expressed the Soviet view when he wrote in 1971 that the Popular Unity victory of 1970 was "second only to the victory of the Cuban revolution in the magnitude of its significance as a revolutionary blow to the imperialist system in Latin America." [13] In late 1971 Boris Ponomarev, the CPSU official in charge of relations with non-ruling communist parties around the world, drew six "basic lessons" from the Chilean experience including these five: (1) contrary to "opportunistic claims," the working class was still the "main moving and guiding force of the revolution"; (2) unity of communist and socialist parties was important; (3) a "consistently democratic government" can "assume power peacefully"; (4) the revolution had to defend itself by effective mobilization of popular support, with major changes coming gradually since the revolution was being carried out in a constitutional framework; and (5) foreign intervention in Chile had been prevented by international solidarity behind the Allende government.[14] Early in the following year, the Popular Unity government was considered the "clearest embodiment" of the task

---

[12] For example, the prominent Venezuelan "castroite" guerrilla, Douglas Bravo; see Chapter 5 below. Also K. S. Karol, *Guerrillas in Power: The Course of the Cuban Revolution* (New York: Hill and Wang, 1970).

[13] V. G. Spirin, quoted in Leon Gouré and Morris Rothenberg, *Soviet Penetration of Latin America* (Miami: University of Miami Press, 1975), p. 97.

[14] See Ponomarev's comments quoted in Gouré and Rothenberg, *Soviet Penetration of Latin America*, pp. 100-101.

14

of the Latin American communists, namely "to rally all progressive, democratic forces and lead them in the fight for an anti-imperialist, agrarian, popular-democratic revolution that will end domination by U.S. imperialism and the power of latifundists and the bourgeoisie." [15]

The military coup that overthrew the Allende government on 11 September 1973 resulted in a break in Soviet relations with the government in Santiago and, over the following year, in an evaluation of the "lessons" of the Chilean events. At first, Soviet analysts merely insisted that the coup did not prove that a "peaceful transition to socialism" was impossible in other countries, as claimed by many critics on the left and "ultra-left." [16] Early in 1974, A. Sobolev, a prominent member of the Soviet Institute of Marxism-Leninism, drew the following conclusions, among others, from the Chilean experience: (1) it is apparently "easier to take power than to hold it"; (2) the election and inauguration of Salvador Allende in 1970 marked the peaceful ascendency of an "anti-imperialist, anti-oligarchic" revolution, the first step toward socialism; (3) the importance of leftist alliances for rallying the "democratic" forces had been reconfirmed, though conflicts within the Popular Unity government showed that the idea of a coalition required more profound analysis; (4) the alliance with the workers and middle classes had been allowed to disintegrate; (5) the Popular Unity government had moved in the right direction but too slowly in setting up crucial "all-embracing mass organizations" such as the soviets in Russia in 1917; (6) when a conflict develops between these mass organizations and the national constitution, priority must be given to the former; (7) opposition from ultra-left forces seriously weakened the revolutionary effort; (8) a confrontation between the revolutionary and reactionary forces was inevitable at some point; (9) the communist party must make the revolutionary process irreversible by creating such mechanisms as are necessary to "compel the exploiter classes to bow to the people's will"; and (10) the proper practical application of these general lines is not always easy to determine. [17]

In an analysis circulated internationally in the *World Marxist Review,* B. Ponomarev, shifting ground somewhat from his 1971 evalua-

[15] *New Times* (Moscow), February 1972.

[16] For example, Yuri Zhukov, the leading political commentator for *Pravda* (Moscow), in a 29 September 1973 interview on Moscow television.

[17] See A. Sobolev's discussion of the experiences and problems of class struggle in Chile, in *Rabochii Klass i Sovremennyi Mir* [The working class and the contemporary world], March-April 1974.

tion, reached the following conclusions, among others: (1) this had been the "first example of 'peaceful' revolutionary development over a long period" and had proved "most valuable to Marxist-Leninists from the point of view of perfecting revolutionary strategy and tactics"; (2) the revolutionary forces must move more decisively than they had moved in Chile to "deprive the old regime of important levers of power," such as the army and the mass information and propaganda media; (3) the peaceful road could be guaranteed only if the communists, acting as vanguard, were prepared to employ the "boldest" forms of struggle against counter-revolutionary actions, thus discouraging the enemy from seeking to terminate the revolutionary process; (4) the opposition forces were the first to violate the constitution and thus the revolutionaries should have used unconstitutional as well as constitutional means to keep them in line; and (5) after the initial political successes have been registered, the economy becomes the "main battlefield for the victory of the revolution." Like Sobolev, Ponomarev was short on specific practical recommendations for application to concrete problems faced by the Chilean revolutionaries.[18]

Latin American events of the early 1970s, particularly the overthrow of the Popular Unity government, led Soviet analysts to issue more militant theoretical statements on the strategy and tactics necessary for achieving socialism in Latin America. At the same time, though these analyses may turn out to be of immediate value to communist parties in Italy, France, and Portugal, they do not reflect the general tendency in Soviet relations toward Latin American governments in the mid-1970s—quite the contrary. Soviet policy toward most countries in early 1976 was not more militant than at the beginning of the decade, and was indeed less so than the policy line of the mid-1960s. Soviet efforts to expand diplomatic and trade relations with Latin American governments, regardless of their ideological inclinations, increased after September 1973. The campaigns against the Chilean government by the Soviet press, and by such international front organizations as the World Federation of Trade Unions, stand in marked contrast to expanding ties with the rightist governments in Brazil and Bolivia and the regime of the Peróns in Argentina.

---

[18] See *World Marxist Review,* vol. 17, no. 6 (June 1974). For a survey of Soviet analyses in the aftermath of the Chilean military coup, see Gouré and Rothenberg, *Soviet Penetration of Latin America,* pp. 107-120.

Soviet leaders have apparently been convinced that significant revolutionary situations are not probable in most Latin American countries in the near future, and that what change does occur is less likely to be initiated by the proletariat and its "vanguard" than by the increasingly radicalized and nationalistic middle class and military. At the same time, ties with the communist parties are being maintained pending an opportunity for them to move into the limelight as was done during 1974 and 1975 by the Communist Party of Portugal.

The People's Republic of China

Between 1959 and 1976 the Chinese communists emphasized a number of themes in their effort to influence (or win the sympathy of) the Latin American people. The two most important, each with a number of variations, were "revolution" (against the domestic reactionaries) and "anti-imperialism" (mainly directed against foreign influence in domestic affairs). Both these subjects were of great interest to Latin Americans of many persuasions during a period of rising nationalism with its attendant calls for "national independence."

Chinese support for revolution in Latin America during the 1950s was generally low-keyed, aimed above all at weakening reactionary positions by applying pressure on existing governments to institute significant political, social, and economic changes. During the 1950s, commentaries emphasized those aspects of the Chinese experience that were related to the construction of socialism: (1) the use of a broad united front to gain the greatest possible support for the proletariat against the chief enemy; (2) the Chinese agrarian reform during its early post-1949 stages; (3) the "four-class" government developed in China during the early 1950s, making use of the developmental potential of the national bourgeoisie; and (4) toward the end of the decade, the contributions of the "Great Leap Forward" and the "people's communes" to the urban and rural development of China. By 1960, the Chinese had begun to make themselves known to Latin Americans of varying political persuasions, chiefly through the application of "people's" or "cultural" diplomacy—the "exchange of information, ideas, persons, and culture as a systematic and unified arm of foreign policy." [19]

---

[19] Richard L. Walker, "The Developing Role of Cultural Diplomacy in Asia," in George L. Anderson, ed., *Issues and Conflicts* (Lawrence: University of Kansas Press, 1959), p. 45.

Armed Struggle and People's War. Armed struggle became the main Chinese line for Latin America during the 1960s, though not before then. In 1957 the Chinese reported Cuban communist (PSP) opposition to the armed struggle of Fidel Castro without critical comment.[20] Four months before the downfall of Batista, an article in China's main foreign affairs journal asserted that armed struggle was "still not the primary form of struggle" in Latin America, though it could become the "leading form of struggle" in countries under "pro-American reactionary regimes" or wherever American imperialism was "directly engaged in military intervention or plotting a reactionary coup." [21] Even Fidel Castro's arrival in Havana in January 1959 did not convince the Chinese that the continent was ripe for guerrilla warfare. In 1959 Chinese theoreticians generally advocated armed struggle only against dictatorial governments, such as those in Haiti, Nicaragua, Paraguay, and the Dominican Republic. In other countries, nonarmed struggle through a broad united front was considered appropriate.[22]

Chinese communist theorists began calling for armed struggle in many Latin American countries in 1960, though for several years they and the Cubans agreed on pushing the Cuban experience as a model for Latin Americans. A joint communiqué issued in Peking in November 1960 by Che Guevara and Chinese Vice-Premier Li Hsien-nien stated in part that

> the Chinese side expressed admiration for and joy over the great victory of the Cuban people who, upholding unity and persisting in their armed struggle, have increased their forces from small to big and from weak to strong and finally succeeded in overthrowing the reactionary dictatorship of Batista. It considers that the Cuban people's struggle and victory have provided abundant experience and set an example for all

---

[20] See Ch'ing Hai, "Tsai chan-tou chung te ku-pa" [In Cuba where the fighting is going on], *Shih-chieh Chih-shih* [World knowledge] (Peking), 20 September 1957, p. 14.

[21] Yen Chin, "Mu-ch'ien La-ting Mei-chou Min-tsu Chieh-fang Yün-tung te T'e-tien" [The characteristics of the Latin American National Liberation Movement], *Shih-chieh Chih-shih,* 20 August 1958, pp. 16-18.

[22] Yüan Wen, "La-ting Mei-chou Min-tsu Tu-li Yün-tung te chi-pen Hsing-shih" [The basic situation in the Latin American National Independence Movement], *Kuo-chi Wen-t'i Yen-chiu* [Research in international problems] (Peking), May 1959, pp. 10-18. After January 1959 the Cuban PSP tried to explain Castro's victory and influence the new Cuban leader's policies by pointing to the Chinese experiences in the seizure of power and construction of socialism; see William E. Ratliff, "The Chinese Communist Domestic United Front and Its Application to Latin America, 1921-1971" (Ph.D. diss., University of Washington, 1974), Chapter 5.

oppressed peoples in the world, particularly the Latin American peoples, in their struggles to win and safeguard national independence.[23]

This was shortly after Guevara had published his own book *Guerrilla Warfare*. For the next three years relations between the Chinese and most Cuban leaders were very close, in part because the Chinese government strongly condemned Soviet violation of Cuban sovereignty during the missile crisis. The Chinese published a series of Cuban revolutionary writings, including Castro's two "Declarations of Havana" and Guevara's later, shorter work *Guerrilla Warfare: A Method,* which the Cubans themselves subsequently admitted had been made available to revolutionaries from all parts of the third world.[24] The Cuban government reported the importation and publication of several hundred thousand copies of Chinese revolutionary works for circulation in Cuba and throughout Latin America.

The November 1964 conference of Latin American communist parties in Havana proved to be a turning point in Sino-Cuban relations and in the Chinese attitude toward revolution in Latin America. Neither the Chinese nor any pro-Chinese groups from Latin America were invited to attend, and the final communiqué demonstrated a sympathy with the Soviet side in the Sino-Soviet dispute by speaking out for the unity of the international communist movement just at the time the Chinese had decided it was essential for true Marxist-Leninists to break away from the "revisionists" who occupied important positions in many of the world's communist parties.

In February 1965 the Albanian Communist Party, China's European ally in the dispute with the Soviet Union, warned the Cubans to beware of "falling into the revisionist trap," [25] and in a speech on 13 March Castro made his first public denunciation of the "Byzantine discords" of the dispute. The crisis in Sino-Cuban relations erupted in January 1966 when Fidel Castro launched an attack on the Chinese during the Tricontinental Conference in Havana in the presence of revolutionary groups from all over the world. After several insulting exchanges between the Chinese and Cuban leaders early in the year, the focus of Chinese criticism shifted to the Cuban road to power. Differences between the Cuban and Chinese roads that had previously

[23] *Peking Review,* 13 December 1960, p. 41.
[24] *El Mundo* (Havana), 7 May 1968.
[25] *Zeri i popullit* (Tirana), 16 February 1965.

been glossed over or minimized (including differences on the role of the communist party, the breadth and importance of the united front, and the strategy of guerrilla warfare) became important points of controversy. Criticism by the Chinese generally came indirectly, in two ways: (1) by their publishing the critical statements of pro-Chinese parties around the world; and (2) by their emphasizing the applicability of their own revolutionary experience for Latin Americans. Typical of the former criticism was a critique of Régis Debray's *Revolution in the Revolution?* (discussed below) by the pro-Chinese Marxist-Leninist Communist Party of France, published on the fifteenth anniversary of the founding of Castro's 26th of July Movement. The book was said to be "anti-Marxist-Leninist," and a "big counter-revolutionary mystification" which served the interests of the "international bourgeoisie" and led "all honest people disgusted with revisionism to a side track, down the drain, to a blind alley." [26] Typical of the latter criticism was the assertion that Marxist-Leninist parties and organizations in Latin America had come to realize that

> the road taken by the Chinese people in seizing political power by force of arms under Chairman Mao's leadership is of general and practical significance for Latin Americans, and is the only correct road of revolution for the Latin American people; that is, to arouse the peasant masses in the countryside under the leadership of the political party of the proletariat to wage guerrilla warfare, unfold an agrarian revolution, build rural base areas, use the countryside to encircle the cities and finally capture them.[27]

During their heavily Mao-centered period in the mid- and late 1960s, the Chinese insisted that the existing governments in Latin America were reactionary semi-feudal "running dogs" of the U.S. imperialists, that the Soviet leaders were "social imperialists," that the pro-Soviet communists were "revisionists" who had capitulated to the deceptive reform-oriented parties, and that the castroite-nationalists were "ultra-leftists" who relied on a "band of swashbuckling three musketeer type bravadoes who are expected to perform miraculous exploits against terrific odds." [28]

---

[26] *Peking Review,* 26 July 1968.

[27] Ibid., 2 February 1968, p. 29.

[28] Final quotation from document of the pro-Chinese Communist Party of Ceylon, a frequent spokesman for Chinese positions during the 1966-1968 period, in ibid., 21 June 1968, p. 14.

For eight years after the victory of the Cuban revolution in 1959, the Chinese communists had a particular sympathy for Che Guevara. The Argentine-Cuban guerrilla expert received warm welcomes on several visits to Peking and had his articles circulated by the Peking Foreign Languages Press in all corners of the third world. Castro's slide into the revisionist camp during the mid-1960s did not damage Guevara's reputation in Peking. While the feud with Castro was at its height in February 1966, a statement published in *Peking Review* for circulation throughout the world said that one of the key ways to judge the "extent or degree to which Cuba has departed from the revolutionary path" was the "exit from the Cuban political scene of one of its foremost leaders, E. Che Guevara." [29] But Guevara's reappearance in Bolivia during 1966–1967 as the "petty-bourgeois adventurist" *par excellence* caused the Chinese to revise their attitude. Guevara's death (October 1967) was not mentioned in China until January 1968, when a prominent official of the *People's Daily,* the official organ of the Chinese Communist Party, reportedly called Guevara an "adventurist" who "cannot be called a Marxist-Leninist." [30] In March 1972 Chou En-lai told Carlos Altamirano, the secretary-general of the Socialist Party of Chile, that he admired Guevara as a revolutionary but considered him strategically incorrect in not seeking a war of the masses.[31]

During 1969 Chinese commentaries began to change and by mid-1972 a new approach to Latin America had emerged. The Chinese became much less concerned with the immediate seizure of power by revolutionaries in most countries than with promoting "third world solidarity" against the two "superpowers"—the United States and the Soviet Union. A major policy statement in March 1971 declared that in Latin America "a new situation has emerged characterized by joint struggle for the defence of national rights and state sovereignty." [32] Chinese leaders noted with satisfaction that many governments, both individually and collectively, were critical of U.S. policy on a number of issues, including economic investments and offshore territorial waters.

[29] Statement by the pro-Chinese Communist Party of Ceylon, in ibid., 25 February 1966, p. 24.

[30] Feng Piao, director of the information department of *Jen-min Jih-pao* [People's daily], reported in the Red Guard paper *Red Seamen,* 24 January 1968, as translated in *Current Background* (Hong Kong), no. 850, p. 9.

[31] Altamirano interview with AFP correspondent, in Peking, 15 March 1972.

[32] By the editorial departments of *Jen-min Jih-pao, Hung Ch'i* [Red flag], and *Chieh-fang Chün-pao* [Liberation army daily], in *Peking Review,* 19 March 1971, p. 7.

Chile and Peru were leading in this criticism in South America in the early 1970s, and Panama was leading in the criticism in Central America.

At the same time, the Chinese argued (even during the Popular Unity period in Chile) that the only truly revolutionary government in Latin America was in Cuba, inasmuch as it was only Fidel Castro who had destroyed the old political structure of his country and founded a revolutionary army to defend the interests of the proletariat. The Chinese still argued that "historical experience shows that the seizure of political power by the proletariat and the oppressed people of a country and the seizure of victory in their revolution are accomplished invariably by the power of the gun." [33] Chou En-lai made this point in a widely publicized interview with the editor of the Mexico City daily *Excelsior* and caused a brief flurry of criticism in several countries. As the expanding relations of the People's Republic of China during this period suggest, however, many Latin American political leaders did not consider these "theoretical statements" a serious threat; they pointed to Chou's statement that "each people must make its own revolution in its own country." [34]

Chinese Impact in Latin America. Chinese policy toward Latin America between 1949 and the early 1960s, policy chiefly directed toward cultural or "people's" diplomacy, was well suited to making an impression on a wide variety of persons in an area traditionally dominated by the United States, where significant political and economic contacts were not yet possible. By 1960 some Latin American leftists looked upon the Chinese experience as a model or inspiration for social and economic development. These and others, many of whom had travelled to China, urged formal diplomatic relations with the People's Republic (PRC) and the admission of the Peking government to the United Nations. Just as this policy was becoming noticeably successful, however, a number of factors (the most important being the growing Chinese dispute with the Soviet Union) led to a shift in the Chinese approach. The increasing Chinese emphasis on armed struggle in the following years and setbacks in Chinese domestic programs such as the

---

[33] Ibid., p. 5.

[34] Interview with Julio Scherer García in *Excelsior* (Mexico City), 5 September 1971. Chinese determination to have formal relations with Latin American countries was made clear in 1973 when China maintained relations with the military rulers of Chile who had overthrown Allende's Popular Unity government. By early 1975 diplomatic relations had been established with Chile, Peru, Mexico, Guyana, and Brazil, in addition to Cuba.

Great Leap Forward and the People's Communes produced a marked decline in broadly based Latin American interest in the People's Republic.

The Chinese communist appeal to a variety of guerrilla-oriented revolutionary groups was greatest during the period from 1960 to 1965. This appeal came from Chinese statements of support for violent revolution and some degree of active support through training and financing guerrilla fighters, generally close relations between the PRC and Cuba, and the disillusionment of those Latin American revolutionaries not tied to the Soviet Union following the Soviet "betrayal" of Cuba during the 1962 missile crisis. By the mid-1960s, however, several factors had produced a disintegration of the Chinese position among revolutionaries in most Latin American countries: the Chinese decision to concentrate on splitting communist parties in Latin America in an effort to weaken the international position of the Soviet Union; the growing dispute with Cuba, which lowered the prestige of the Chinese in the eyes of most Latin American guerrillas, and led to the exclusion of pro-Chinese groups from hemispheric revolutionary meetings; and Chinese insistence on the preparation for and waging of "people's war" according to the Chinese prescription, thus ruling out immediate armed struggle in most countries and precluding participation in certain castroite activities.

The effort to split the pro-Soviet parties began in the early 1960s, and became the primary Chinese objective after the middle of the decade. It shook up some of the communist parties and made an impression on students in several countries, but most Latin American communists remained in the pro-Soviet parties and the pro-Chinese factions often proved to be unstable and ineffective domestically. They did, however, constitute "evidence" for the Chinese claims of "Marxist-Leninist" opposition to "Soviet revisionism" throughout the hemisphere and were available to serve as spokesmen for the Chinese position in the Sino-Soviet dispute.

After the end of the Cultural Revolution in the late 1960s, the PRC moved from the depths of isolationism to an unprecedented involvement in international affairs. Although the Chinese communist position improved throughout the world, the rate and degree of improvement were perhaps greater in Latin America than anywhere else. The three most important factors in this change were (1) the rebirth of Chinese communist interest in conventional foreign relations at a time

23

of rapidly increasing international acceptance of the Peking government; (2) the increasingly independent attitudes of many Latin American governments, resulting from rising nationalism and other causes, and their interest in developing trade and other relations in all parts of the world; and (3) the sudden shift in U.S. policy toward China which, on the one hand, removed long-felt pressures against substantive Sino-Latin American relations, and, on the other hand, encouraged Latin American governments to act independently of the United States so as not to get caught again in the backwash of U.S. policy.

Chou En-lai told several Latin American visitors to the PRC in the early 1970s that China would continue to support peoples fighting for their national liberation.[35] As the decade progressed it became clear that this did not generally mean the organizations the PRC had been supporting in the 1960s, but rather those governments that demonstrated some degree of independence from the United States and that joined, no matter how loosely, the "third world united front" against the two "superpowers."

By early 1976 the Chinese maintained relations with a wide variety of South American countries, ranging from the leftist military regime in Peru under Francisco Morales Bermúdez to the rightist military in Chile under Augusto Pinochet. Yet most Latin American political leaders agreed with former Chilean presidential candidate Radamiro Tomic who said in 1972 that few Latin Americans would want to exchange a spokesman in Washington for one in Peking.[36] Chinese relations with several Latin American countries were somewhat clouded after 1973 as a result of the PRC's close ties with the military government in Chile.

Sino-Cuban ties, after improving from their low point in 1966, took a decided turn for the worse in the mid-1970s as a result of immediate Chinese recognition of the Pinochet government in Chile and Chinese opposition to the Popular Movement for the Liberation of Angola (MPLA) in Angola. On the latter, the Chinese in fact charged that the Soviet Union had sent "mercenaries from Latin America [i.e., the Cubans] to invade Angola."[37]

---

[35] Ibid.; and Carlos Altamirano, *El Dia* (Mexico City), 16 March 1972.

[36] Interview with the author, Santiago, 24 May 1972. For more on this subject see my articles, "Chinese Communist Cultural Diplomacy toward Latin America, 1949-1960," *Hispanic American Historical Review,* vol. 46, no. 3 (February 1969), pp. 53-79, and "Communist China and Latin America," *Asian Survey,* vol. 12, no. 10 (October 1972), pp. 846-63, from which portions of this chapter were taken.

[37] *Peking Review,* 12 March 1976, p. 21.

Conclusions

In Latin America, the period from 1959 to 1976 was characterized by sometimes gradual and sometimes sudden shifts in the policies of the Soviet Union and the People's Republic of China and therefore by shifts in their relationships to each other, Cuba, and the assorted Marxist-Leninist organizations of the hemisphere. The party lines were formulated in part on the basis of studies of the actual conditions in Latin America. Despite lofty claims of scientific validity and revolutionary altruism, however, policies were often determined largely by the fluctuating self-interests of the powers involved. International and domestic preoccupations led to superficial analyses of revolutionary potential in the area and to shifts in revolutionary loyalties. In general, the different analyses and national interests of the two powers were reflected chiefly in attitudes toward allies and toward roads to power.

Soviet analyses of Latin America were overall more realistic—less determined by ideological and revolutionary preconceptions—than those of the Chinese (or those of the Cubans). This resulted in part from the general Soviet international line promoted during the Sino-Soviet dispute and from domestic tranquility in the Soviet Union greater than obtained in China, but it was also (apparently) the result of the higher quality of Soviet appraisals both of Latin American conditions and of the degree of communist strength or potential in the various countries. Chinese (and Cuban) analyses and policies were least realistic during their most distinctive years in the mid- and late 1960s. During these years a combination of domestic and international conditions led China (and Cuba) to proclaim the international applicability of an oversimplified model of its own revolutionary experience. By the mid-1970s these international powers, to varying degrees, had adopted more flexible lines that permitted them to place primary emphasis on conventional diplomatic and economic relations with an increasing number of Latin American governments, while at the same time continuing covert activities throughout the area and maintaining a degree of verbal—and sometimes material—support for revolutionaries seeking to overthrow governments in selected Latin American countries.

2
International Marxism-Leninism: Cuba

Cuban policies toward Latin America have passed through several stages in response to changing domestic and international conditions. From the time of their own victory in 1959, the Cuban leaders urged revolutionaries in Latin America to seize power in their countries by armed struggle. The urgency of this call and the breadth of its applicability varied considerably from one period to another. The advocacy of rural guerrilla warfare was strongest in two periods. First, it was strong during the early 1960s, when it was expounded most forcefully in Che Guevara's *Guerrilla Warfare* (1960) and Castro's "Second Declaration of Havana" (1962). Cuban enthusiasm for armed struggle was curtailed somewhat by the meeting of the CPSU and Latin American communist parties in Havana at the end of 1964, though it returned with more vigor than ever before during the next two years. The second and most intense period of support for armed struggle in Latin America occurred between 1966 and 1968. This support was propounded most dramatically in Fidel Castro's speeches of 13 March and 10 August 1967 and in the statements of the Latin American Solidarity Organization (OLAS) conference in Havana during July and August of that year. Its chief theoretical development came in a semi-official political tract by Régis Debray entitled *Revolution in the Revolution?* (1967) and in several short writings by Che Guevara. This theoretical line was carried out most memorably by Guevara in Bolivia in 1966–1967. During the years that followed, Castro was increasingly selective in his support for guerrillas and guerrilla warfare in Latin American countries.

Origin and Early Development of Castroism

The first period of what has been called "castroism" as a road to power (the period between 1959 and 1968) was dominated by the leaders of the Cuban revolution. The most important early statement, still in crude outline form, was Guevara's *Guerrilla Warfare*. According to Guevara, the Cuban revolution had made "three fundamental contributions" to the "mechanics of revolutionary movements in Latin America," these being the demonstration (1) that "the forces of the people can win a war against the army"; (2) that "it is not always necessary to wait until all the conditions for revolution exist; the insurrectionary center [*foco insurreccional*] can create them"; and (3) that "in underdeveloped America the field of the armed struggle must be fundamentally in the countryside." [1] The first two were said to contradict the defeatist attitude of revolutionaries and pseudo-revolutionaries who were afraid to begin the struggle; the third was a strategic concept putting the crucial role of the rural population of the Americas into its proper perspective. Several paragraphs later, Guevara wrote that "where a government has come to power through any form of popular consultation, fraudulent or not, and maintains at least an appearance of constitutional legality, it is impossible to bring about a guerrilla outbreak inasmuch as all the possibilities of civic struggle have not been exhausted." [2] Whereas the first three points remained crucial to castroism as it was developed during the 1960s, the warning was disregarded almost as soon as the book was off the press, only to be revived without reference to Guevara in the 1970s.

Fidel Castro's most important statement of the Cuban road during the early years was his "Second Declaration of Havana," on 4 February 1962. This speech was a declaration of revolution and contained many important "castroite" elements, though, like Guevara's book, it was in some respects different from the fully developed formulations of 1967. Castro argued here that revolution was "inevitable" in many countries of Latin America. But, he asked, under what conditions?

> It happens inevitably that in those nations where the control of
> the Yankee monopolies is strongest, where the exploitation of
> the oligarchy is most merciless and the conditions of the

---

[1] Che Guevara, *La guerra de guerrillas* (Bogotá: Juventud Combatiente, 1960), p. 11.
[2] Ibid., p. 12.

masses of workers and peasants most unbearable, political power becomes more vicious, states of siege become habitual, all manifestations of mass discontent and democratic channels are closed off completely, revealing more clearly than ever the brutal dictatorial character assumed by the power of the dominant classes. That is when the revolutionary breakthrough of the people becomes inevitable.[3]

On the question of what road to take, Castro commented:

Wherever the roads are closed to the peoples, where the repression of the workers and peasants is fierce, where the domination of the Yankee monopolies is strongest, the first and most important thing is to understand that it is neither just nor correct to divert the peoples with the vain and accommodating illusion that it is or will be possible to uproot the dominant classes by legal means.[4]

These two statements seem to parallel Guevara's warning about the need to exhaust all possibilities by civic struggle before turning to guerrilla warfare. The crucial difference, however, is that by 1962 the Cuban government was already actively supporting guerrillas who were trying to overthrow Castro's erstwhile ally, the democratically elected president of Venezuela, Rómulo Betancourt.

Castro noted further that in the underdeveloped countries of America the working class was "in general relatively small," but that the peasants constituted a potential force of "decisive importance." Yet the peasants, uncultured and always kept in isolation, "require the revolutionary and political leadership of the working class and revolutionary intellectuals, without whom they would not be able to launch the struggle and win the victory."[5] There is no clear reference to the role of Marxism-Leninism or of a Marxist-Leninist party.

In some respects Guevara's most comprehensive and sophisticated analysis of revolutionary strategy and tactics in Latin America was *Guerrilla Warfare: A Method* (1963). Here he laid the groundwork for his analysis by restating the three fundamental lessons of the Cuban revolution (from his *Guerrilla Warfare*) and quoting at length from Castro's "Second Declaration." He then went on to argue that guerrilla

---

[3] Fidel Castro, "Segunda declaración de la Habana: del pueblo de Cuba a los pueblos de América y del Mundo," in *Obra Revolucionaria* (Havana), vol. 5 (1962), pp. 16, 22.

[4] Ibid., p. 23.

[5] Ibid., p. 22.

warfare is a "people's war" (*guerra de pueblo*) which requires a "people's army" and mass support to be successful. Guevara believed that the objective factors were highly favorable in nearly all Latin American countries, though not all were yet ready for guerrilla warfare.[6] He quoted Castro's "Second Declaration" to the effect that the revolutionary struggle could not be led by the national bourgeoisie. Rather, it had to be led by the working class and revolutionary intellectuals. Guevara went on with a reference to "Marxist-Leninist party leaders," thus adding two essential elements—Marxism-Leninism and Marxist-Leninist party leadership. He discussed the role of the guerrilla *foco* in getting the revolution started and pointed out the need for guerrilla bases.[7]

Many of Guevara's and Castro's ideas were developed (or, some say, distorted) in Régis Debray's *Revolution in the Revolution?*, published in Havana in January 1967 by the government-backed Casa de las Américas. According to the introduction to the Cuban edition, Debray visited revolutionaries in several Latin American countries and spent more than a year in Cuba just before the book's publication. While in Cuba he had access to unpublished documents and talked at length with Fidel Castro and other revolutionary leaders. "No one else who has written on the Cuban revolution has had access to such a wealth of material and data for historical research." [8] In the introduction to the French edition, Debray stated that the principles put forward were, above all, those of Fidel Castro.[9]

Debray's declared aim in this book was to disprove the "dangerous cliché"—a view which he himself had once held—that the Cuban revolution could not be repeated in the Western Hemisphere. According to Debray, the technical, tactical, and even strategic truths of the Cuban revolutionary struggle provided a revolutionary model for other

---

[6] "Guerra de guerrillas: un método," *Cuba Socialista* (Havana), vol. 3, no. 25 (September 1963), pp. 1-17. Commenting in a CBS interview in December 1964, Guevara said: "In America, the road to liberation of the peoples, which will be the road to socialism, will be opened by armed struggle in nearly all countries." Quoted in Michael Lowy, *The Marxism of Che Guevara* (New York: Monthly Review Press, 1973), p. 86.

[7] Guevara, *La guerra de guerrillas,* pp. 10, 13-14.

[8] Roberto Fernández Retamar, "Introduction," in Régis Debray, *¿Revolución en la revolución?* (Havana: Casa de las Américas, 1967), pp. 9-10. According to K. S. Karol, Debray wrote his book "after long private discussions with Fidel Castro, who . . . himself revised and corrected the proofs." Karol, *Guerrillas in Power,* p. 374.

[9] *Revolution dans la revolution?* (Paris: Maspero, 1967), p. 10.

Latin American countries seeking national liberation. The Cubans had proceeded "by means of the more or less slow construction, through guerrilla warfare carried out in the most favorable rural zones, of a *mobile strategic force,* nucleus of the People's Army and of the future Socialist State." [10]

Much of the book was devoted to a condemnation of *"imported* political plans, disguised as military lines, and applied to historic conditions very different from those in which the conceptions had their roots. Such were the conceptions of armed self-defense, a particular way of understanding armed propaganda and the guerrilla base, and, finally, the subjection of the guerrilla force to the party as just one piece added to its peacetime organization." [11] According to Debray, Fidel Castro was able to lead the Cuban revolution effectively because he avoided these "imports," and invented "on the spot, starting from his own experience, the rules of a military doctrine in conformity with the terrain." [12] His single-minded effort to hold up the Cuban model for Latin Americans led Debray into serious distortions of the events of the Cuban revolution on the one hand and the writings and experiences of the Chinese communists and other third world revolutionaries on the other. When on one occasion he acknowledged the applicability of a non-Cuban writing to Latin America (Mao's *Problems of Strategy in Guerrilla War against Japan*) he considered it a "stroke of good luck" that the Cubans had acted in ignorance of this formulation and learned the principles elaborated therein on their own by trial and error.[13]

Near the end of his book, Debray concluded that

> the Latin American revolution and its vanguard, the Cuban revolution, have thus made a decisive contribution to international revolutionary experience and to Marxism-Leninism: *Under certain conditions, the political process is not distinct*

---

[10] Debray, *¿Revolución en la revolución?*, p. 20; emphasis in original.

[11] Ibid.; emphasis in original.

[12] Ibid., p. 16.

[13] See ibid., p. 16, and passim. Debray is a polemicist with generally undisguised contempt for those who are mistaken or disagree with him. When the editors of the U.S. publication *Monthly Review* interpreted the experiences of the Peruvian MIR in a way he did not like, he wrote it was not clear whether their work was "more sinister or ridiculous," adding that their "persevering naïveté" approximated the "fine art of misinformation." Ibid., p. 49. In fact, this judgment applies much more accurately to Debray himself. Guevara was not nearly so contemptuous of learning from non-Latin American experiences; see 1959 Guevara interview in Rolando Bonachea and Nelson Valdés, *Che: Selected Works of Ernesto Guevara* (Cambridge, Mass.: MIT Press, 1969), p. 368.

from the military; both form one organic whole. This orga-
nization is the People's Army, whose nucleus is the guerrilla
army. The vanguard party can exist in the form of the guerrilla
foco itself. The guerrilla is the Party in gestation.[14]

This emphasis on military over political concerns does not imply the total absence of a unified political outlook among the guerrillas. Debray states that, in contrast to what had been the situation in Cuba, the ideology of the new guerrilla commands is clearly Marxist, and the majority of the fighters come from communist ranks. Those whose Marxist-Leninist backgrounds are underdeveloped will learn from the enemy in face-to-face confrontation during the people's war. When Debray concludes that "at the present juncture, the principal stress must be put on the development of guerrilla warfare and not on the strengthening of existing parties or on the creation of new parties," he is faithfully stating Fidel Castro's position during 1967.[15]

For Castro in 1967 the "true revolutionary" in Latin America was distinguished by his attitude toward guerrilla warfare and his efforts to move the masses. Thus the true revolutionary either participated in or supported guerrilla warfare in his own country and elsewhere, or supported guerrilla warfare abroad while actively preparing for its use at home. The "false revolutionary" (and for Castro this designation applied to most of the communists in Latin America, and in particular to the leadership of the Communist Party of Venezuela, a point that will be made in more detail later) opposed, held back, or actively betrayed the guerrilla activities in his country and to varying degrees tried to cooperate with the "oligarchs" and "imperialists." The false revolutionary was satisfied to put off positive revolutionary action until after the masses as a whole had acquired adequate awareness.[16] However, while maintaining that "seizing power by peaceful means" was impossible in any Latin American country, Castro conceded on 10 August

---

[14] Debray, *¿Revolución en la revolución?*, p. 90; emphasis in original.

[15] Ibid., pp. 99, 90, 94, 97. The best collection of commentary on Debray and his formulation of the castroite road, by individuals who are generally in agreement with his long-term socialist objectives, is *Régis Debray and the Latin American Revolution,* ed. Leo Huberman and Paul Sweezy (New York: Monthly Review Press, 1968); and Lewis Feuer, "Neo-Primitivism: The New Marxism of the Alienated Intellectuals," in his *Marx and the Intellectuals* (Garden City, N.Y.: Anchor Books, 1969), pp. 216-28.

[16] See speeches of 13 March and 10 August 1967, in *Granma* (Havana), 19 March and 20 August, respectively. Castro emphasized the importance of revolutionary initiative in an interview published in the Italian communist weekly *Rinascita,* 22 September 1967, quoted below.

1967 that "no one can be so sectarian, so dogmatic, as to say that, everywhere, one has to go out and grab a rifle tomorrow." [17]

According to Castro, the guerrilla force, which was bound to be the nucleus of the revolutionary movement, must unite in itself both the political and the military commands. Above all, political leadership must not be confined to party officials in the cities, though, as the Cuban report to the Latin American Solidarity Organization (OLAS) conference stated, "the fact that the revolutionary army is organized in the countryside . . . does not mean that the leadership of the struggle should not be oriented by the ideology of the proletariat. On the contrary, the ideas of the proletariat, and even its best cadres, should be at the head of this struggle." [18]

On 13 March 1967, in the course of his discussion of guerrilla activities in Venezuela and his condemnation of the Communist Party of Venezuela, Castro observed that not all parties of the proletariat had taken their revolutionary obligations to heart. Thus he warned that

> if in any country those who call themselves communist do not know how to fulfill their duty, we will support those who, without calling themselves communist, conduct themselves like real communists in action and in struggle. For every true revolutionary, who bears within him the revolutionary spirit, revolutionary vocation, will always come to Marxism! . . . Many, the immense majority of those who today proudly call themselves Marxist-Leninists, arrived at Marxism-Leninism by way of the revolutionary struggle.[19]

Emphasis on the specifically Latin American nature of the "anti-imperialist struggle," often overriding the Marxist-Leninist element, was evident on many occasions throughout the OLAS conference. The long report of the Cuban delegation to the conference discussed Marx and Lenin, but laid great stress on the history of "colonialism" and "imperialism" in Latin America, and on Latin American revolutionaries, beginning with Simón Bolívar and passing through José Martí to Che Guevara. Cuban President Osvaldo Dorticós gave his opening address before a large picture of Bolívar and Castro, and, in closing the meeting, spoke before one of Guevara.

---

[17] *Granma* (Havana), 20 August 1967.

[18] Quoted from official English-language translation released by the OLAS conference.

[19] *Granma* (Havana), 19 March 1967.

The convening of the OLAS conference drew attention to the international perspectives of castroism during this period, but neither the meeting in Havana nor most of the statements emanating from Cuba during 1967 brought out with unmistakable clarity one of Che Guevara's chief concerns during this period just before his death. That concern was directed toward the continental proportions of the struggle against imperialism and for socialism in the hemisphere. More than any other theorist, Guevara was responsible for developing and popularizing the concept of a continental revolution, both through his writings and his personal efforts to turn Bolivia into the Vietnam of the Americas. The strategy had been proposed earlier by guerrillas and theorists of armed struggle in Latin America (by Douglas Bravo and Abraham Guillén, among others), though Guevara's insistence on this line in 1967 no doubt came in large part from his own experiences and evaluations of international developments—particularly his contacts with Africa in the mid-1960s, the U.S. intervention and the concomitant revolutionary setback in the Dominican Republic in 1965, and the phenomenon of the Vietnam War. As Guevara saw it, the struggle for socialism necessarily involved an international army of fighters whose revolutionary successes, through the implantation of guerrilla *focos* in critical strategic areas, would liberate the continent as a whole.

Cuban Retreat from Castroism

A slightly more flexible line began to emerge in 1968, and the glorification of the guerrilla was modified, in spite of the fact that 1968 in Cuba was officially designated the "Year of the Heroic Guerrilla." The change can probably be accounted for by Castro's need to devote most of his time and resources to Cuba's increasingly faltering economy, to his wish to avoid further conflict with the Soviet Union (which might endanger continuation of vital Soviet economic and military aid), and to his recognition of the repeated failures of the castroite line in the Latin American countries. What is more, the death of Guevara removed that passionate advocate of the *foco* line from active participation in policy formation.

In April 1968 Castro said that too little credit had been given to the role of urban groups during the Cuban revolution. In reference to those whose efforts had been underestimated, he commented: "We

34

believe that, as time goes on, all of these things should be made clear, that everything should be put in its proper place." [20] Later in the year, explaining that "special circumstances" prevented their criticism from being "more timely," Simón Torres and Julio Aronde (identified only as two "Cuban revolutionaries") roundly denounced many of Régis Debray's formulations which had been supported by official and unofficial spokesmen for Cuba up to that time.[21] On Debray's juxtaposition of the "bourgeois" city and the "revolutionary" countryside, they stated:

> There never was such a thing as "the city" and "the Llano" taken as a homogeneous entity where everybody appeared alike. Far from it. The "city" was the place where the class contradictions became sharpest; and if Debray, who claims to have studied the Cuban experience (he had ample time to do so), is unaware of this factor, then one must say that he has not understood anything.

They also attacked Debray's neglect of political activities and his conclusion that "the people's army will be the nucleus of the party, not vice versa." According to Torres and Aronde, this was not what had happened in Cuba: "In Cuba the guerrilla *foco* did not create the party, but rather a political organization with very definite characteristics which distinguished it from the traditional Marxist parties, the July 26 Movement, formed the guerrilla force." [22]

In September 1968 Debray himself began his retreat from the more extreme positions taken in *Revolution in the Revolution?* In a letter from his cell in Camiri, Bolivia, he stated that his controversial work had been merely a "political tract" which had "only one ambition: to play a part in breaking down a mental, theoretical, and practical block hindering the upsurge of the revolutionary armed struggle where, and only where, it was then underway." He acknowledged that

---

[20] Ibid., 14 April 1968.

[21] Torres and Aronde, "Debray and the Cuban Experience," in Huberman and Sweezy, eds., *Régis Debray and the Latin American Revolution,* pp. 44-62. An editorial note says that while the authors are Cuban revolutionaries, "the views they express in this critique are their own and are not intended to present the position of the Cuban Communist Party or the Cuban leadership" (p. 44). Such a disclaimer, coming from Cuba at that particular time, when freedom of expression on revolutionary policy was severely restricted (to say the least), is very nearly the government's unofficial stamp of approval. Even in the United States such disclaimers are frequently made by government agencies when it is common knowledge that they are untrue.

[22] Ibid., pp. 50-51, 57.

the "so-called *foco* theory in its simplest, most skeletal form" was "certainly a utopian notion," but insisted that "people's war" was not.[23] In his prison cell in Bolivia it came to Debray that revolutionaries had a great deal to learn about alliances from Mao Tse-tung. After discussing the Chinese historical experience, Debray concluded:

> While every situation, every historical junction must be grasped as a whole, it must also be analyzed in terms of the numbers two and three: the strategic two and the tactical three. It is here that we find the fundamental error of *gauchisme*: it sees the two so clearly as to be blind to the three. For if there are only two camps: there is a struggle between two entities—labour and capital, and two classes—bourgeoisie and proletariat, but nothing between the two. True, there *are* only two camps, but there are three forces, and if the revolutionary camp is to win the day, it must of necessity be extended to include the pivotal forces, those upon whom victory or defeat hinges—it may be the peasants, it may be the petty bourgeoisie, it may be both. *Gauchisme*—dualist and Manichean—is incapable of achieving a successful policy of alliances. The basis for the right policy is this: "To develop progressive forces, win over the intermediate forces, and to isolate the forces of the extremists." [24]

In an interview published after his release from jail in 1971, Debray acknowledged that *Revolution in the Revolution?* smacked of superficial polemics and admitted that the Latin American situation required much more serious analysis than he had presented.[25]

Cuba's retreat from insistence on guerrilla warfare throughout Latin America became clearer in 1969. At mid-year, in a statement which could not have been imagined just two years before, Fidel Castro declared:

> We are far from being impatient. We are in no hurry whatsoever. We will wait and watch as, one by one, those countries [in Latin America] break away from the past; as, one by one, they make their revolutions. . . . How long will we have to wait? We will wait as long as it is necessary: 10, 20,

---

23 Letter to Huberman and Sweezy, published in *Monthly Review* (New York), February 1969.

24 Régis Debray, *Prison Writings* (New York: Random House, 1973), pp. 125-26; the final quotation is from Mao's "The Present Situation and Our Tasks," 25 December 1947, in Mao Tse-tung, *Selected Works of Mao Tse-tung* (Peking: Foreign Languages Press, 1961), vol. 4, p. 171.

25 *Punto Final* (Santiago), 5 January 1971.

30 years if necessary. Of course, nobody should be misled into believing that we will have to wait that long.[26]

This position—verbally similar to that taken by several pro-Soviet communist parties in Latin America and attacked by Castro in 1967—was probably behind the mid-year termination of regular radio broadcasts from Havana to revolutionaries in Venezuela and Chile.

After such single-minded support for guerrilla warfare during the OLAS period, and such unrestrained condemnations of those who did not follow their line, the Cuban leaders were obviously ill at ease for several years during their retreat. They felt themselves on the defensive, just as the leaders of the Communist Party of Venezuela (PCV) had felt themselves on the defensive during their "tactical retreat" from guerrilla warfare after 1966. Ironically, the Venezuelan guerrillas figured in the embarrassment this time too. Douglas Bravo, probably the best known guerrilla leader in Latin America and long a favorite of the Cubans, turned on Castro as he had turned on the PCV several years earlier, accusing the Cuban leader of selling out to the Soviet Union. After similar charges had been made by several other lesser castroite guerrillas, Castro shot back in April 1970:

> Cuba has not refused nor will she ever refuse support to the revolutionary movement. But this is not to be confused with support for just any faker [or for] destroyers of revolutions, men who had the opportunity to wage a revolutionary war, [but] instead sabotaged it and destroyed it. . . .
> That kind of pseudorevolutionary cannot count on any kind of help from Cuba, of course. Ah! But revolutionaries like Che, revolutionaries like Che who are ready to fight and die, this kind of revolutionary can always count on receiving aid from Cuba.[27]

Then he opened the door to Cuban support for very different kinds of movements and for existing Latin American governments by saying that

> as long as imperialism exists and as long as there are fighters ready to fight for the liberation of their peoples from that imperialism, the Cuban Revolution will lend its support. . . . When we speak of supporting a revolutionary movement we should say that that support does not necessarily have to be expressed exclusively in favor of guerrilla movements, but

---

[26] Speech of 14 July 1969, in *Granma* (Havana), 20 July 1969.
[27] Ibid., 3 May 1970.

37

includes any government which sincerely adopts a policy of economic and social development and of liberating its country from the Yankee imperialism yoke; no matter by what path that government has reached power, Cuba will support it.[28]

An editorial in *Granma* in mid-June 1972 set forth the Cuban attitude toward Latin American governments which remained in effect into the mid-1970s: "Our country is willing to establish relations with those governments that are independent and are willing to express and to show their conduct in real steps of sovereignty and national independence." [29]

The Fidel Castro talking to Mexican reporters in Havana in January 1975 was but a pale image of the fiery revolutionary of the OLAS days. The Cuban revolution, he claimed, had shown Latin Americans that it was possible to "resist imperialism." However, there were no immediate prospects for a thoroughgoing revolution in Latin America, such as had occurred in Cuba, since, though the objective conditions were present, the subjective were not, albeit there were "positive, progressive changes" taking place in several countries, including Mexico, Panama, Peru, and Venezuela. Unequivocal Cuban alignment with pro-Soviet policies in Latin America came at the June 1975 conference of communist parties in Havana and in Fidel Castro's address to the 25th CPSU Congress in Moscow in February 1976.[30]

Cuban Support for Revolution

The so-called "exportation of revolution" became a major controversial aspect of castroism as soon as the guerrillas took power in Cuba. On 14 February 1962, only ten days after Castro delivered his "Second Declaration of Havana," Venezuelan President Rómulo Betancourt, on the third anniversary of the beginning of his administration, condemned Venezuelan guerrillas who "receive arms and money from Communist Russia, through the branch office they have set up in Havana." [31] An OAS committee, which in December 1963 investigated charges against Cuba by the Betancourt government, reported in

---

[28] Ibid.

[29] Ibid., 18 June 1972.

[30] See *Excelsior* (Mexico City), 10 January 1975, and *Granma* (Havana), 7 March 1976, respectively.

[31] Quoted in Special Consultative Committee on Security, Organization of American States (OAS), *Initial General Report* (Washington, D.C.: OAS, 1962), p. 41.

early 1964 that "the Republic of Venezuela has been the target of a series of actions sponsored and directed by the Government of Cuba, openly intended to subvert Venezuelan institutions and to overthrow the democratic Government of Venezuela through terrorism, sabotage, assault, and guerrilla warfare." [32] This report led the OAS ministers of foreign relations to impose diplomatic and economic sanctions against Cuba in July 1964, resulting in a break in formal relations between Cuba and all Latin American countries except Mexico.

The first formal OAS move to reconsider this decision came in November 1974. Though the representatives of Uruguay and several other countries charged then that Cuba continued to support all forms of subversion, the majority of the ministers concluded that the sanctions were no longer justifiable. The resolution to lift the sanctions failed to gain approval of the two-thirds required for passage, however, and thus the 1964 decision remained in force at the end of 1974, though increasingly disregarded by Latin American governments. Sanctions were officially lifted by the OAS in July 1975.

In January 1975 Cuban Deputy Prime Minister Carlos Rafael Rodríguez tried to draw a distinction between exporting and aiding revolution:

> We have always talked about aiding revolution, never about exporting it. Cuba shall never renounce its right and its duty to cooperate with those who wish to change society, whenever such change is impossible by democratic means and above all whenever such change is deterred by the intervention of the United States and the CIA. In Paraguay's case, for example, we can give aid to the revolutionaries without sending armed forces. In Chile's case, naturally, we shall aid the revolutionaries with all our strength, to overthrow Pinochet's government. [33]

While Rodríguez was correct in saying that Cuban leaders have not talked about exporting revolution, the fact is that they have tried to do it. The first rather naive and unsuccessful efforts, in 1959, were directed

---

[32] "Resolutions Adopted at the Ninth Meeting of Consultation of Ministers of Foreign Affairs," in U.S. Congress, Senate, Committee on Foreign Affairs, *Inter-American Relations* (Washington, D.C.: U.S. Government Printing Office, 10 October 1972), pp. 189-93.

[33] *El Dia* (Mexico City), 26 January 1975. At the 25th Congress of the CPSU, Fidel Castro stated: "Nobody can export revolution or impose it by means of war," adding, however, that "nobody can prevent the peoples from making it, either, and the future belongs entirely to socialism and communism." *Granma* (Havana), 7 March 1976.

against dictators in Nicaragua, the Dominican Republic, and Haiti. The most important attempt was the Guevara-led insurgency in Bolivia in 1966 and 1967. In his introduction to Guevara's diary, Fidel Castro wrote that Che wanted beside him a "small nucleus of experienced guerrilla fighters, almost all of whom had been his comrades in the Sierra Maestra." The leading role of Guevara and the Cubans is made clear by all of the guerrilla diaries captured and published since 1967.[34] Furthermore, the one thing the major competing Bolivian leftists have agreed on is that Guevara gave them and other Bolivians no opportunity to lead the operation. Guevara's diary itself shows that for much of the time the majority of the guerrillas in the National Liberation Army (ELN) that Guevara established in Bolivia were Cubans (seventeen out of twenty-five in early June, for example) and that there was no support from the peasants and little from any other group in Bolivia.

At the same time, it is true that Cuban aid for foreign revolutionaries was much the more important issue over the years. In general terms Cuban leaders have long acknowledged giving aid to foreign revolutionaries. The November 1964 conference of Latin American communist parties, for example, promised "active aid" to guerrillas in several countries. On 18 May 1967, after several Cubans were found participating in a guerrilla landing on the coast of Venezuela, the Central Committee of the Cuban Communist Party, in one of the few statements it has ever made, issued a document that said: "We are accused of helping the revolutionary movement, and we, quite so, are giving and will continue to give help to all revolutionary movements that struggle against imperialism in any part of the world, whenever they request it." The statement argued that the United States was the real aggressor in Latin America and that Cuban help was merely to enable Latin Americans to liberate themselves from imperialism and its puppets.[35] On 22 April 1970, in response to charges from Douglas Bravo and other Latin American guerrillas that Cuba had stopped giving aid to revolutionaries, Castro argued (in the passage quoted earlier) that true revolutionaries could always count on receiving aid from Cuba. The most important Cuban contacts with Latin American guerrillas during the next few years occurred in Chile during the Allende period.

[34] See Daniel James, ed., *The Complete Bolivian Diaries of Che Guevara and Other Captured Documents* (New York: Stein and Day, 1968), which includes the complete diaries of Guevara and three of his Cuban aides.
[35] *Granma* (Havana), 21 May 1967.

Cuba's (to many observers unexpected) demonstration that it would honor this commitment to true revolutionaries came in late 1975 when the country sent some 12,000 troops to Angola to assist the revolutionary struggle of the People's Liberation Movement of Angola (MPLA). Referring to this Cuban assistance to the MPLA, the Cuban ambassador to the United Nations told that body's General Assembly in early October 1975 that as a result of the "scandalous interference" by "imperialists, colonialists and racists" in Angola, it was Cuba's "elementary duty to offer the people of Angola whatever aid is necessary to guarantee true independence and full sovereignty of their country." [36] As this action was under way in Angola, the "Constitution of the Republic of Cuba" was promulgated (February 1976), giving Cuba's official position on aid to revolutionaries around the world. According to the new constitution (Article 12), Cuba "espouses the principles of proletarian internationalism and of the combative solidarity of the peoples" and "recognizes the legitimacy of the wars of national liberation, as well as armed resistance to aggression and conquest; and considers that its help to those under attack and to the peoples for their liberation constitutes its internationalist right and duty." [37] Carlos Rafael Rodríguez elaborated on the new Cuban policy in a press conference in Mexico in late May 1976. According to the Mexico City daily *Excelsior* on 27 May Rodríguez said that Cuba would send troops to Latin America only if asked to do so by a government suffering from foreign invasion. He added that Cuba was not obliged to intervene even when this situation occurred. Before making its decision, the Cuban government would examine the type of aggression, who was being attacked, the problem in its international configuration, and what the repercussions of Cuban action would be.

Guerrilla training camps were set up in Cuba during the early 1960s, the main center being at Minas del Frio in the Sierra Maestra. The U.S. Central Intelligence Agency reported in April 1965 that the Cuban General Directorate of Intelligence (DGI), with Soviet advisors, had provided more than $1 million to Venezuelan guerrillas alone during the period from 1960 to 1964; at the time of the OLAS conference in 1967, the *Washington Post* reported that the DGI "is now spending $1.1 million a month to support stepped-up guerrilla warfare in Latin America," adding that "most of the money [is used] to train insurgents, with some

---

[36] Ricardo Alarcón, in ibid., 26 October 1975.
[37] *Granma* (Havana), 7 March 1976.

3,000 latinos already trained in Havana and returned to their native countries since Castro came to power."[38] Beginning in the mid-1960s serious attention was also given to training African revolutionaries.[39]

At the end of the decade, a defector from DGI, Orlando Castro Hidalgo, reported that that organization, under the leadership of Manuel Piñeiro, was responsible for providing money, intelligence training, false documents, travel arrangements, and contacts for trainees, while the Cuban Revolutionary Armed Forces (FAR) gave military instruction.[40]

According to Castro Hidalgo, potential students—from Africa as well as from Latin America—were screened more carefully after the guerrilla setbacks of 1967 and 1968, and Cuban officials, under increasing Soviet influence, decided not to send Cuban military leaders to assist revolutionary groups in foreign countries until a significant level of development had been reached and the Cubans had been invited to come by local leaders. As was noted earlier, Fidel Castro himself said on 22 April 1970 that a more careful and rigorous examination of self-professed revolutionaries would be necessary than in the past since some "fakers" had managed to get considerable Cuban assistance without deserving it.[41] A Cuban intelligence official who defected in London in late 1971 stated that Santiago (Chile) was the new base for Cuban support of Latin American revolutionaries, though this was immediately denied by the Allende government. Chile was nevertheless a center for castroite activity during the Allende period, in part because of the influential Chilean Movement of the Revolutionary Left (MIR) and in part because of the influx of castroite-nationalists from nearby Latin

---

[38] CIA report in U.S. Congress, House, Subcommittee on Inter-American Affairs, *Communism in Latin America* (Washington, D.C.: U.S. Government Printing Office, 1965), pp. 120-23. *Washington Post* account, by Carl T. Rowan, published on 18 June 1967. Also see the Juan de Onís article in *New York Times,* 2 August 1967. Some estimates of the number of guerrillas trained are several times 3,000.

[39] Che Guevara himself went to Africa before embarking on his Bolivian campaign. By early 1976, Cuban forces were reportedly located in varying numbers in Angola, the Congo (Brazzaville), Tanzania, Guinea, Equatorial Guinea, Guinea-Bissau, Somalia, and Sierra Leone; see *Washington Star,* 23 January 1976.

[40] The account of the former DGI official, Orlando Castro Hidalgo, is found in testimony before the U.S. Senate Internal Security Subcommittee, 16 October 1969, in *Communist Threat to the United States through the Caribbean,* Part 20 (Washington, D.C.: U.S. Government Printing Office, 1969), and in the more popularized story, *Spy for Fidel* (Miami: University of Miami Press, 1971). In December 1974 Piñeiro was appointed head of the Cuban Communist Party Central Committee Americas Department.

[41] *Granma* (Havana), 3 May 1970; see above.

American countries—particularly Uruguay, Argentina, Bolivia, and Brazil.

Cuba and the Socialist World

Cuban relations with the so-called socialist world between 1959 and 1976 were more complex than Cuban relations with countries in Latin America. These complexities, however, are not of major concern to the present study except insofar as they affected Cuba's Latin American policies and insofar as they affected Marxist-Leninist parties and strategies in Latin America. These relations will therefore be discussed only briefly here and again in other relevant parts of the volume.

Cuban attitudes toward the socialist world in general grew increasingly warm between 1959 and the missile crisis of October-November 1962, except for some Soviet-Cuban tension in early 1962 over Castro's purging of the old Soviet-line communist Aníbal Escalante. The Soviet response to the United States blockade of ships carrying offensive weapons to Cuba, with the removal of missiles installed on the island, had several important repercussions: (1) The Cuban government was deeply offended by the unilateral Soviet decision, and a suspicion of Soviet commitments and intentions seems to have colored Cuban judgments and policies throughout the remainder of the decade. However, Cuba's increasing dependence on the Soviet Union and Eastern Europe, and recognition that more support would be needed in the future, prevented a break even after this humiliating experience. (2) The reputation of the People's Republic of China was enhanced in the eyes of many Cubans by China's extensive and outspoken support for Castro's policies during and after the missile crisis. However, although many Cubans favored the general Chinese line on revolution over that of the Soviet Union, the Chinese were unable to meet the economic and military needs of the Cuban government. (3) The Soviet "betrayal" of the Cuban government also disillusioned many Latin American revolutionaries (including some in communist parties) on the subject of Soviet revolutionary commitments. For several years this strengthened the positions of both the castroite and emerging pro-Chinese revolutionary forces in Latin America.

During the next fifteen months, Castro took two trips to the Soviet Union (in April-May 1963 and January 1964), while taking none to China, and received Soviet commitments for substantial economic aid, high fixed prices on sugar purchases, and guarantees on defensive aid: in the Soviet Union he signed his name to ideological statements which could be interpreted as favoring the Soviet position in the Sino-Soviet dispute. In spite of this, the Cuban position on the dispute remained ambivalent until the November 1964 conference of communist parties in Havana. Here Cuba adopted a pro-Soviet stance by inviting only communist party members acceptable to the Soviet Union, by welcoming Soviet but not Chinese observers, and by accepting the Soviet-sponsored communiqué issued after the meeting.[42]

After Castro's two visits to the Soviet Union and the 1964 Havana conference, the Chinese grew more and more suspicious of his own commitments, despite his refusal to declare himself openly in favor of one side or the other. (From the Chinese perspective, refusal to join the conflict and denounce "revisionists" who had infiltrated the ranks of the revolutionaries was in itself a pro-Soviet position.) The serious split with the Chinese, described in the previous chapter, occurred during 1966. China and Cuba recalled ambassadors in 1967 and for four years there were no high-level diplomatic relations between the two countries. Cuban-Soviet relations also began to go downhill in 1966 and reached a low point in 1967–1968, as indicated elsewhere.

It is worth putting these problems of Soviet-Cuban and Sino-Cuban relations into perspective by noting the increasingly suspicious attitudes of Cuban leaders in international affairs in general during this period. These attitudes were reflected most clearly in Castro's speech to the OLAS delegates in Havana on 10 August 1967, when the Cuban prime minister attacked a wide variety of groups around the world that he said were plotting against him, against the Cuban revolution, and against Latin American guerrillas such as those represented that day in his audience. His condemnations were directed at (1) the U.S. government, allegedly responsible for sending CIA agents to subvert the Cuban revolution and assassinate him (eight Cubans charged with being such agents were put on display at the conference); (2) all Latin American countries (except Mexico) which in the OAS condoned "U.S. aggression" in the hemisphere while condemning "Cuban aggression," most recently in response to charges made in June 1967 by Venezuelan President Raúl Leoni; (3) the Communist Party of Venezuela, which had "betrayed" the Venezuelan revolution and allegedly

---

42 The communiqué was first released by TASS on 18 January 1965; the text is found in Appendix A.

44

was spearheading the attacks of other Latin American communist parties against Cuba; (4) other unnamed Latin American communist parties, whose ideas were so antiquated and dogmatic that they had ceased to be revolutionary; (5) the "socialist" governments (unnamed, but understood to be those of the Soviet Union and Eastern Europe) that gave aid to the "oligarchs" in Latin America and thus made the activities of the guerrilla forces more difficult; and (6) a "microfaction" in Cuba which had been "systematically opposed to all the concepts of the Revolution, to the deepest, sincerest, purest revolutionary attitudes of our people, to our concepts of socialism, of communism, of everything." [43] On 10 August Castro did not even bother to restate his ongoing objections to the anti-Cuban policies of the People's Republic of China.

Then in August 1968, to the discomfort of many of his followers around Latin America, Castro began his reentry into the pro-Soviet camp with his critical approval of the Soviet-led invasion and occupation of Czechoslovakia. On 23 August Castro defended his position as follows: (1) "Anything that begins to receive the praise, support or enthusiastic applause of the imperialist press naturally begins to arouse our suspicions." (2) "Czechoslovakia was moving toward a counter-revolutionary situation, toward capitalism and into the arms of imperialism. . . . We consider that it was absolutely necessary, at all costs, in one way or another, to prevent this eventuality from taking place." (3) "The decision made [by the Soviet Union and participating East European countries] concerning Czechoslovakia can only be explained from a political point of view, not from a legal point of view. Not the slightest trace of legality exists. . . . The sole justification can only be the simple political fact that Czechoslovakia was moving toward a counterrevolutionary situation and that this seriously affected the entire socialist community." [44]

At an international communist meeting in mid-1969, only a few weeks after the Sino-Soviet border clashes on the Ussuri River, a prominent Cuban leader placed his government more firmly behind the Soviet Union than ever before, though still without condemning China by name: "We declare from this rostrum that, in any decisive confrontation—whether concerning Soviet action in the face of the danger of the tearing off of members from the socialist system by imperialist

---

[43] *Granma* (Havana), 20 August 1967.
[44] Ibid., 25 August 1968.

maneuvers or concerning a provocation or aggression against the Soviet people, come from where it may—Cuba will unyieldingly be at the side of the USSR." [45]

In general international policies during the late 1960s, the Cubans agreed much more frequently with Chinese than with Soviet leaders, though this was seldom pointed out by any of the parties concerned. For example, on the international level, the Chinese and Cubans shared opposition, in varying degrees, to the Soviet views and positions on (1) the use of the nonarmed road for revolution in most countries; (2) on "peaceful coexistence"; (3) on the fundamental contradiction in the world, arguing that it was between "imperialism" and the national liberation movements of the underdeveloped world and not between imperialism and socialism, as the Soviet Union maintained; (4) on international agreements on limiting and banning of nuclear weapons, at least under existing conditions; and (5) on aid to Latin American "oligarchies." The Cuban refusal to side with the Chinese seems to have derived largely from the need for extensive economic and military aid, which the Chinese could not provide, and from Cuban concern lest advocates of armed revolution in Latin America might find their example in the Chinese rather than in the Cuban road.

As indicated elsewhere, Cuban relations with the Soviet Union became the closest ever during the period from 1970 to this writing in early 1976. This closeness was formalized in a five-point economic agreement announced by Fidel Castro on 3 January 1973. The agreement (1) stipulated that repayment of Soviet credits to Cuba between 1959 and January 1973 (estimated at over $4 billion, military aid excluded) was to be postponed until 1986, then repayable over a twenty-five year period without interest; (2) provided credits to cover Cuba's projected unfavorable trade balance with the Soviet Union over the period from 1973 to 1975, repayment due over twenty-five years without interest, beginning in 1986; (3) listed bilateral trade and extensive economic and technical assistance and collaboration; and (4) pledged that from 1973 to 1980 the Soviet Union would buy Cuban sugar at eleven cents per pound and buy Cuban nickel-cobalt products at $5,000 per ton. Further, new credits were made for investments, particularly in the nickel industry, repayable in twenty-five years at a

[45] Carlos Rafael Rodríguez, at the International Meeting of Communist and Workers' Parties in Moscow, May 1969; see ibid., 15 June 1969.

"very low interest rate." [46] Cuba's signature on the June 1975 statement of communist parties from Latin America marked Castro's complete political reentry into the Soviet camp. Addressing the 25th CPSU Congress on 25 February 1976, Fidel Castro said that Soviet society is "optimistic, victorious and confident" and that it "constantly progresses materially, socially and morally." He lauded the Soviet Union for inspiring all true revolutionaries around the world, defending the independence of small nations, upholding world peace, and generating humanitarian hopes for all mankind. In its international relations, the Soviet Union was a "model of internationalist practice, understanding, respect, and mutual confidence." Never in its dealings with the Cuban government had it demanded anything, put down any conditions, or tried to tell the Cubans what to do. "Never before in the history of international relations, long governed by self-interest and force, have such fraternal links been known to exist between a mighty and a weak nation. Only socialism can make possible this kind of ties between people." [47]

If by early 1976 Cuban praise of the Soviet Union was uncommonly ardent, criticism of the People's Republic of China was unrelenting. The June 1975 statement by Latin American communist parties contained, among other points, the first unequivocal condemnation of China by name to be endorsed by the Cubans since the height of the Sino-Cuban conflict in 1966. But it was Chinese policy toward Angola in late 1975 and early 1976, even more than Chinese relations with the military government in Chile, that set Cuban critics against the PRC. A *Granma* editorial on 27 January 1976 stated that "events in Angola have, with irrefutable facts, demonstrated to the world the disgraceful alliance between Maoists and the sworn enemies of the peoples' independence, sovereignty, equality, and progress." An editorial on 17 February argued that at last "the masks have fallen" and the entire world sees that "in word and in deed the Maoists coincide with the most rabid of imperialists, with dogged counterrevolutionaries and with the enemies of peace and of the liberation and progress of the peoples." In his talk to the CPSU Congress, Castro declared that "true history

---

[46] Ibid., 14 January 1973; also see ibid., 21 January. The estimate on Cuban economic indebtedness to the Soviet Union comes from *New York Times,* 5 January 1973. On 22 April 1970 Fidel Castro acknowledged that in ten years Cuba had received military aid from the Soviet Union valued at $1.5 billion; *Granma* (Havana), 3 May 1970.

[47] *Granma* (Havana), 7 March 1976.

47

will not be written by reactionaries, calumniators, intriguers or traitors, whether they go by the name of fascists, bourgeois or Maoists, because history itself will sweep them all away." [48]

Conclusions

Cuban analyses of Latin America, like the Chinese analyses, moved from broad support for guerrilla wars in the early 1960s through dogmatic insistence on a single national model in the middle and late 1960s to a much more flexible line in the 1970s. Policies during the first decade were in part the result of international pressures (by the United States) and rivalries (within the communist world), but above all they were a reflection of Fidel Castro's own revolutionary outlook. The Cuban leader was an impatient revolutionary. (The pro-Soviet and pro-Chinese communists frequently described his approach as typically "petty-bourgeois.") Despite their common advocacy of armed struggle, Castro's approach to revolutionary war was in marked contrast to the approach of Mao Tse-tung. The subtleties of revolutionary struggle (the importance of political training, clearly formulated political leadership of military operations, use of united front techniques to enhance mass support and isolate enemies) that helped to bring the Chinese communists to power in the world's most populous country were frequently brushed aside by Cuban revolutionaries. [49] In Marxist-Leninist terminology, "subjective" factors (such as consciousness, personal determination, boldness of action) were more strongly emphasized than "objective" factors (such as political, economic, and social conditions, available resources, and the like). For example, Castro stressed the importance of revolutionary initiative in an interview published by an Italian Communist Party weekly in September 1967, stating that a true revolutionary could probably start a revolution in a given country even if favorable objective conditions were missing. (In Cuba, he said, not all objective conditions had been favorable.) Conversely, if a

---

[48] The editorials of 27 January and 17 February are in ibid., 8 February and 29 February, respectively; Castro's speech is in ibid., 7 March.

[49] This tendency was manifested in Castro's nationalization of domestic as well as foreign industries in Cuba during 1959-1960. The communist People's Socialist Party (PSP), pointing to the Chinese communist example, argued that the skills of the bourgeois sectors of society should be utilized in the early stages of socialist transformation and construction. See, for example, Carlos Rafael Rodríguez, "Unidad Revolucionaria, Unidad Popular y Lucha de Clases," *Hoy* (Havana), 19 August 1960.

country had altogether favorable objective conditions, but lacked true revolutionaries, there would be no revolution.[50]

There is an important element of truth in this position. In a national situation characterized by dislocation and crisis, a well-organized elitist revolutionary group (which the castroites sought to be) acting with a decisiveness unmatched in other political sectors may indeed have a profound impact. (The prospects of this revolutionary course are improved if the group makes an appeal for mass support by proposing a moderate short-term program just as Lenin and the Bolsheviks did in 1917 and as Castro himself did during the late 1950s.) But the castroites pushed the revolutionary initiative line too far, particularly in 1967. Cuban leaders virtually disregarded individual national conditions and offered up what Venezuelan guerrilla leader Douglas Bravo correctly labeled "dogmatic little recipes" for revolution. None of the castroite spokesmen urged the use of moderate appeals (in which they did not then believe) to win the temporary support of a broad cross-section of the population, supporting instead a line that must be recognized as straightforward and honest if demonstrably ineffective. On this united front issue, the Cuban stand contrasted sharply with the stands of the Soviet Union and the Chinese, both of whom rejected the immediate use of armed struggle in most countries of Latin America during this period. The Soviet line called for broad participation in national affairs wherever possible; the Chinese line (even during its most dogmatic period) recognized the need for building a mass base through political actions; whereas the Cuban strategy was unambiguously elitist in expecting a little band of guerrillas (the small motor) to carry out armed vanguard actions that would set the masses (the large motor) in motion.

It is worth noting that during the period covered by this study, there was a great fluctuation in Cuban attitudes toward united fronts and cooperation with various sectors of Latin American society. Castro's own strategy before 1959 had called for and won broad support among the Cuban people. By the time of the "Second Declaration of Havana" (1962), however, Castro had turned on most members of that much-discussed sub-class, the national bourgeoisie. This sector had been nationalized out of existence in Cuba, against the strong recommendations of the communist PSP. Internationally, Cuba had begun its support for armed factions seeking the violent overthrow of the demo-

---

[50] *Rinascita* (Rome), 22 September 1967.

49

cratically elected national bourgeois government of Rómulo Betancourt in Venezuela; Castro's distrust of most members of the national bourgeoisie was expressed theoretically in the "Second Declaration."

The second half of the decade was the heyday of the rural guerrilla *foco,* an acknowledged elitist vanguard—Lenin had proclaimed the need for such a vanguard as early as 1902—which did not originally have but sought to attract mass support. The goal was to win the backing of the masses of the Latin American people, but the under-developed "objective" and "subjective" conditions in Latin America cast an aura of unreality about the Cuban objectives. The OLAS conference, which was intended to bring together representatives of all the "true revolutionaries" in Latin America—those who could rally mass support—very nearly degenerated into a case study of paranoia with Castro's concluding speech. As Castro's perception of Latin American conditions changed between the late 1960s and 1975, and as his government came under increasing domestic and international pressures, particularly at the turn of the decade, the Cuban government saw some revolutionary potential in a much broader cross-section of Latin Americans than before.

The exclusively rural-oriented OLAS castroism, which had its origins in the Cuban revolution (though it was a distortion of the Cuban experience), proved ineffective in some countries and in others disastrous for the guerrillas themselves. The castroite rural guerrillas were nonetheless one of several important influences on the urban guerrillas who emerged in Uruguay, Brazil, Argentina, and several other countries during the late 1960s, providing examples of productive and unproductive modes of operation. Urban-oriented guerrilla struggle, which was developed largely by South American fighters themselves, drew varying degrees of support from Fidel Castro. By 1976 the castroite element in Cuban foreign policy seemed insignificant in comparison to the OLAS years, which is not to deny Cuba's openly hostile attitude toward several Latin American governments during the mid-1970s.

The Cuban intervention in Angola was not so much exportation of revolution (as had occurred in Bolivia under Guevara) as massive assistance, similar in principle but not scope to the aid provided to Venezuelan guerrillas in the early 1960s. Indeed, the intervention was in many respects similar to North Vietnamese involvement in South Vietnam during the 1960s and early 1970s, except that the Cubans in

Angola (like the Americans in Vietnam) were an ocean away from home. By early 1976 Cuban participation in this foreign "war of national liberation" had caused quiet concern among many Latin Americans and, along with Cuban support for the independence of Puerto Rico, had led to a renewal of open tensions between the governments of Cuba and the United States.

3

Pro-Soviet Parties in Latin America

Every Marxist-Leninist group in Latin America was influenced directly or indirectly by the policies and activities of the Soviet, Chinese, and Cuban governments during all or part of the period from 1959 to 1976. Their own positions, successes, and failures were, however, determined in large part by conditions in their individual countries. This chapter will pull together the international and domestic factors in an examination of the development and activities of the various self-professed communist organizations in Latin America during the 1960s and early 1970s.

Background

The pro-Soviet communist parties were the most numerous and varied, though not always the most important, of the Marxist-Leninist groups in Latin America between 1959 and 1976. In most countries they were essentially the pre-1959 communist parties in organization and leadership. During the 1950s Chinese communist efforts to win the friendship of the Latin American communists had been remarkably successful without causing overt anti-Soviet manifestations. But, with the emergence of the Sino-Soviet conflict, several years of ties with the Chinese Communist Party (CCP) could not offset decades of close relationship with the CPSU and the numerous advantages the close relationship brought with it.

Throughout their histories, the outstanding characteristics of the Latin American communist parties had been their loyalty and subservience to the Soviet Union on international relations and their willingness to accept Soviet tutelage in domestic affairs when it was provided. In 1951 a prominent Brazilian communist novelist wrote that "love for the Soviet Union is like a grandiose summation of all that a man can love on earth, a summation of all the great sentiments, the purest and most noble. . . . I do not know how one can conceive today of a true patriot who does not at the same time love the Soviet Union with the deepest love." [1] Such obsequiousness, common enough before 1945, did not emerge often during the period from 1959 to 1976, though Uruguayan Communist Party (PCU) support for the Soviet invasion of Czechoslovakia in 1968 was such as to lead Giuliano Pajetta, a member of the Central Committee of the Italian Communist Party who had just visited Uruguay, to write that the PCU was "more Catholic than the Pope." [2] Luis Corvalán, secretary-general of the Communist Party of Chile, said he preferred the term "sovietinchas" to "prosovieticos" in describing the PCCh and its relations with the Soviet Union, the former term suggesting the relationship of a fan or supporter.[3] Although there have been a few examples of opposition to the Soviet line within pro-Soviet parties, the exceptions tend mainly to emphasize the high degree of overall conformity. Only the parties of Mexico and the Dominican Republic, the former demonstrating a strong tendency toward independence and the latter toward castroism, refused to endorse the Soviet-led occupation of Czechoslovakia, though the occupation did eventually lead to a split in the Communist Party of Venezuela. The Dominican Communist Party alone refused to sign the main document of the 1969 International Meeting of Communist and Workers' Parties, though several other parties expressed reservations on certain points.

It is probably accurate to say that Latin American communists were generally free to determine their own domestic strategy and tactics during the period from 1959 to 1976, but this statement must be seen in its proper perspective. Almost all prominent communist leaders in Latin America owed their positions to training and support received from the CPSU. They knew very well the extent—sometimes considerable—of their freedom and did not usually go beyond it. When they went too far, the CPSU interfered to assure their contrition or expulsion

---

[1] The novelist was Jorge Amado, in *O mundo da paz* (Rio de Janeiro: Vitória, 1952), pp. 16-17; the translation is from Poppino, *International Communism in Latin America*, p. 167.

[2] Pajetta's comments were published in *Acción* (Montevideo), 6 November 1968.

[3] *El Siglo* (Santiago), 1 February 1973.

from the party. The most frequent cases of disciplining were those of pro-Chinese dissidents, and, in practice, these elements, finding the majority of the party leaders unresponsive to their efforts, often withdrew on their own to form a rival party—a point discussed below. In some countries, such as Brazil and Peru, important party members were among those rejected for pro-Chinese sympathies. Two other situations require special attention: the incidents in Paraguay during the mid-1960s and in Venezuela between 1968 and 1970.

In 1965 the CPSU backed the organization of a commission of pro-Soviet Paraguayan communists which in 1967 expelled the Paraguayan Communist Party (PCP) secretary-general, Oscar Creydt, from the party. The long-time leader was accused of being too lenient with dissident pro-Chinese members of the party and of acting in a high-handed and dictatorial manner in the conduct of party affairs. In February 1968 Creydt released a message to Fidel Castro expressing his support for Castro's prosecution of the pro-Soviet "microfaction" in Cuba, taking the opportunity to condemn Soviet intervention in his own party.[4] Following the endorsement of the 1968 occupation of Czechoslovakia by the Communist Party of Venezuela (PCV), the conflict within the party came into the open, appearing first in two books by Teodoro Petkoff, popularly dubbed the Venezuelan Roger Garaudy. Petkoff condemned the Soviet Union for its invasion of Czechoslovakia, for the crushing of a fruitful experiment in decentralized, flexible, and nationally oriented socialism. He wrote that the PCV was bureaucratic and authoritarian ("Stalinist") and called upon the party to modify or abandon its erroneous interpretation of the stages of revolution, class alliances, the vanguard role of the communist party, freedom of discussion, and democratic centralism. By the end of 1970, when the PCV split, Petkoff had been joined by five members of the PCV Politburo, twenty-two members of the Central Committee, a substantial portion of the party membership, and the vast majority of the communist youth. The CPSU actively supported the "loyal" PCV members led by the party's secretary-general, Jesús Faría.[5]

[4] On the Creydt affair, see *Yearbook on International Communist Affairs* [hereafter *YICA*] *1966* (Stanford: Hoover Institution Press, 1966), pp. 243-44; *YICA 1968*, pp. 463-65; *YICA 1969*, pp. 659-63. On the Cuba "microfaction," see *YICA 1969*, pp. 191-92.

[5] The most important of several Soviet attacks on the dissenters was a long article by A. Mosinev, published in *Pravda* (Moscow), 20 October 1970, and reprinted in the PCV paper *Tribuna Popular*, 5 November. The *Pravda* article appeared immediately after the arrival in Caracas of Rudolf Shlyapnikov, a man Raúl

When splits occurred in the Latin American communist parties in the 1960s, most old-time communist leaders—and old-timers led most of the parties—had a variety of reasons for retaining their allegiance to the Soviet Union. The vast majority had a decided preference for the moderate domestic strategy generally encouraged by Soviet leaders, rather than the more radical strategies proposed by the Chinese and the Cubans. This preference derived from their own training in the Soviet Union and from their experiences in Latin America. Furthermore, some leaders had held important positions in the Communist International and the Communist Information Bureau or, more recently, in several of the Soviet-controlled international front organizations (such as the World Federation of Trade Unions or the World Peace Council). Most high- and some intermediate-level party members had taken or expected to take all-expense-paid trips through Europe and the Soviet Union. When in trouble at home, party leaders in the past had found comfortable refuge in Soviet bloc countries. The CPSU had in the past provided training and other forms of tangible aid to their parties. Thus, Latin American communists had little incentive to turn against the Soviet Union when the Sino-Soviet and Cuban-Soviet disputes erupted.

Party Organization

During the years under consideration, Latin American communist parties maintaining relations with the Communist Party of the Soviet Union—most of them outspokenly pro-Soviet in the Sino-Soviet dispute—existed in all of the Caribbean, Central American, and South American republics, including Guyana (until 1966 the British dependent territory of British Guiana). Variations in size, strength, and success

Castro had accused of interfering in Cuban affairs in 1968. His presence in Venezuela was widely interpreted as Soviet interference in PCV affairs. Eleazar Díaz Rangel—until December 1970 a member of the central committee of the PCV and the executive committee of the Soviet-front International Organization of Journalists—wrote that PCV leaders had taken the signal from the Soviet Union in their moves against Petkoff. See my article in Ratliff, ed., *Yearbook on Latin American Communist Affairs* [hereafter *YLACA*] (Stanford: Hoover Institution Press, 1972), pp. 158-67.

For examples of Soviet interference in Latin American communist affairs between 1919 and the 1950s, see Robert J. Alexander, "Impact of the Sino-Soviet Split on Latin American Communism," in Donald L. Herman, ed., *The Communist Tide in Latin America* (Austin: University of Texas Press, 1973), pp. 35-38.

over the years were great from one country to another and within a single country from one time to another.

Legal status was often a meaningless measure for pro-Soviet communist parties in Latin America during the period from 1959 to 1976. Some parties were legal and active during all or most of the period, while others were illegal and forcibly suppressed. Most parties were somewhere in between. Several were legal all or part of the period but restricted in electoral and other activities; others were illegal, proscribed, outlawed, yet relatively free to participate in national affairs. Consider these few examples:

(1) The communist parties of Mexico and Colombia, which were legal throughout the period but prevented from participating fully in national affairs by national legislation.

(2) The communist parties of Chile and Uruguay, the most active and important in South America during most of the seventeen-year period, both of which were legal until 1973.

(3) The communist parties in Venezuela, Argentina, Bolivia, and Ecuador, all of which were legal for approximately half the period, though the practical significance of legality varied greatly. (Contrast, for example, the numerous restrictions placed on the party in Argentina during the early 1960s with the freedom exercised by the party in Venezuela in the 1970s.)

(4) The communist parties in Costa Rica, Brazil, and Peru, illegal for all or most of the period, which nonetheless acted at times with considerable freedom and effectiveness—the Brazilian party during the early 1960s and the other two during the 1970s.

(5) The communist parties in Haiti, Guatemala, and Paraguay, which were actively suppressed throughout the period.

It is particularly difficult to determine the size of the Marxist-Leninist parties examined in this volume. Most do not publish their membership figures and if they do the claims must be viewed with considerable skepticism. Any party seeking to extend its influence and enhance its national reputation is tempted to inflate its membership figures. At times published claims are obviously contradictory or imprecise, or highly improbable, or a combination of these.[6] Even when

---

[6] For example, Luis Corvalán claimed the Communist Party of Chile had "250,000 or so" members in early 1972 (*El Siglo* [Santiago], 13 February), while Orlando Millas claimed 120,000 three months later (ibid., 21 May).

Table 1
ESTIMATES OF COMMUNIST PARTY SIZE, BY COUNTRY

Country	1959	1963	1966	1969	1973
Argentina	70–80,000	40–50,000	60,000	60,000	70,000
Bolivia	4,000	4–5,000	4,000	4,000	1,500
Brazil	50,000	30,000	20,000	15,000	6,000
Chile	20–25,000	25–30,000	30,000	45,000	120,000
Colombia	5,000	10–12,000	10,000	8,000	10,000
Costa Rica	300	300	450	600	1,000
Ecuador	1,000	2–3,000	1,000	750	500
El Salvador	1,000	500	200	200	125
Guatemala	1,200	1,300	1,000	750	750
Honduras	400	2,000	1,300	300	300
Mexico	5,000	3,000	5,000	5,000	5,000
Nicaragua	200	2–300	200	200	100
Panama	—	3–500	500	250	500
Paraguay	500	3–4,000	5,000	5,000	3,500
Peru	6,000	8–9,000	2,000	2,000	2,000
Uruguay	5,000	10,000	15,000	21,000	22,000
Venezuela	40,000	30,000	10,000	5,000	8,000

Source: U.S. Department of State, *World Strength of the Communist Party Organizations* (Washington, D.C., 1960, 1964, 1967, 1970, 1974).

the figures are accurate, they undoubtedly include many persons (perhaps a majority) who are only nominal members. Often a party simply states that membership went up "X" percent from an unspecified figure, or that "Y" number of persons joined during a given period. The Bureau of Intelligence and Research (INR) of the U.S. Department of State published annual estimates of communist party memberships during most of the period covered by this book. Though the INR figures are only informed guesses and have been questioned by some qualified observers—even within the State Department—they furnish the best systematic impression available of communist party size at various times in individual countries between 1959 and 1974.[7]

---

[7] *World Strength of the Communist Party Organizations,* published annually for twenty-six years, was terminated in 1974. Some current estimates are found in the *YICA,* published since 1966 by the Hoover Institution, Stanford University, and in the Central Intelligence Agency's *National Basic Intelligence Factbook.*

These parties, like other "vanguards of the proletariat" discussed in this volume, were led mainly by petit-bourgeois intellectuals. They were based in urban centers and sometimes reported that a substantial portion of their rank and file was made up of workers. (In 1970 the communist parties of Chile and Uruguay claimed to have membership that was respectively 68 and 73 percent made up of workers.) Most theorized about the peasants but did not work extensively or effectively with them, in part because non-communist or anti-communist influence was often strong in the countryside and political organization there more difficult than in the urban areas.

Party Activities

Most Latin American communist parties directed their greatest attention toward workers and intellectuals, particularly in the labor unions and the universities. Considering the size of the communist parties, these efforts were impressively effective in several countries and showed varying degrees of marginal success in others.

Labor. A number of generally interrelated factors determined the success of the labor activities of the pro-Soviet communist parties in Latin America. These were (1) the extent of industrialization in a country or region of a country; (2) the movement of persons from rural areas to the cities; (3) the level of "proletarian consciousness" among workers; (4) the extent of unionization; (5) the absence or presence of a powerful non-communist or anti-communist labor movement as an alternative; (6) the unity or conflict within the communist movement in a given country; (7) the degree of freedom granted the communist party and its labor leaders by the existing governments; (8) the productivity of a communist-dominated labor organization once it reached an influential national position; and (9) the nature and extent of international support for or opposition to its labor activities.

Pro-Soviet communist party participation in formally organized labor activities during this period was most extensive and effective in Chile, Uruguay, and Peru; it was of less importance but worthy of note in Argentina, Bolivia, Colombia, Ecuador, Venezuela, Guyana, and Costa Rica. Though pro-Soviet labor activities may become important in some other countries (such as El Salvador) in the future,

59

during the years from 1959 to 1976 in these countries they were difficult to isolate and measure with any accuracy.

In Uruguay, the Communist Party of Uruguay (PCU) dominated the major labor confederations operating throughout the period from 1964 to 1973—both the Workers' Center of Uruguay (CTU) and, after its formation in 1966, the National Convention of Workers (CNT). Though most CNT members were not communists, the PCU dominated the decision-making offices. Before being outlawed in mid-1973, the CNT was active in opposing government economic and labor policies, chiefly through calling nationwide strikes and labor stoppages. During the years of greatest guerrilla activity in Uruguay, particularly between 1969 and 1971, a militant faction challenged but never took control away from the PCU leaders. In 1966 and 1968 the Uruguayan government expelled Soviet embassy officials for their alleged involvement in labor affairs. In 1969 CNT Secretary Enrique Pastorino was made president of the Soviet-front World Federation of Trade Unions (WFTU), the first Latin American to hold this position. He retained the office into 1976.

In Peru, the Communist Party of Peru (PCP) formed the General Confederation of Workers (CGTP) in 1968. By 1972, the CGTP was probably nearing the size of the older Confederation of Workers of Peru (CTP). The CGTP, which claimed some 350,000 members in 1973, faced a government-sponsored rival in the newly formed Central Organization of Workers of the Peruvian Revolution (CTRP) and some extremist opposition within the CGTP. Following the PCP lead, the CGTP generally supported the policies of the Peruvian military government, but expressed serious reservations about the CTRP and the government's older and by 1976 virtually defunct National System of Support for Social Mobilization (SINAMOS), both of which were clearly regarded as competitors for influence among the Peruvian people.

Pro-Soviet communist parties in several other countries had a more limited effect on their national labor movements. In Argentina, the major trade union organization, the General Confederation of Labor (CGT), was run by the Peronists. The Communist Party of Argentina (PCA) controlled the much smaller Movement for Trade Union Unity (MUCS), which was active chiefly in Córdoba and Mendoza. In Bolivia, the two major unions rose and fell in influence as more or less sympathetic presidents seized control in the country. The Communist Party of Bolivia (PCB) was active in both the Mineworkers Federation of Bolivia (FSTMB) and the Bolivian Workers' Center (COB) but did not control either. In Colombia, the Communist Party of Colombia (PCC) controlled the Confederation of Workers of Colombia (CSTC), whose claimed membership increased from some 150,000 in the mid-1960s to more than 200,000 in 1975, though it should be noted that by the mid-1970s there was considerable dissension within the CSTC, having its origins in the Chinese-oriented Independent Revolutionary Workers Movement (MOIR).[8]

In Venezuela, the Communist Party of Venezuela (PCV) controlled the United Workers Confederation of Venezuela (CUTV), a small but often active member of the national union movement. The CUTV was weakened by the split within the PCV in 1970. In Ecuador, the Communist Party of Ecuador (PCE) was the main force in the Confederation of Ecuadorian Workers (CTE), which claimed 60,000 members in the mid-1970s, and in several small rural unions. In Costa Rica, the People's Vanguard Party (PVP) controlled the small General Confederation of Costa Rican Workers (CGTC). And in Guyana, labor activities of Cheddi Jagan's People's Progressive Party (PPP) were carried out chiefly among workers in the sugar industry by the Guyanan Agricultural Workers' Union (GAWU).

Youth. Marxist-Leninists in Latin America paid close attention to the youth of their countries, particularly to the university students. Not only were these students the national leaders of the future, but in some cases they were influential in national affairs during their student days. During the 1960s and early 1970s their activities ranged from leading guerrilla struggles to serving in national legislatures. Furthermore, a significant minority of university students, especially in the state (as contrasted to private and Catholic) universities, were political activists who thought in leftist—often Marxist-Leninist—terms. These students were frequently idealistic, intolerant of delay, and unencumbered by inhibiting responsibilities.

Students of varying shades of Marxism-Leninism were assisted in many countries by several additional factors. The autonomy of state universities in some countries, an outgrowth of decades of university reform throughout Latin America, made the campuses havens which could not be entered by law enforcement officials. Also, because of

---

[8] See Daniel Premo, "Colombia," *YICA 1976*, p. 457.

the principle of "co-government" at most universities, which gave students strong representation on governing bodies, Marxist-Leninist activists were sometimes able to advance their own interests by intimidating faculty members or by preventing the expulsion of "professional students" who remained on campus for a decade or more mainly as political agitators.

The receptivity of students to Marxism-Leninism was noted by Latin American Marxist-Leninists in their writings and in practice. The late pro-Soviet communist and poet from Central America, Roque Dalton García, observed in 1966 that whereas Latin American workers had often been slow to take part in the revolutionary struggle, students had shown a "high degree of socio-political activity." [9] This phenomenon made some orthodox members of the "vanguard of the proletariat" uneasy, and Dalton himself noted some of the problems. Yet, potential problem or not, Latin American communists exploited this human resource on every possible occasion. A prominent pro-Soviet communist in Venezuela even went so far as to brag that his party could mobilize 20,000 students in Caracas and "move them to all battle fronts" in twenty-four hours.[10]

Pro-Soviet communists were most consistently effective in reaching the youth of Chile, Venezuela, and Uruguay, though there were periods and pockets of influence in Colombia and several other countries. The high and low points of the activities toward students (usually undertaken by the parties' youth organizations) were frequently determined as much by cooperation or conflicts with other Marxist-Leninist groups as by competition with non-communist groups in the universities.

Venezuela presented an important example in the mid-1960s when the communist party was carrying out a guerrilla war against the Betancourt and Leoni governments. During these years the Venezuelan Communist Youth (JCV) attracted young persons, particularly university students, who supported armed struggle in the countryside; it controlled much of university politics at the Central University in Caracas in alliance with the youth of the Movement of the Revolutionary Left (MIR). During the late 1960s, after the PCV had abandoned the guerrilla road, the JCV split with the MIR youth and, alone or in alliance with other leftist groups, retained a dominant position in

---

[9] In "Student Youth and the Latin-American Revolution," *World Marxist Review,* vol. 9, no. 3 (March 1966), p. 55.
[10] Eduardo Machado, *Nueva Voz Popular* (Caracas), 30 May 1968.

the universities. At the end of 1970 the JCV controlled the Federations of University Centers (FEU) in five of the country's eight universities. When the PCV split at the end of 1970, however, most of the young people abandoned the pro-Soviet PCV and joined the dissidents in the Movement toward Socialism (MAS).

In Uruguay, the Union of Communist Youth (UJC) played an important and sometimes dominant role in the Federation of University Students of Uruguay (FEUU), worked among secondary school students, and supported labor strikes and work stoppages. Like its parent party, the UJC was mildly critical of the urban guerrillas who were active in Uruguay during the late 1960s and early 1970s. Its activities were curtailed by the government in 1973.

In Colombia, the Communist Youth of Colombia (JCC) exerted some influence in university politics but at times found its effectiveness lessened by disputes among its own members and differences with the parent Communist Party of Colombia (PCC). Many of the youth objected to PCC support for the Soviet occupation of Czechoslovakia in 1968, and in 1970 the influence of "ultra-left" youth caused the JCC to oppose the PCC on other issues, including electoral participation. During the 1970s, the JCC repeatedly criticized disunity among leftist youth, aiming its attacks mainly at so-called Trotskyists and Maoists.

Pro-Soviet youth groups were present in other Latin American countries, though their effectiveness was often limited by their small size or by dissension among students of the left. In Argentina the Communist Youth Federation (FJC) was torn by fierce internal struggles in the late 1960s; by 1975 it had recouped its forces somewhat, and claimed nearly 60,000 members, but remained largely overshadowed by the Peronist youth. Pro-Soviet communist youth were important in carrying out and ending the student strikes in Mexico in 1968. A degree of influence was present in Guyana, where the Progressive Youth Organization was always a major source of personal support for Cheddi Jagan, and in Costa Rica and Panama.

Strategy and Tactics

The strategies and tactics of the communist parties in Latin America were determined in varying degrees by the international policies of the Soviet Union, the People's Republic of China, and Cuba, and by the enormously contrasting conditions and revolutionary opportunities existing at different times in the area. Considering the complex problems of political, economic, and social change in the individual countries, and the diverse assumptions and levels of Marxist-Leninist understanding of the revolutionaries and the people at large, it is not surprising that a variety of contrasting and often conflicting analyses came from the pro-Soviet and other groups.

The differences were usually played down during the early 1960s for several reasons: (1) the Soviet Union was willing to endorse armed struggle in some countries and prepared to condone it in others, while pro-Soviet parties at times took an active part in guerrilla operations; (2) the Chinese endorsed the "Cuban road" for revolution in Latin America and had not yet begun calling for the formation of pro-Chinese (Marxist-Leninist) splinter parties; and (3) the Cubans had not yet become so all-encompassing as they later became in their calls for armed struggle in Latin America. Between the mid-1960s and the early 1970s each group set forth its own distinctive strategy while virtually excommunicating the other two groups from the revolutionary camp. Intra-Marxist-Leninist conflicts decreased but did not disappear in the mid-1970s.

Throughout the years of maximum feasible dissension, the pro-Soviet parties generally demonstrated a greater degree of theoretical and practical flexibility than any of the other Marxist-Leninists. They were quicker to adapt their policies to new conditions or (from a hostile perspective) it might be said they sometimes flip-flopped from one line to another, lacking the persistence, confidence, and devotion to principle apparently reflected in the policies of the Maoists and the castroites. In the pages that follow, the pro-Soviet communist positions will be presented through an examination of attitudes and activities with respect to four fundamental issues: the nature and stages of revolution, the roads to power, revolutionary leadership, and the united front.

Stages of Revolution. The pro-Soviet parties almost always called for a revolution in two stages: the first to overthrow imperialism and domestic reaction (that is, the oligarchic, semifeudal, and monopoly-capitalist forces)—a bourgeois democratic or national liberation revolution—and the second to establish socialism. A typical statement of this line was presented in the general resolution of the 20th Congress of the Communist Party of Uruguay (in December 1970), which declared that the socioeconomic transformation in Latin America was to be understood as "consisting of two stages, anti-imperialist and socialist," which must be differentiated from each other, but which formed part of a "single and continuous revolutionary process." [11]

Roads to Power. According to the pro-Soviet parties, the first stage of the revolution could be carried out, and the second stage reached, through armed struggle, nonarmed struggle, or a combination of the two. Party officials were frequently put on the defensive by Maoist and castroite groups when they opted for the nonarmed road, prompting them to warn repeatedly against automatically discounting any particular form of struggle.

Nonarmed struggle. The nonarmed road for the most part involved labor and student activities (described above) and electoral participation. Pro-Soviet parties almost always took part in elections when they were permitted to do so. When their open participation was prevented by legal barriers, they often went to great lengths to work with other political groups (usually only small ones were willing) in electoral alliances; thus communist candidates often sought and occasionally won office under some other banner than their own. Communists held elected offices at one time or another during the period from 1959 to 1976 in about half the Latin American countries, though they rarely gained more than token representation in local, departmental, or national councils or legislatures.

Though many pro-Soviet communist parties followed what was basically a nonarmed line with little or no success, two parties could regularly count on a substantial amount of popular support in national elections and three made concerted and relatively effective efforts to employ the nonarmed road in carrying out the national liberation revolution. The most important Latin American communist party experiences with the nonarmed road are reviewed below, with the exception of the Chilean party, which is covered in detail in Chapter 7.

The People's Progressive Party (PPP) of Guyana, founded in 1950 by Cheddi Jagan and others, occupies a unique position among pro-Soviet parties in Latin America. At its first congress in 1951 it declared itself a nationalist party committed to national independence and the construction of socialism. Within two years, however, ideological and ethnic divisions began to split the organization, leading to the formation of the rival People's National Congress (PNC) under

---

[11] *Estudios* (Montevideo), January-February 1971.

the leadership of Forbes Burnham. From 1957 to 1964 the PPP was the ruling party in British Guiana. In the 1964 election the PPP won a plurality of the votes (46 percent). However, a new law passed by the government of Great Britain required a legislature determined by proportional representation. Since no other party would work with the primarily East Indian PPP, the PNC, now the chief opposition party, formed a united front government with the conservative United Force Party. The PNC presided over independence celebrations in 1966 (when the country became Guyana) and has ruled without interruption into 1976. The PPP won 37 percent of the vote in 1968 and 26 percent in 1973, though Jagan charged that innumerable electoral irregularities had occurred and until mid-1976 boycotted all parliamentary activities. Though some PPP leaders admitted to being Marxist-Leninists from the beginning, and party policy on international affairs always paralleled that of the Soviet Union, most of the rank and file were not Marxists. The PPP was not officially affiliated with the international communist movement until 1969 when Cheddi Jagan made an unequivocal move to align the party with the CPSU. After that Soviet leaders recognized the PPP as a bona fide communist party. Jagan's move was apparently made without the knowledge or approval of most other PPP officials and it led to some defections and expulsions from the party.

A number of communist parties in other countries have put up candidates for political office. The following data give some idea of the nature and importance of communist electoral activities.

The two most important experiments with the nonarmed road after Guyana were in Chile and Uruguay. The Communist Party of Uruguay (PCU) won 2.6 percent of the vote in 1958 and slowly increased its number of supporters over the next thirteen years. In 1962 the party led in the formation of the Leftist Liberation Front (FIDEL), a grouping of small leftist organizations that served as the main vehicle for the party's participation in national elections before the formation of the Broad Front (FA) in 1971. FIDEL never drew many votes away from the National (Blanco) and Colorado parties which had dominated Uruguayan politics for decades; in 1962 FIDEL won 3.5 percent of the vote and in 1966 5.7 percent. Inspired in large part by the Chilean Popular Unity experience of 1970, the PCU turned to broad united front participation in 1971 when it joined the FA—an alliance of leftist parties, movements, and individuals that was much more broadly representative of the Uruguayan people than FIDEL had ever been by itself. In 1971 the PCU adopted the FA program as its own minimum program. Among its objectives were (1) the lifting of government security measures against the Tupamaro guerrillas; (2) full autonomy for all educational establishments; (3) agrarian reform; (4) nationalization of banks and foreign trade; (5) termination of dealings with the International Monetary Fund; (6) establishment of commercial and diplomatic relations with all countries; (7) an end to prices and income control; and (8) return of the police force to its "civilian" functions.[12] At the beginning of 1971 a survey by the University of the Republic showed that between 25 and 30 percent of the electorate contemplated voting for the FA. However, after a campaign which gained the tacit support of the Tupamaros, the election on 28 November found the FA winning only 18 percent of the vote, still a respectable total in an electoral system that discourages voting for candidates on minority party tickets. FIDEL's share of the vote was 6.1 percent; several top PCU officials, including Secretary-General Rodney Arismendi, were elected to the national congress.

The Communist Party of Argentina (PCA) did not have many congressional seats between 1959 and 1976 since civilian government in Argentina was sporadic and the party was rarely free to run its candidates in elections. In February 1958 the party supported the presidential candidacy of Arturo Frondizi (in power from 1958 to 1962), though it turned against the new president shortly after his inauguration when he reversed his electoral promises. The party supported Peronist candidates in the March 1962 election and called on the people to abstain in the presidential election of July 1963 which brought Arturo Illia to power. (Illia was in power from 1963 to 1966.) The next election, held in March 1973, found the PCA a part of the Revolutionary People's Alliance (APR), which won 7.4 percent of the vote. Two communists won seats in the Chamber of Deputies, though their membership in the PCA was not widely known before the election. At its 14th National Congress in August 1973 the PCA decided to support the candidacy of Juan Perón in the presidential election the following month.

The Communist Party of Venezuela (PCV) was active in efforts to overthrow the government of Marcos Pérez Jiménez that proved

---

[12] See FA program in *El Popular* (Montevideo), 18 February 1971, and statement by FA presidential candidate General Líber Seregni, in ibid., 26 August.

successful in January 1958. The party was strongly opposed to the Democratic Action (AD) party's presidential candidate in the December 1958 election and, in an unsuccessful effort to bring about his defeat, supported the candidacy of Admiral Wolfgang Larrazábal, the head of the provisional junta that had ruled the country during 1958. In the December election the PCV won 4.8 percent of the vote nationwide, but took a high 16.5 percent in the Federal District, a better showing there than was registered by the AD. PCV relations with the Betancourt government (1959–1964) went from bad to worse. Together with dissidents from the AD, known as the Movement of the Revolutionary Left (MIR), the PCV engaged in urban terrorism, which led to "suspension" of its legal status in May 1962, and soon thereafter openly adopted the road of guerrilla warfare against the government. In April 1967 the party decided on a "temporary" retreat from guerrilla warfare and set out to regain its legal position, which it did in March 1969. The PCV participated in the 1968 election under the banner of the Union for Advancement (UPA), drawing only 2.8 percent of the popular vote. The PCV was seriously weakened in 1970 by internal conflict, a large group of dissidents breaking away to form the Movement toward Socialism (MAS).[13] In the December 1973 election the PCV took 1.1 percent of the vote and the MAS received 5.2 percent.

In Colombia, the Communist Party of Colombia (PCC) was disqualified from running its own candidates by the National Front agreement, implemented in 1958 and binding until 1974, which stated that only a member of the Liberal or Conservative Party could hold elected office. The agreement was amended in 1968 to allow other parties to run members on their own tickets for departmental assemblies and municipal councils. During the early 1960s the PCC sought to influence elections through the left wing of the Liberal Party, particularly within the Liberal Revolutionary Movement (Movimiento Revolucionario Liberal, or MRL) which operated separately from the Liberal Party between 1962 and 1967 under the leadership of Alfonso López Michelsen. When López Michelsen rejoined the Liberals in 1967, taking most of the MRL with him, the PCC was left to work with a rump of dissidents, the Liberal Revolutionary Movement of the People (Movimiento Revolucionario Liberal del Pueblo, or MRLP). Though the PCC could contest departmental and municipal elections on its own

---

13 On the 1970 split, see my chapter on Venezuela in *YLACA,* pp. 158-67.

ticket in 1970 (but did not do so in every case), it had to seek national office within the MRLP, which passed as a splinter of the Liberal Party. The MRLP, with some non-communist support, won 2.1 percent of the vote, giving the PCC only 3 (of 204) seats in the national congress, 6 (of 406) in departmental assemblies, and 100 (of 7,697) in municipal councils. The party urged abstention in the presidential election. In 1972 the PCC won 8 departmental and 104 municipal seats. The party ran candidates at all levels in the 1974 elections through the National Opposition Union (UNO), which took 2.6 percent of the vote, giving the PCC 2 seats in the lower chamber.

In Mexico, the Communist Party of Mexico (PCM) could not contest elections since its membership (approximately 5,000) fell far below the minimum required to qualify for electoral participation (75,000). Pro-communist seats were held in the legislature mainly by some members of the Socialist People's Party (PPS), led until his death in 1968 by Vicente Lombardo Toledano, an "independent" Marxist who was long the head of the Soviet-front Confederation of Latin American Workers (CTAL). Between 1959 and 1974 the PPS averaged approximately 1 percent of the vote, in a system which provides dubious voting statistics, its most impressive total being 2.3 percent in 1968.[14]

In Costa Rica the illegal communist party, the People's Vanguard Party (PVP), supported other parties and fronts during the early 1960s and had one sympathizer elected to the national legislature in 1962. The PVP tried to set up a front for the 1966 election, but the Legislative Assembly proscribed it before the voting took place. Manuel Mora, the PVP founder and secretary-general, was elected to congress in 1970 on the ticket of the Socialist Action Party (Partido de Acción Socialista, or PASO); his bid for the presidency in 1974 on the PASO ticket drew about 2 percent of the vote.

In Peru, communists participated in elections under other party affiliations or through fronts (with little success) until the coup that overthrew the popularly elected (but no longer popular) government of Fernando Belaúnde Terry in 1968. The strategic objective of the pro-Soviet communist party (the PCP) after the coup was the creation of a popular government that would take the first steps toward socialism. The PCP statutes published in early 1969 said the party sought to "free

---

[14] On the problem of Mexican voting statistics, see Donald Mabry, *Mexico's Acción Nacional* (Syracuse: Syracuse University Press, 1973), pp. 170-73.

Peru from imperialist domination, mainly by the U.S.A.; to eliminate all feudal remnants; to end racial and national discrimination; and to liquidate the economic and political power of the large landholders and capitalists." [15] After early criticism of the coup led by General Juan Velasco, the PCP found that the policies of the military leaders were ordinarily what they would expect from a "popular government." Consequently, beginning in 1969, the pro-Soviet communists in Peru actively supported most of the "anti-imperialistic and anti-oligarchic revolution" launched by the Velasco government and carried on under the leadership of Francisco Morales Bermúdez in late 1975 and early 1976. Wide-ranging PCP support for the military government was stated at the party's 6th Congress in November 1973 and continued into 1976.

Armed struggle. Whereas the communist parties of Chile, Guyana, and Uruguay were the leading practitioners of the nonarmed road, the leading spokesmen for the armed road were the parties in Guatemala, Venezuela, and Colombia, particularly during the middle 1960s. At the end of 1965, a high-ranking Guatemalan communist wrote that increasingly brutal resistance to change by Latin American rulers and the United States imperialists "obviously leaves most of the Latin American countries only one realistic way of furthering the revolution today—that of armed struggle against the violence and reaction of U.S. imperialism." [16] The secretary-general of the Guatemalan Party of Labor (PGT), in a major analytical article published in late 1966, said that the Guatemalan communists believed that there existed in Guatemala the objective conditions for armed struggle, though the subjective conditions had not yet "fully matured." The latter, however, would develop during the armed struggle. In March 1965, the official reported, the PGT Central Committee had concluded that the armed struggle would take the form of

> a revolutionary people's war and not a brief armed insurrection or the creation of pockets of guerrilla resistance with no prospect of further development of war. . . . A revolutionary people's war presupposes the existence of definite conditions which mature as the war develops and make it possible organi-

---

[15] See *Unidad* (Lima), 1 November 1968; and *Statutes of the Peruvian Communist Party* (Lima, 1969).

[16] Jose Manuel Fortuny, "Has the Revolution Become More Difficult in Latin America?" *World Marxist Review,* vol. 8, no. 8 (August 1965), pp. 39-40.

zationally, politically and militarily to prepare the popular forces for the eventual uprising and victory.

Further, the Central Committee resolution pointed to two features of armed struggle in the country: the *protracted* nature of the war that will pass through successive stages, and the *popular* character of the war that the people, conscious of the justice of the cause, will increasingly support and gradually join.[17] A resolution adopted by the Central Committee in June 1966, however, called for the "proper combination of political, armed, economic and social struggle."[18] The adoption of both peaceful and violent tactics led to disputes among PGT members themselves and between leaders of the PGT and the two main guerrilla groups in the country—the Rebel Armed Forces (FAR) and the 13 November Revolutionary Movement (MR-13). PGT cooperation with (and to a considerable degree during the mid-1960s control over) the FAR was lost at this time and a clear distinction between pro-Soviet and castroite lines in Guatemala first became evident.[19]

The experience of the Communist Party of Venezuela (PCV) with armed struggle lasted only a few years but proved to be of extraordinary significance for Marxist-Leninists in general in Latin America during the late 1960s. The Venezuelan communists, who had been relatively important in national affairs during and immediately after the overthrow of Marcos Pérez Jiménez (January 1958), were opposed to the elected government of Rómulo Betancourt (1959–1964) from the day it took office. After several years of bitter verbal criticism and urban terrorism, the PCV decided in April 1964 that rural guerrilla or partisan warfare should be the main form of struggle in Venezuela. Writing in late 1964, Carlos López reported that at its April 1964 plenum the PCV Central Committee

> carefully examined concepts which regard armed struggle and other forms of mass struggle as mutually exclusive, and came to the conclusion that this was a superficial, scholastic, and not a dialectical approach. The experience of class struggle makes

---

[17] Bernardo Alvarado Monzón, "Some Problems of the Guatemalan Revolution," ibid., vol. 9, no. 10 (October 1966), p. 42; emphasis and omission in original.

[18] Jose Manuel Fortuny, "The Political Situation and Revolutionary Tactics," ibid., vol. 10, no. 2 (February 1967), p. 61.

[19] The split is discussed in Chapter 5. Régis Debray praised only one communist party in Latin America other than the Cuban—the PGT, which he said had been "renewed and rejuvenated" in 1965; see Debray, *¿Revolución en la revolución?*, p. 34.

this quite clear. Strikes, the peasants' fight for credits, or protest campaigns against particular measures may begin in the most peaceful manner and end in violence—as a rule imposed by the enemy.

According to López,

> it is essential to utilize a thousand and one forms of struggle, to employ all the means at our disposal with a view to the combined effect of all forms of struggle promoting the main form, namely, armed struggle. At the same time, we emphasize that armed struggle, too, must be primarily mass struggle, that it should be understood as the highest expression of mass struggle.[20]

The PCV, in cooperation with the Movement of the Revolutionary Left (MIR), carried out military activities through the Armed Forces of National Liberation (FALN), at first with significant success. However, by the end of 1965, some PCV leaders began to believe that emphasis on guerrilla warfare was not advancing communist objectives. The retreat from guerrilla warfare that followed took several years to complete and created some conflicts within the politburo and lower levels of the party. The PCV lost control of the main FALN forces in April 1966 when five guerrilla leaders, including PCV politburo member Douglas Bravo, assumed all decision-making prerogatives for themselves. Bravo was removed from the politburo in May 1966 and expelled from the party at the PCV plenary meeting in April 1967.

Quotations from Lenin were used in public statements to justify the retreat, while the authority of Mao Tse-tung and the Chinese communists was used in internal documents to try to convince guerrillas in the field.[21] In 1968, Teodoro Petkoff assured Venezuelans that for the PCV "armed action is still the main way, for no revolution or democratic change can be attained without it," but that, with a lack of popular support for guerrilla warfare, the PCV had decided to "accentuate struggle in the political context, chiefly through the electoral campaign." [22]

---

[20] López, "The Communist Party of Venezuela and the Present Situation," *World Marxist Review,* vol. 7, no. 10 (October 1964), pp. 25, 26.

[21] For an example of the former, see Juan Rodríguez, ibid., vol. 10, no. 9 (September 1967), p. 81; for the latter see *Confidencial* (Caracas), no. 38 (February 1967).

[22] "Pre-election Climate in Venezuela," an interview with Teodoro Petkoff, *World Marxist Review,* vol. 11, no. 4 (April 1968), p. 62.

Although several pro-Soviet communist parties, such as those of Haiti and Paraguay (most of whose members were in exile), still emphasized the need for immediate armed struggle during the 1970s, most of the communist parties in Latin America turned primarily or entirely to nonarmed struggle.

Armed and nonarmed struggle. The simultaneous use of "all forms of struggle" was vigorously defended by some pro-Soviet communists—especially for revolutionaries in other countries than their own—though it often brought problems in its wake. At the 23rd Congress of the CPSU in Moscow (March-April 1966) Rodney Arismendi argued that

> throughout our continent, the peoples are engaged in struggle, utilizing all its methods, combining them simultaneously or alternately, depending on the circumstances—legal or illegal, action in parliament or outside of it, rebel action or guerrilla warfare. . . . As the struggle extends the peoples are overcoming the stereotyped counterposing of different forms of struggle [realizing that Lenin demanded] mastery of all forms of struggle in conformity with the circumstances.[23]

The Communist Party of Colombia (PCC) urged the use of all forms of struggle for most of the period studied here.[24] The PCC had its own military arm in the Revolutionary Armed Forces of Colombia (FARC) from 1966 to 1976, though during the later years the party's emphasis on armed struggle decreased. The FARC even urged participation in the 1970 national elections, returning to sporadic military action two days after the voting was completed.[25] Several other parties tried at times to follow this line as well.

Revolutionary Leadership and Alliances. Just as there were shifting positions among pro-Soviet parties regarding the road to power, so there was considerable flexibility as to leadership and composition of the revolutionary forces. The problems were to avoid "rightist" and "leftist" extremes, the former involving such broad alliances that the communists might lose influence over the direction of the revolution,

---

[23] *Information Bulletin,* nos. 74-77 (in one volume) (1966), pp. 103-104.

[24] For representative statements, see articles by PCC Secretary-General Gilberto Vieira: "Growth of Militarism in Colombia and the Line of the Communist Party," *World Marxist Review,* vol. 6, no. 4 (April 1963), pp. 17-19; and "Lenin, Greatest Revolutionary Strategist of All Time," ibid., vol. 13, no. 5 (May 1970), esp. p. 22.

[25] See FARC call for electoral participation in *Voz Proletaria* (Bogota), 9 April 1970.

and the latter resulting in the political isolation of the communists and their inability to form a broad revolutionary front. In the early 1960s most Latin American parties much more often found themselves isolated from significant movements for revolution or even reform than leading them. Communist recognition of this isolation came out repeatedly at a discussion organized by the editorial board of the *World Marxist Review* during the summer of 1962 and attended by officials of the communist parties of Argentina, Bolivia, Brazil, Chile, Colombia, Cuba, Ecuador, Paraguay, Peru, and Uruguay. Many of the leaders openly acknowledged that intra-party disputes over the road to power and the united front, the lack of revolutionary perspective among the masses, and a reluctance of other leftist parties to cooperate with communists made prospects for communist leadership of a broad revolutionary movement remote. A general survey of the discussion at the end emphasized the communists' responsibility to set up a broad front of "democratic forces." While repeating that the most reliable allies of the workers were the peasants, it called as well for recruits from among the students, professional people, the urban petit-bourgeoisie, and the national bourgeoisie (industrial and commercial), depending on specific national conditions. The working class must lead the united front, but it must be unified to do so; the prestige gained from hard battle would ultimately lead to proletarian hegemony.[26]

An article by a prominent Guatemalan communist in early 1964, clearly intended to apply in many respects to Latin America as a whole, acknowledged the lack of communist strength among workers and peasants in most countries. After conceding that in Guatemala the most revolutionary actions in recent years had been carried out by the urban middle sectors, he concluded: "The urban middle sections who are petty-bourgeois in thinking and in status will, evidently, as the Cuban experience has shown, play an important revolutionary role in Latin America, and not only in the anti-imperialist stage of the revolution." At the same time, these sectors brought with them typically petit-bourgeois concepts and methods of action; this being the case, they could not remain allies indefinitely.[27]

---

[26] See abridged transcript of conference talks in *World Marxist Review* (Prague), vol. 6, no. 1 (January 1963), pp. 67-83; concluding remarks by A. M. Rumyantsev, pp. 81-82.

[27] Hugo Barrios Klee, "The Revolutionary Situation and the Liberation Struggle of the People of Guatemala," *World Marxist Review*, vol. 7, no. 3 (March 1964), p. 19.

The mood of self-criticism reached a peak in 1965. Guatemalan communist leader José Manuel Fortuny tried to explain why the vanguard of the proletariat was "lagging behind" and generally ineffective in Latin America. Some reasons, he wrote, were historical: for example, the Comintern (particularly between 1928 and 1935) had forced a stereotyped pattern on Latin American communists, resulting in "dogmatism and narrow-mindedness." Though the 7th Congress of the Comintern in 1935 had advanced a more creative line, Latin American communists were still bound down by the "Stalin personality cult." Many Latin American communist policies were mistakenly directed entirely toward the immature and underdeveloped urban working class "to no purpose," paying little or no attention to agricultural laborers and the middle sectors. They did not recognize that the working class was simply not ready to play the leading role in the anti-imperialist revolution. Furthermore, the party still had failed to convince Latin Americans that socialism was in their interests and had been unable to deal with questions of religion, treatment of intellectuals, art, and literature.[28] A Brazilian leader added that in Latin America, perhaps more than anywhere else in the world, "the charge that the communists are supporters of totalitarian and undemocratic rule remains a central, and not always ineffectual, argument of anti-communist propaganda." [29]

Several of the same points came out in another article a year later, this time by a prominent communist from El Salvador. Roque Dalton, writing on student youth in the Latin American revolution, argued that in a "broad historical sense" the working class was the social vanguard of modern society and thus was "always the most progressive class, regardless of the present level of its political consciousness or actual participation in the concrete political struggle at any particular time." In many Latin American countries, however, the working class had not yet become the leading class. At the same time, it was becoming increasingly clear that the bourgeoisie would not play the role it had played in Europe. Thus, there existed a "vacuum of public leadership" which allowed the army, intelligentsia, students, bureaucracy, and (to a lesser degree) the peasants and urban middle classes to play a "*bigger* and more *independent* political role over a longer period of time" than

---

[28] Fortuny, "Has the Revolution Become More Difficult in Latin America?" pp. 42-44. Also see Luis Figueroa, "Some Problems of the Working Class Movement in Latin America," *World Marxist Review*, vol. 9, no. 3 (March 1966), p. 64.
[29] Pedro Motta Lima, "The Revolutionary Process and Democracy in Latin America," ibid., vol. 8, no. 8 (August 1965), p. 50.

they had in Europe. In the upper Andean and Caribbean countries, students "often comprise the most active and mobile section of the revolutionary vanguard [and] emerge as a kind of *social detonator* (or catalyst), which extends the revolutionary tension of the moment to other social groups and classes objectively interested in the struggle." The radical intellectual youth "awakens, enlightens and organizes the working class movement." When the vanguard role is temporarily assumed by the students or any other non-proletarian group, the masses must be incorporated in the struggles very soon in order to avoid isolation and even defeat. The vanguard is "the 'small engine' that sets the 'big engine' of mass struggle into motion." [30] The difference between actual proletarian leadership, as contrasted to theoretical proletarian leadership, was raised at the same time by a prominent Chilean communist labor leader.[31]

Over the next few years many pro-Soviet communists became increasingly outspoken in their opposition to national bourgeois leadership when significant structural revolution was wanted. In March 1968 Victor Volsky, the director of the Latin American Institute of the Soviet Academy of Sciences, published an article on the "new stage" reached in the struggles of the Latin American peoples. The article, which originally appeared in *Pravda* on 19 March, was reprinted in whole or in part and endorsed in pro-Soviet publications around Latin America. It stated that

> the liberation movement of the peoples of Latin America is now entering a new stage. In the 1950s, when the struggle of the general crisis of capitalism was developing, the working people still believed in the possibility of progressive social changes under the leadership of the national bourgeoisie and in the latter's constructive potential and were still willing to support it in many ways and to follow it. Now the national bourgeoisie, which in some countries had been crushed by the oligarchic cliques and the military and in others has been frightened by the Cuban revolution, is incapable of independently implementing any serious social and economic trans-

---

[30] Dalton, "Student Youth and the Latin-American Revolution," pp. 53-61. Compare Debray's reference to Raúl Castro's description of the guerrilla *foco* as "the 'small motor' that sets the 'big motor' of the masses into motion." Debray, *¿Revolución en la revolución?*, p. 69.

[31] Figueroa, "Some Problems of the Working Class Movement in Latin America," p. 64. The president of the Single Center of Chilean Workers warned communists against repeating "should be" so frequently and so categorically as to fool themselves into thinking what "should be" had actually come to pass.

formations. It is becoming still more obvious that this can be accomplished only through the struggle of the popular masses. In the present stage, as never before, the progressive forces, first of all the Communist Parties, are setting themselves the primary task of assuming full leadership in this struggle of the peoples and of rallying around themselves all forces that in one form or another oppose the oligarchies and imperialism and stand for progress and democracy.

Needless to say, Volsky continued, the conditions for implementing this task are far from identical in the various countries of Latin America; this gives rise to a great diversity of methods and techniques so that the vanguard of the working people in each country can take specific national features into account. In some countries of Latin America (Chile, Mexico, Uruguay, Costa Rica, and others) an activation in the struggle of the democratic forces can be observed, a process of their consolidation is taking place, albeit slowly, and stubborn class battles are developing. In other countries, especially following coups d'etat, reactionary and pro-imperialist forces have succeeded in bringing about a temporary weakening in the liberation movement.[32]

Attacks on Critics

Many of the pro-Soviet communist parties were challenged on domestic policy by a number of Marxist-Leninist groups: the Maoists, the castroite-nationalists, the Trotskyists, and the communist-nationalists. Disputes with the first three groups generally were reflected most clearly in differences over the proper road to power, though other related issues were involved. The Maoists and castroites in particular, joined by dissidents from some prominent nationalist parties (such as the Acción Democrática in Venezuela and the Apristas in Peru) which soon became "castroite," insisted on pursuing armed struggle as the primary or only form of struggle on an almost continent-wide basis during much of the period from 1959 to 1976—a line the pro-Soviet parties were not about to endorse. The arguments and actions of these groups proved attractive to many young members of the universities and even of the communist parties and communist youth organizations. When sympathy for armed struggle was strong in a communist party, as it was during the early

---

[32] V. V. Volsky, "New Stage of the People's Struggle," in J. Gregory Oswald and Anthony J. Strover, eds., *The Soviet Union and Latin America* (New York: Praeger, 1970), p. 69.

1960s in Venezuela, disputes with castroite groups were delayed and in at least two countries (Venezuela and Guatemala) pro-Chinese elements within the parties were discouraged from setting up dissident groups of their own.

The pro-Soviet parties in the various countries reacted in different ways to the challenges of local Marxist-Leninist groups, the reaction depending largely on the origin and strength of the rival organization. In most countries Trotskyists were ineffective or nonexistent, and the term "Trotskyite" was thrown about as little more than a pejorative epithet, aimed at Maoists, castroites and others with whom the communists disagreed. At times brief comments on the undertakings of true Trotskyist groups were offered. These were generally critical, as in the case of comments on the People's Revolutionary Army (ERP) in Argentina made by that country's pro-Soviet party, but occasionally they indicated guarded support, as when the Communist Party of Peru encouraged some of the early peasant organization and land occupation activities led by Hugo Blanco in the Valley of La Convención (department of Cuzco).[33]

The pro-Chinese groups presented a very different problem. In most countries they had originated, to a large extent, in the ranks of the established (and eventually "pro-Soviet") parties. Dissident members usually advocated a Chinese line within the party until they were expelled or they themselves "expelled" their pro-Soviet rivals. The two resulting parties differed over the basic issues raised in the Sino-Soviet dispute, some of which had nothing whatsoever to do with the domestic conditions in their countries. The most important disagreements were over the proper road to power, the nature of the party leadership required for a successful revolution, and the scope of the united front. At times the pro-Soviet parties tried to refute Maoist contentions— which they said spread confusion among the people—but often they merely ignored them or responded by attacking their rivals personally. In Peru and several other countries, for example, Maoists were accused of harboring visions of grandeur (like Mao Tse-tung), or promoting personal ambitions, absconding with party funds, and informing to the police. In 1970 the secretary-general of the Communist Party of Chile described the pro-Chinese Revolutionary Communist Party of Chile as a tiny "micro-group" which had "no significance in spite of the fact

---

[33] For the former, see *New Times* (Moscow), no. 28 (1972), and for the latter, see *Unidad* (Lima), 7 November 1962.

that the four wretches who make it up keep on yapping out against the communists." [34]

The pro-Soviet communists generally considered the castroite-nationalists to be a more serious threat than were the Maoists, as indeed they were. Differences with Fidel Castro and the fledgling Cuban-inspired groups in several countries developed early but did not lead immediately to a serious public dispute between advocates of the two lines.[35] Divergent views on the applicability of armed struggle were discussed at the November 1964 meeting of Latin American communists in Havana and, as indicated earlier, a modus vivendi of sorts was reached when the pro-Soviet parties agreed that "active aid" should be given to "freedom fighters" in Venezuela, Colombia, Guatemala, Honduras, Paraguay, and Haiti. But the modus vivendi did not last.

In June 1965, the Peruvian Movement of the Revolutionary Left (MIR), a castroite splinter of the APRA party with some Maoist overtones, launched several guerrilla operations which lasted only six months and resulted in heavy guerrilla casualties. The Peruvian Communist Party, after criticizing the MIR for adopting an anti-communist attitude, concluded that

> in a country whose people suffer from poverty and landlord violence, guerrilla struggle can win popular sympathy. But *this sympathy cannot be utilised and cannot develop into active support unless there are more or less mature objective conditions for revolution.* The second condition for the successful growth of the guerrilla movement is *a relatively high level of organisation and consciousness on the part of the political organisation heading the guerrilla struggle.*[36]

The high point in continent-wide tension between the pro-Soviet parties and the castroites, including Fidel himself, came in 1967.[37] At first the pro-Soviet parties simply tried to ignore the attacks leveled at them by the Cubans, Debray, and the castroites in their own countries. However, after Castro's stinging speech of 13 March 1967, the

---

[34] Luis Corvalán, *El Siglo* (Santiago), 15 December 1970.

[35] For early guarded criticism see Gilberto Vieira, "Growth of Militarism in Colombia and the Line of the Communist Party," *World Marxist Review* (Prague), April 1963, pp. 18-19; and Hugo Barrios Klee, "The Revolutionary Situation," *World Marxist Review*, vol. 7, no. 3 (March 1964), esp. p. 22.

[36] César Levano, "Lessons of the Guerrilla Struggle in Peru," *World Marxist Review*, vol. 9, no. 9 (September 1966), p. 50. Emphasis in original.

[37] The castroite positions are presented in the following chapter.

Communist Party of Venezuela (PCV), the main target of Castro's wrath, responded with a will. On 15 March the party's politburo issued a statement condemning Castro's "irresponsible arrogance" and saying that the Venezuelan communists "do not admit tutelage from anyone, no matter how great his revolutionary merits may be." The statement strongly objected to Castro's charge that the Venezuelan communists were "cowards" and chided the Cuban leader for his "irritating tendency" to think he had a "monopoly of valor and courage." The politburo then proclaimed that it rejected "the role of 'Pope' which Fidel Castro has arrogated to himself. We categorically reject his pretension that it should be he and no one else but he who decides what is or is not revolutionary in Latin America." And finally, the PCV regretted that, because of Castro's insolence, the dispute had turned into a "disagreeable polemic [which] undoubtedly will please the enemy." [38]

Some Latin American communists tried to cool the growing dissension. In July 1967 the secretary-general of the Communist Party of Chile (PCCh) wrote that the Cuban revolution "demonstrated that the petty-bourgeoisie has a potential of revolutionary courage in battling for national liberation and socialism." He continued:

> There is, then, a distinct bond between the revolutionary trends of the proletariat, on the one hand, and those of the petty-bourgeoisie, on the other. There is much that unites them, but also much that divides them. Petty-bourgeois revolutionaries tend at times to under-rate the workers and the Communist parties, to gravitate towards nationalism, recklessness, terror and, at times, even anti-communism and anti-Sovietism. Also, they are more susceptible to despair and subjectivism. But they are revolutionary all the same and the proletariat must put the accent on unity with them rather than on fighting their mistakes. The two trends are competing for leadership of the movement; to a certain extent, their rivalry is ideological. But if anything is done to accentuate this rivalry or precipitate a "fight for the destruction" of either trend, the sole beneficiary will be imperialism.[39]

But one month after Corvalán's article, the Latin American Solidarity Organization (OLAS) conference convened in Havana and the

---

[38] Politburo statement quoted in Robert J. Alexander, *The Communist Party of Venezuela* (Stanford, Cal.: Hoover Institution Press, 1969), pp. 203-204.

[39] Luis Corvalán, "Alliance of Anti-imperialist Forces in Latin America," *World Marxist Review*, vol. 10, no. 7 (July 1967), p. 48.

pro-Soviet parties were on the receiving end of the criticism for almost two weeks.[40] After that, pro-Soviet responses began to come rapidly, some directed toward the Cuban leaders themselves but most (in hardly disguised Aesopian language) aimed at "petty-bourgeois nationalists." An Argentine communist leader, Rodolfo Ghioldi, condemned the "petty-bourgeois nationalists" for insisting that Latin American countries "proceed directly to socialism, spurning the preliminary stages of agrarian, anti-imperialist and democratic revolutions." He condemned the "extreme adventurism" of "Maoism and related currents," the latter in reference to the castroites.[41] The Venezuelan communists criticized terrorist activities of "factionalist adventurists and other Leftist groups" in Venezuela for trying to "create artificial stimuli in order to set the masses in motion from the top, solely through vanguard actions" and for "denying that real revolutionary work consists in providing political and organizational conditions, both objective and subjective, for bringing the masses into the fight."[42] Two longer and more detailed critiques were Rodolfo Ghioldi's *There Cannot Be a Revolution in the Revolution,* an attack on Debray's book emphasizing the importance of mass support for the revolution and the role of the proletariat and the communist party, and Gerardo Unzueta's "La Revolución en América Latina," which concluded:

> In their totality, Debray's ideology and conceptions attempt to push us back to stages in the labor and revolutionary movement that have already been surpassed, to pre-Marxist stages; to a socialism that is not class socialism. And anyone who in our age proclaims a non-class politics and non-class socialism deserves, as Lenin said, "to be exhibited alongside an Australian kangaroo."[43]

Of all the pro-Soviet communist parties, only the party in Uruguay (PCU) avoided open criticism of Castro and the castroites during the OLAS period. This may be accounted for in part by the peculiar circumstances of Uruguay—an urban nation in which rural guerrilla

---

[40] On the OLAS conference, see Appendix B.

[41] *Pravda* (Moscow), 25 October 1967. The insult was double-barreled when the "related currents" were linked to Maoism.

[42] Politburo statement of January 1967, in *Information Bulletin,* no. 94 (1967).

[43] Unzueta, *El Siglo* (Santiago), 4 February 1968; the long critique by Unzueta, the chief theoretician of the Mexican Communist Party, was published in the Chilean Communist Party paper *El Siglo* in three installments: 21 and 28 January, and 4 February 1968. Ghioldi's book, *No puede haber revolución en la revolución,* was published by Editorial Anteo in Buenos Aires in September 1967.

81

warfare seemed highly unlikely. Also, it is probable that during the period of greatest Soviet-Cuban tension, Arismendi was trying to bridge the gap between the positions of the Soviet Union and the pro-Soviet parties, on the one hand, and Cuba and the castroite groups, on the other.

The dispute between the pro-Soviet communist parties and Castro began to decline during 1968, particularly after the Cuban leader endorsed the Soviet-led invasion of Czechoslovakia. But not all of the communist parties were yet free of the problems caused by castroites at home, as will be shown in the chapter devoted to Chile.

Such "ultra-leftist" actions as terrorism, assassination, and kidnapping, frequently employed by some castroite-nationalist groups, were regularly rejected and sometimes condemned by pro-Soviet communist parties, chiefly on the grounds (if grounds were given) that such activities were repellent to the masses of the people and thus counterproductive. The politburo of the Communist Party of Venezuela, in a statement typical of pro-Soviet parties, asserted in January 1967 that "individual terror" is "resorted to by those who have lost faith in themselves, in their ability to carry on a protracted struggle." Such methods are "completely alien to revolutionary tactics [and] contradict Marxism-Leninism," and they are "extremely harmful to the popular movement." Then the politburo commented: "Decades ago Lenin, in keeping with the dialectical method typical of genuine revolutionaries, demonstrated the negative aspect of terrorism. 'We cannot kill the system by killing the tsar,' he said. 'They can always find a worse tsar.' " [44] Even Rodney Arismendi, whose support for armed struggle in most countries was noted above, argued in 1970 that Lenin himself "exposed terrorism as futile tactics, opposing it to the Marxist revolutionary tactics of *mass* action." [45]

Conclusions

Among Marxist-Leninist organizations in Latin America, the pro-Soviet communist parties were notable for their longevity, relative flexibility

---

[44] *Information Bulletin*, no. 94 (1967). Also see resolution of the Communist Party of Argentina (PCA), *Nueva Era* (Buenos Aires), December 1975, p. 411.
[45] "Lenin, Revolutionary Communist and Revolutionary Leader," *World Marxist Review*, vol. 13, no. 5 (May 1970), p. 95. Emphasis in original. Arismendi was undoubtedly referring indirectly to the kidnappings and assorted terrorist activities recently carried out by the Tupamaro guerrillas in his country, as well as making a general observation.

in strategy and tactics (during the period from 1959 to 1976), and general ineffectiveness. After the Cuban revolutionary victory in 1959, several communist parties (for example, those in Guatemala and Venezuela) carried out armed struggle which was similar to, and at times made in cooperation with, the struggle of the castroite organizations; many professed to believe that armed struggle would have to be employed at some point in the future. During the 1960s and early 1970s, however, most pro-Soviet parties emphasized nonarmed struggle—chiefly labor, student, and electoral activities—in their efforts to gain national influence and eventually to seize political power.

Recognizing that they did not have enough popular support to take power independently, the pro-Soviet parties generally advocated the formation of broadly based united fronts, a strategy followed most successfully in Chile between 1956 and 1973, first in the Popular Action Front (FRAP) and then in the Popular Unity (UP) alliance. This policy was summarized in early 1971—immediately after the inauguration of President Allende—at a Santiago conference of communist party leaders from Argentina, Brazil, Colombia, Peru, and Venezuela. Chilean Communist Party theoretician Orlando Millas told the officials that some features of the Chilean experience should be "taken into account regardless of the distinctive characteristics of the revolutionary movement in each particular country." These features, as summarized from Millas's comments by the *World Marxist Review,* included

> the guiding political role of the Communist Party, the Communist-Socialist alliance, the unification of the working class in one trade union center, the mobilization of the peasantry to win a radical agrarian reform, the formation of a broad democratic, national revolutionary coalition on the basis of an anti-imperialist and anti-oligarchic program, the consolidation of mass organizations of the population (such as house committees) uniting various segments of the people in the fight for pressing demands, and the campaign for an educational reform.[46]

In reality, the Chilean experience was only marginally relevant to most other Latin American communists during this period. No other communist party in the area, and only the parties of France and Italy in the non-communist world, had comparable influence and experience

---

[46] "Latin America: Liberation Struggle and the Working Class," ibid., vol. 14, no. 7 (July 1971), pp. 75-76.

operating within a highly developed and sophisticated political system. Only in Uruguay, where a fairly strong communist party played a leading role in labor and student affairs, was anything resembling a serious parallel possible. A so-called Broad Front (FA) of leftist individuals and organizations, in large part inspired by the Popular Unity success in Chile, was formed in Uruguay at the end of 1970 to participate in the presidential election of 28 November 1971. Though the Broad Front—a unique force in Uruguayan political history—made a respectable showing (winning 18 percent of the vote), it fell far short of duplicating the Chilean victory. In other countries talk of united fronts remained largely theoretical, and even after united front activities were stepped up during the 1970s—in the wake of the Popular Unity triumph—truly broad fronts with communist participation failed to materialize in other countries. The overthrow of the Allende government in September 1973 did not, however, bring an end to the united front activities of other pro-Soviet parties in Latin America.

Most Latin American communist parties did not have an important degree of influence in their countries during the period from 1959 to 1976. The reasons for this were many, among them (1) an ideology promising a better (indeed "scientific") understanding of political, economic, and social conditions, situations, and forces than it could produce; (2) an inclination to overestimate the existing revolutionary consciousness in some sectors of society—and thus to blur distinctions between present reality and future expectations; (3) opposition from powerful traditional sectors of society, particularly the military and the church; (4) existence of other organizations with more popular and impressive leaders offering reform programs of wider appeal; (5) hostility, suspicion, or indifference of the majority of the middle and lower sectors of society, including the proletariat for whom the communists presumed to speak; (6) popular apprehension regarding possible Soviet intervention in the hemisphere, as seen in the 1962 missile crisis and in the increasing degree of Soviet influence on Cuban domestic affairs, particularly after the economic setbacks and dislocations connected with the 1970 sugar harvest; (7) criticism and competition of "super-revolutionaries" of the castroite and Maoist varieties; and (8) opposition of foreign non-communist economic and political interests, particularly those based in the United States.

On the other hand, their activities were not entirely without effect. Efforts to achieve a measure of influence, most successful among work-

84

ers and university students, were aided in varying degrees by national and international conditions, including (1) the absence of any agreed-upon and demonstrably effective non-communist solutions to many of the innumerable problems facing the Latin American people; (2) the general atmosphere following in the wake of Fidel Castro's victory in 1959; (3) Castro's efforts to eliminate the long-standing inequalities and build socialism through communist-style programs; (4) successful Cuban defiance of the "U.S. imperialists"; (5) Soviet willingness to aid the Cuban economy and defense when faced by "Yankee" threats; and (6) the rising level of nationalist sentiment and independent action by Latin American governments in general, especially during the 1970s.

The Soviet-oriented communist parties have been relatively adept (among the Marxist-Leninist organizations of Latin America) at adjusting strategy and tactics to shifting national and international conditions while seeking to avoid what they consider the extremes of moderate reformism of the right and ultra-revolutionism of the left. Their positions regarding potential long- and (especially) short-term allies have changed from one time and place to another, and have opened them up to the charge of opportunism by their enemies and rivals of the right and ultra-left.

The accusation of opportunism, of adapting themselves to different conditions without regard to principle, is more complicated than many enemies of the communists seem to allow. Over the decades, some communist parties have indeed been willing and relatively able to get along with a wide variety of political leaders, from caudillos and military dictators of the right to reformists or revolutionaries of the left. It is the "without regard to principle," the commonly accepted negative characteristic of opportunism, that causes the trouble. Though many critics generally assert that communist party leaders form alliances simply to "save their necks" or reap some of the benefits of the existing society, it is not always easy to determine without question the motives behind any specific communist position. No doubt there is an important element of self-preservation and self-aggrandizement in many communist decisions, but these qualities are hardly unique to the communists. Communists are not necessarily more venal than other political leaders, though their loud professions of revolutionary objectives and morality often make them seem more hypocritical.

To a considerable extent, the communists have a built-in answer to their critics. It has frequently been noted that the communists, by their very opportunism (among other things), have been uncommonly successful in maintaining their political organizations during the most unfavorable of circumstances. If the long-term objective, indeed the historical mission, of a communist party is to bring communism to a country, then the preservation of the party when threatened, by whatever means necessary, is not so much an option as a duty of the party's leaders. In the past this rationale has led communists all over the world to work with those they labeled "fascists." For example, the Soviet and German communist parties contributed substantially to the rise of Hitler in the early 1930s, while the Chinese communists formed a united front in the late 1930s and early 1940s with Chiang Kai-shek, the Nationalist Party leader they had for years called the "running dog of Japanese imperialism." In the end, the opportunism practiced by the true Marxist-Leninist need not be considered opportunistic; rather than abandoning his principles (an abandonment which he invariably denies has taken place, whatever the circumstances), he can argue with some support from historical experience that he is preserving his party for that inevitable showdown. Those who cast aspersions at him are merely demonstrating that morally they are (in Marxist-Leninist jargon) "bourgeois" to the core.[47]

---

[47] The deliberate tactic of opportunism, as applied in Latin America, was described several decades ago by Eudocio Ravines, a former Comintern agent in Chile. Writing for an audience that had little understanding of communist tactics and morality, Ravines offered what was perhaps an excessively sordid picture of communist deception, blackmail, intimidation, and corruption when dealing with non-communists; the essence of his critique, however, is sound. See Eudocio Ravines, *The Yenan Way* (New York, 1951, reprinted Westport, Conn.: Greenwood Press, 1972), pp. 148-58, published in Spanish as *La Gran Estafa* (Santiago: Pacifico, 1954), pp. 72-88. In a letter to the author (dated 20 September 1970), Ravines withdrew his controversial claim that he had learned these tactics from Mao Tse-tung, but maintained his position regarding Chinese influence.

4

Pro-Chinese Organizations
in Latin America

Many Latin American communist leaders were on good terms with their counterparts in the People's Republic of China during the 1950s. However, as was indicated earlier, during the 1960s a combination of the Sino-Soviet conflict and conditions in their own countries forced the Latin American leaders to choose between continued friendship with the Chinese communists and an acceptance of the Soviet line in the international communist dispute. Most lined up with the Soviet Union, but a few did not.

Background

The first pro-Chinese party was founded in Brazil in 1962, even before the Chinese communist call in late 1963 for the establishment of "Marxist-Leninist" parties around the world. During the next few years pro-Chinese parties and organizations were formed in Ecuador (1963), Chile (1964), Peru (1964), Bolivia (1965), and Colombia (1965). In the late 1960s and early 1970s there were, at any given time, somewhere between twelve and twenty-five groups that were defiantly pro-Chinese (pledging their loyalty to "the invincible thought of Mao Tse-tung") or clearly sympathetic toward China and the advocates of Maoist policies. Most of the parties were, however, small, ranging from a dozen to several hundred members, and even these small parties sometimes split into two or three factions. Only in the Dominican Republic and Peru did pro-Chinese militants ever seem to outnumber the pro-Soviet militants.

In general the Maoist organizations were formed by young members of established communist parties or their youth groups who had become frustrated with the domestic strategies and tactics of their parties and discouraged by the international policies of the Soviet Union, particularly the Soviet "capitulation" in the 1962 missile crisis. Some incorporated members of other leftist groups. In one case a pro-Chinese party (Brazil) and in another a party with strong sympathy for the Chinese (Paraguay) developed under the leadership of communist officials who had lost Soviet backing and been removed from long-held party leadership positions. In several incidents, nonideological and nontactical factors seem to have been important in party splits, the Maoist orientation being little more than a convenience. Two communist parties known to have had strong pro-Chinese contingents, the Communist Party of Venezuela (PCV) and the Guatemalan Party of Labor (PGT), emphasized the armed road for some years during the 1960s and avoided a split along Sino-Soviet lines; in general they remained neutral or only mildly critical of the Chinese in the dispute.[1]

Maoist organizations had their greatest successes among youth and especially among student groups. They generally controlled major university student federations in Ecuador and Peru during the late 1960s and early 1970s; they were influential in the Dominican Republic and occasionally showed signs of life in Colombia and several other countries. But most of these pro-Chinese students gave few indications of serious interest in Mao's theories or in the Chinese communist experience, apparently looking upon the designation "Maoist" as roughly equivalent to "super-revolutionary" (not in a pejorative sense). Pro-Chinese parties formed two guerrilla organizations, the People's Liberation Army (EPL) in Colombia during 1967 and a group in Bolivia during 1969–1970; the Colombian party formed the first all-feminine guerrilla front in 1968 with the María Cano Unit of the EPL. Several small Venezuelan guerrilla groups began assuming a pro-Chinese coloring in 1970.

At the turn of the decade, as was explained earlier, the Chinese Communist Party began showing decreased interest in most of the pro-Chinese communist parties in Latin America. Maoist parties and organizations remained in a number of countries, but in an increasingly

[1] Splits in these parties, discussed elsewhere, came during 1966-1968 along pro-Soviet and castroite lines. The most important Venezuelan communist to become a castroite in this period, Douglas Bravo, became increasingly Maoist in attitude during the late 1960s and early 1970s.

unstable form. They continued to be hostile to their governments, insisting that no revolution has ever succeeded by the nonarmed road, and maintained an enthusiastic core of slogan painters, particularly in the universities.

Strategy and Tactics

The theoretical positions and critiques put forward by the pro-Chinese political parties and organizations are easily described, largely because the Maoist groups had a short life span and with only a few exceptions adhered closely to a single revolutionary strategy propounded by the Chinese Communist Party.

Maoist groups, without exception, called for a revolution in two stages. The interrelationship of this apparently insignificant theoretical assumption and the positions regarding the proper road to power, leadership, and the united front came out more clearly in pro-Chinese writings than in the works of the pro-Soviet parties. The Maoist conviction that a successful socialist revolution could come only by stages, after a patriotic, anti-imperialist, anti-feudal, anti-oligarchic, people's democratic revolution, was the theoretical assertion upon which the pro-Chinese parties based their insistence on all other matters. "The central objective of the revolution in its popular-democratic stage," said the Revolutionary Communist Party of Chile (PCRCh), is "to seize power from the most reactionary sectors and to establish a form of dictatorship of the proletariat, in alliance with other anti-imperialist, anti-latifundist, anti-monopolist forces." [2] Opponents needed to be eliminated in stages, beginning with the elimination of the principal enemies. This application of "salami tactics" called for the making of a clear distinction between the fundamental enemies, on the one hand, and the lesser enemies and short- and long-term allies, on the other. An inflexible revolutionary line during a period of vulnerability would drive too many groups into the camp of the fundamental enemies and lead to the defeat of the revolutionary forces. As explained in a widely circulated 1967 pamphlet of the PCRCh, what was essential was "to prevent the principal adversaries from pulling together in their turn the numerous intermediate sectors isolated from the proletariat and its most loyal ally, the peasantry. If this happened, through a sectarian policy

[2] *Programa del Partido Comunista Revolucionario de Chile,* 2nd ed. (Santiago, 1969), pp. 69-70.

such as that advocated by the Trotskyists, it would be impossible to defeat [the principal enemies]." [3]

Thus a pro-Chinese party of the proletariat would follow Mao's orientation, applicable in all countries where the proletariat was relatively weak and the enemies extremely powerful—that is, it would base itself on the support of the progressive forces, win the intermediate forces over to the revolutionary front, and isolate the recalcitrant and reactionary forces. Once the fundamental enemies had been defeated in the people's democratic revolution, the dictatorship of the proletariat would be established, in alliance with the anti-imperialist, anti-latifundist, and anti-monopolist forces that opposed the fundamental enemies, in order to carry out the socialist revolution and the elimination of the lesser oppressors and oppressions. The transformation to socialism would take place under a provisional government—modeled on Mao's people's democratic dictatorship—made up of the proletariat, semi-proletariat, petit-bourgeoisie, and portions of the middle or national bourgeoisie which did not support the counterrevolutionaries. These classes would have all political rights for themselves and would impose a socialist order on the country.[4]

The pro-Chinese groups repeatedly asserted that a true revolution was possible only under the leadership of the party of the proletariat—that is, an authentic Marxist-Leninist party.[5] According to the pro-Chinese Communist Party of Bolivia (PCB-ML):

> It is necessary to have the leadership of the working class and its Party, and to establish a broad front of the people's forces based on the worker-peasant alliance and to direct the spear-

[3] Partido Comunista Revolucionario de Chile, *Una línea pequeño-burguesa y una línea proletaria* (Santiago: Espartaco, 1967), pp. 30, 31.

[4] See Galvarino Guerra, "El pensamiento de Mao Tse-tung," *Causa Marxista-Leninista* (Santiago), no. 17 (April 1970), pp. 16-30; "Extractos de la resolución política del Tercer Pleno de Comité Central del Partido Comunista de Colombia (ML), sobre la línea de masas," ibid., pp. 67-68; *Programa del Partido Comunista Revolucionario,* pp. 44-45, 69-70; Partido Comunista Marxista-Leninista del Ecuador, "La lucha de la clase obrera y su unidad con el pueblo," *En Marcha* (Quito), 30 April-6 May 1972; interview with José Camargo, Partido Comunista do Brasil, *A Classe Operaria*, Spanish ed., probably published in Santiago, December 1971.

[5] See "Extractos de la resolución . . . del Partido Comunista de Colombia (ML)," pp. 74-75; *Programa del Partido Comunista Revolucionario,* pp. 56-65. The Revolutionary Communist Party of Chile went so far as to claim it was the first party in Chilean history to truly represent the interests of the masses of workers and peasants. "Entrevista al Partido Comunista Revolucionario de Chile," *Causa Marxista-Leninista* (Santiago), July-August 1971, p. 34; and *El Pueblo* (Santiago), 1 May 1972.

head of the struggle at the imperialists and the rulers they sustain. The only road for national-liberation struggle is armed struggle and the fundamental prerequisite for winning the people's war is to rely firmly on the peasants under the leadership of the proletarian party.

Thus in Bolivia, as elsewhere, the "worker-peasant alliance" was seen as a "pillar in the national liberation struggle" and the foundation for a broad front comprised of the majority of the Bolivian people. The task of the Bolivian Maoists, working from a "clear and definite program" with emphasis on the "peasant problem," was to carry out "political and military work among the masses." The party's "Draft Peasant-Agrarian Programme," stressed that "people's war" was the road to the liberation of the proletariat, the peasantry and the other people's revolutionary forces, and warned against underestimating the importance of the peasants: "The principal error of the guerrilla force [led by Che Guevara in 1967] was that it neglected the role of the peasants, failed to win their support and did not carry out intensive political work among them." On the other extreme, the "peaceful means advertised by the revisionists" could only "lead the people away from their true revolutionary objectives." [6]

At times it was argued that the proletariat, the semi-proletariat, and the petit-bourgeoisie were the fundamental forces of the Maoist united front, though at other times it was acknowledged that the petit-bourgeoisie was reluctant to join with the proletariat. According to Maoist groups, members of the national bourgeoisie (sometimes called the middle bourgeoisie or the upper petit-bourgeoisie) wanted to improve their positions in society and, though dependent upon and influenced by North American imperialism, they were at the same time impeded by imperialist forces. Under certain conditions and for a limited time they might join the proletariat in the revolutionary struggle. Nevertheless, they feared the socialist outlook of the people's democratic revolution, resisted the leadership of the proletariat, and vacillated between the revolution and counterrevolution. Maoists had to adopt a flexible attitude toward these groups, drawing them in or excluding them from the united front according to the circumstances at a given time. [7]

---

[6] Partido Comunista de Bolivia–ML, "Draft Peasant-Agrarian Programme," *Peking Review,* 6 June 1969.

[7] See "IV Conferencia nacional del Partido Comunista Peruano: Resolución sobre el Informe Político" (18-19 January 1964), *Bandera Roja* (Lima), 10 February

As will be seen later, most Maoist groups never joined, much less led, the broad united fronts they constantly advocated. The pro-Chinese party in Chile, working within the Chilean context, explained why this was so:

> The proper construction of the united front is a process that passes through diverse stages. This alliance would not accomplish anything while the working class and its most intimate ally, the peasantry, are not mobilized and carrying out armed struggle against the principal exploiter. Thus we don't look for this alliance at present, when it could only be led by the bourgeoisie or its agents. We believe that the principal task at present is to build the party that will lead the proletariat in its revolutionary struggle. Only when the working class is fighting in a revolutionary manner, directed by its party, and when it has won over the peasantry to this struggle, will it then be possible to draw together the other forces for the struggle to the death against imperialism, the latifundists and the most reactionary sectors of the bourgeoisie.[8]

Pro-Chinese parties claimed to maintain their own adherence to principle and the revolution's correct line through the practice of "unity and struggle," particularly toward the bourgeois sectors of the front. As the Maoist party in Peru stated in its first major public resolution, there would be "unity in what signifies progress, development and national sovereignty, and open struggle against capitulation, treason, and surrender." [9] The pro-Chinese party in Chile was a bit more circumspect regarding the "struggle," maintaining that "with the non-proletarian allies it is necessary to practice a policy of unity and struggle, graduating the two factors according to the political circumstances, according to their magnitude as exploiters, in relation to their conduct with respect to the principal enemies and the proletariat, and in accordance with other tactical considerations." [10] The parties should not, however, seek unprincipled reconciliations with the vacillating elements, even in the short term since to do so would bankrupt and defeat the

---

1964; "Extractos de la resolución . . . del Partido Comunista de Colombia (ML)," pp. 69-70; and *Programa del Partido Comunista Revolucionario,* pp. 24-26; Movimiento de Izquierda Revolucionaria (Uruguay), "No Soñar con la democracia burguesa," *Causa Marxista-Leninista* (Santiago), no. 13 (November 1969), pp. 10-11; and *Línea Política del Partido Comunista de Bolivia Aprobada por el Primer Congreso Extraordinario* (Llallagua, Bolivia: Siglo XX, 1965).

[8] *Una línea pequeño-burguesa y una línea proletaria,* pp. 27, 28.

[9] "IV Conferencia nacional del Partido Comunista Peruano."

[10] *Una línea pequeño-burguesa y una línea proletaria,* p. 24.

revolutionary proletarian movement itself. Nor should there be un-restrained struggle against the short-term allies who do not fully agree with the proletariat and peasantry since such activities might drive them into the arms of the fundamental enemies and tip the power balance in favor of the latter. According to the Maoists, the two extremes were the "rightist" or "revisionist" approach of such false revolutionary groups as the pro-Soviet communist parties and the "ultra-leftist" approach of the castroites and some Trotskyists. At the same time, Maoists argued that the fundamental enemies were only the first to be subdued, as indicated above, the short-term allies becoming the targets after the first stage of the revolution had been completed.[11]

And, finally, the Maoists maintained that a truly broad united front was possible only during wartime, and thus at all times "people's war" was one of their main concerns. The leader of the Bolivian Maoists explained the strategy this way:

(1) To place politics first in the conduct of people's war. That is to say, it is essential to depend on Marxist-Leninist leadership, eliminating all counterrevolutionary trends such as contemporary revisionism.

(2) People's war is the armed political struggle of the masses for their liberation. For it, political work among the masses, particularly the workers and peasants, is inseparable from its military activity; this political work must be carried out before and during the armed struggle.

(3) People's war is developed in the following three stages: (a) guerrilla war, linked with peasant uprisings; (b) mobile warfare; and (c) the war of positions, or taking of the cities from the countryside.[12]

Critiques of Marxist-Leninist Rivals

In view of the fact that the pro-Chinese parties themselves are a mani-festation of the Sino-Soviet dispute, it is hardly surprising that virtually

---

[11] See, for example, *Que es el Partido Comunista Revolucionario?* (Santiago, n.d.), pp. 23-26.

[12] Oscar Zamora M., "Partido Comunista de Bolivia (ML) responde a Fidel Castro," *Causa Marxista-Leninista* (Santiago), no. 5 (January-February 1969), p. 36. Also see Zamora, "Guerra Popular: Unico Camino para la Liberación Nacional," in *El pensamiento político Boliviano despues de la nacionalización del petroleo* (Cochabamba, Bolivia: Universitaria, 1970), pp. 105-44; and Partido Comunista de Colombia–ML, *Triunfa la guerra popular en Colombia* (Monte-video, 1969). Robinson Rojas, *Colombia: surge el primer Vietnam en américa latina* (Montevideo: Nativa, 1971); and Partido Comunista Revolucionario, "Resoluciones Políticos aprobadas en el congreso del P.C.R.," *Espártaco,* 2nd fortnight of July 1966.

every important general statement they made attacked "revisionism" in one way or another. Though the pro-Soviet parties accused the Maoists of deliberately trying to split and weaken the left, the pro-Chinese responded, in the words of a Chilean Maoist, that separation from the pro-Soviet parties was "not a break among the workers, but one between workers and the bourgeois agents who have infiltrated their ranks." [13]

In some circumstances, Maoist attitudes toward electoral politics were flexible. In general the party system was considered a device by which leftists of one organization were set against leftists of another organization. However, the decision whether to participate in an election had to be made each time on the basis of tactical considerations. Most pro-Chinese parties encouraged participation in student elections, and (less often) in labor elections. They were much less willing to participate in the national political system itself. In Chile during the late 1960s, the pro-Chinese party looked upon congressional elections as frauds perpetrated by the bourgeoisie and the imperialists, with the complicity of the revisionists. The same was true of the "electoral circus" in September 1970 that led to the election of Salvador Allende as president of Chile.[14] The pro-Chinese Movement of the Revolutionary Left in Uruguay took precisely the same position toward the presidential election in November 1971.[15]

In general terms, the pro-Chinese critique of the "revisionist" communist parties was that they had sought (1) to restrict the activities of revolutionaries to those that fell within the bounds of "bourgeois legality"; (2) to prevent the theoretical and practical training of the masses in armed struggle, even for purely defensive purposes; and (3) to render the masses impotent by giving leadership of the united front

---

[13] "Entrevista al Partido Comunista Revolucionario de Chile," *Causa Marxista-Leninista* (Santiago), no. 3 (September-October 1968), p. 10; also, Movimiento de Izquierda Revolucionaria (Uruguay), "Lucha obrero-estudiantil: ¿Porque?," *Voz Obrera* (Montevideo), October 1971. For typical attacks, see Raimundo León, "La 'Via Pacifica' de Corvalán: camino contra-revolucionario," *Causa Marxista-Leninista* (Santiago), no. 17 (April 1970), pp. 3-15; and "IV Conferencia nacional del Partido Comunista Peruano."

[14] Partido Comunista Revolucionario, *Las elecciones y la lucha de nuestro pueblo* (Santiago, 1969), and *Derrotemos el sectarismo y coloquemos el partido a la cabeza de la lucha de las masas* (Santiago, 1970); and "Las elecciones presidenciales: una siembra de ilusiones para impedir la revolución," *Causa Marxista-Leninista* (Santiago), no. 16 (February-March 1970), pp. 2-6.

[15] See "¿Que significa noviembre para el pueblo?," *Voz Obrera* (Montevideo), 23 November 1971.

and the revolutionary movement over to the bourgeoisie and its representatives on the grounds that it was necessary to have them as allies and that they would be allies only on these terms.

Maoists in Latin America have been much more openly critical of Fidel Castro than have the Chinese communists and have directed some of their longest and most colorful critiques at Régis Debray and the castroites in their own countries.[16] In their view, the fundamental misconceptions of the castroite line were (1) its origins in "petty-bourgeois," adventurist, romantic, individualistic, ultra-left, and anti-Marxist thought and experience; (2) its reliance on a small clique of non-proletarian leaders to the exclusion of the masses, the latter a class the castroites feared and did not much respect; (3) its determination to take on all enemies at once, as reflected in the call to bypass the people's democratic revolution and to move immediately to the socialist revolution; (4) its rejection of Marxist-Leninist proletarian party leadership; and (5) its rejection of the fundamental Maoist understanding that "the party must command the gun"—that is, that politics must come before military action. This adventurist line, the "focoist" line, had been advocated for the continent by the Cuban leaders, in large part by the circulation of Régis Debray's book *Revolution in the Revolution?* It had failed repeatedly in the past, according to the Maoists, and was bound to do so in the future. Even if it were successful in overthrowing an unpopular government, it would not—since the leadership and orientation were non-proletarian—produce a socialist state but merely lead to a different group in power, a group that would eventually be transformed into a new oppressor.[17]

The most widely circulated attack on a Maoist party was made by Fidel Castro in his "Necessary Introduction" to the Cuban edition of Che Guevara's diary. According to Castro, Oscar Zamora, the leader of the pro-Chinese Communist Party of Bolivia, "had once promised to work with Che on the organization of an armed guerrilla fight in Bolivia," but subsequently "withdrew his commitments and cowardly folded his arms when the hour for action arrived, becoming one of the most poisonous critics in the name of 'Marxism-Leninism' after Che's

---

[16] For example, see *Carta Abierta a Fidel Castro del Partido Comunista de Brasil* (Santiago: Entrecerros, 1966).

[17] Important statements on the petit-bourgeois adventurist line are: *Programa del Partido Comunista Revolucionario*, pp. 81-84; and the pamphlet *Una línea pequeño-burguesa y una línea proletaria.*

death." [18] Zamora responded with a long "open letter" to Castro in July 1968, his main points being (1) that Guevara nowhere in the diary made or implied any such criticism of Zamora or the Maoist Communist Party of Bolivia; (2) that in September-October 1964 Zamora and some other Bolivians decided to form a revolutionary vanguard separate from the Communist Party of Bolivia to liberate Bolivia and that Zamora, on a trip to Cuba at the end of that year, won Guevara's backing in this venture; (3) that Castro then "sold out" to the "revisionists" at the November 1964 conference of Latin American communist parties in Havana, decided to break contacts with Marxist-Leninist parties in Latin America, and persuaded Guevara to go along with him; and (4) that from that time onward the pro-Chinese communist party knew nothing of Cuban plans for Bolivia, including the decision to send Guevara, the time of his arrival, or his whereabouts after arriving. Thus, said Zamora, he had not withdrawn his support but rather been shut out by Castro and not allowed to participate.[19]

The Maoists rejected the "focoist" line in the countryside and in the city—that is, in rural guerrilla warfare as attempted by Che Guevara in Bolivia in 1966–1967 and in urban guerrilla warfare and terrorism. The rural focoist approach was described as one of typical "petty-bourgeois" impatience. Rather than trying to win the support of the rural population so that they could carry on their own protracted war of liberation, the castroites tried to wage war on their own in order to win the support of the masses for themselves. The castroites did not try to raise the level of consciousness of the masses by instructing them in the ideology of the proletariat so that they could form their own liberation army for both offensive and defensive purposes; rather, they formed a small military nucleus (the *foco*) of their own which then undertook heroic actions to win the support of the masses. The castroite approach might, on the one hand, win no support and drag on indefinitely as with the National Liberation Army (ELN) in Colombia, or it might be crushed, as was the National Liberation Army (ELN) in Bolivia. In either case the government might launch a cam-

---

[18] *The Diary of Che Guevara*, p. 14. Inti Peredo, in his *Mi campaña con el che* (Buenos Aires: Edibol, 1971), p. 47, writes that Zamora was "as opportunistic and false as the other self-proclaimed vanguardists."

[19] Zamora, "Partido Comunista de Bolivia (ML) responde a Fidel Castro," pp. 30-37.

paign of oppression against the masses and they, left untrained by the castroites, would be left at the mercy of the national repressive forces.[20]

The Maoist organizations were equally critical of the urban guerrillas. Though they did not automatically rule out struggle in the cities, the pro-Chinese groups did insist that the main field of battle was in the countryside. The urban guerrilla warfare of the castroites, best represented by the National Liberation Movement (the Tupamaros) in Uruguay or the Trotskyists, the most representative of which was the People's Revolutionary Army (ERP) in Argentina, was un-Marxist. The Uruguayan Movement of the Revolutionary Left (MIR) was particularly vocal in its criticism of the Tupamaros.[21] Only weeks after the MLN had kidnapped and murdered U.S. security advisor Dan A. Mitrione in the summer of 1970, the MIR published a long condemnation of the castroite Tupamaros. They were described as the "natural expression of the focoist doctrine," influenced primarily by the Cuban revolution. The focoist doctrine of the Tupamaros was based on a "deformation of the Cuban experience." It was characterized by adventurism, subjectivity, leftist opportunism, and terrorism and was, consequently, "totally at odds with Marxism." The Tupamaros were mistaken about the role of the people and of the party in the revolutionary struggle.[22]

The difference between the revolutionary roads of the Maoists and the castroites was summed up by the pro-Chinese Revolutionary Communist Party of Chile:

> People's war is an expression of proletarian ideology just as "focoism" and urban terrorism are the expression of petty-bourgeois ideology. Our differences with the MIR [the Chilean castroites] are not, as they claim, those of following or sympathizing with this or that country, but very profound ones corresponding to the different classes which we represent.[23]

[20] For a typical developed statement of this line, see *Una línea pequeño-burguesa y una línea proletaria.*

[21] "Movement of the Revolutionary Left" was a popular name for revolutionary organizations in Latin America during the period from 1960 to 1976. In Uruguay the MIR was pro-Chinese, but that was not so anywhere else. The name MIR was generally adopted by castroite groups (as in Chile and Peru), though these groups sometimes originated as splits from major political parties (as in Venezuela and Peru).

[22] See *Tupamaros, ¿Conspiración o Revolución?, Repuesta de los Marxistas-Leninistas del Uruguay* (Montevideo: Ediciones Voz Obrera, 1970).

[23] *Una línea pequeño-burguesa y una línea proletaria*, p. 47.

Conclusions

The Maoist road emphasized by the Chinese Communist Party (CCP) and its admirers in Latin America was substantially different in important respects from the roads propounded by the pro-Soviet parties and the castroite guerrilla organizations in their rural or urban forms. What is more, contrary to Chinese assertions at the time, the Maoist road of the 1960s was not an accurate distillation of the Chinese communists' own rich historical experience, an experience which could indeed prove instructive to Latin American revolutionaries. Rather, it was a distortion (appealing in theory but too narrow and inflexible in practice) designed to serve the interests of dominant Chinese leaders during the 1960s, first in the conflict with the Soviet Union and then in the domestic upheaval of the Great Proletarian Cultural Revolution.[24] This road never drew a significant number of active followers in Latin America though more Latin Americans sympathized with the general strategic line than joined the pro-Chinese organizations.

The pro-Chinese communist parties and organizations of Latin America, never serious contenders for political power in any country at any time, were chiefly a phenomenon of the Sino-Soviet dispute. By the mid-1970s, most of them had declined from their original insignificance or disappeared altogether, though a generally nondescript "Maoism" was still advocated by pockets of students, workers, and guerrillas in a number of countries.

---

[24] See Ratliff, "The Chinese Communist Domestic United Front and Its Application to Latin America, 1921-1971," Chapter 2.

5

Castroism: Rural Guerrilla Warfare

If the pro-Soviet and pro-Chinese communist parties generally turned fully toward Moscow and Peking, respectively, the castroite-nationalist groups usually turned half way toward Havana. They had a strongly nationalistic streak, yet at the same time were fascinated by the Cuban revolution and its leaders; during the later years of our period they were usually convinced that the revolution would have to be continental in scope. Throughout the period from 1959 to 1976 the castroites were the main representatives of what Robert J. Alexander has called the Jacobin Left, characterized by their elitism, anti-democratic bias, and determination to destroy the existing political, economic, and social structures of their countries in order to achieve immediate national liberation and socialism.

Background

Castroite tendencies developed during the 1960s in several parties that had been established long before the victory of Fidel Castro, among them the socialist parties of Uruguay and Chile. The latter, an important force in Chilean politics for several decades before September 1973, had a castroite wing (led by Carlos Altamirano) that was dominant in the party and influential in national affairs during most of the Popular Unity government (1970–1973), a point which is discussed in Chapter 7.

Most castroite groups, however, were newly formed during the 1960s. Like the leaders of the Cuban revolution, castroites came to these groups from a variety of political and social positions. Some had been Marxist-Leninists before their castroite days; among these were prominent leaders of the Bolivian National Liberation Army (ELN) and the Venezuelan Armed Forces of National Liberation (FALN). Many may not have begun as Marxist-Leninists but by the late 1960s they professed the Marxist-Leninist ideology. No doubt it was in part this phenomenon that led Fidel Castro to comment on 13 March 1967 that "many, the immense majority of those who today proudly call themselves Marxist-Leninists, arrived at Marxism-Leninism by way of the revolutionary struggle." [1] In early 1964 Luis de la Puente, originally a young leader of the Peruvian Aprista party, who formed Peru's first important castroite group, said that "the ideology of the true left— Marxism-Leninism—is the proletarian ideology, the ideology of the working class that, allied with the peasantry, can lead the liberation process in our country." [2]

De la Puente's Movement of the Revolutionary Left (MIR) was only one of several castroite groups to grow out of tensions within some of the most important leftist-reformist parties in Latin America. The Venezuelan MIR was founded by dissidents from President Rómulo Betancourt's Democratic Action (AD) party, and the Chilean Movement of United Popular Action (MAPU) and Christian Left (IC) both were formed by internal critics of the Christian Democratic Party (PDC). These dissidents, impatient with the policies and actions of their reform-oriented parties, became convinced that armed revolution was essential. Over varying periods of time, they concluded that the castroite version of Marxism-Leninism gave the best theoretical explanation of contemporary conditions in their countries and in Latin America generally and offered the most productive (often they insisted, the only) guide to revolutionary victory. Accustomed to handling the complexities of political doctrines, they assimilated castroite Marxism-Leninism with greater ease, and articulated it more clearly, than many less sophisticated persons. Among the latter were several other groups, including the Colombian National Liberation Army (ELN), which were clearly castroite yet which for years had leaders who demonstrated only a

---

[1] *Granma* (Havana), 19 March 1967. Debray wrote that "the best teachers of Marxism-Leninism are the enemies met face-to-face." He noted that in contrast to the Cuban experience, where "the ideology of the Rebel Army was not Marxist, the ideology of the new (guerrilla) commands clearly is, just as the revolution they seek to carry out is clearly socialist and proletarian." Debray, *¿Revolución en la revolución?*, pp. 94, 90.

[2] Rogger Mercado, *Las guerrillas del Peru* (Lima: Fondo de Cultura Popular, 1967), p. 84.

passing acquaintance with Marxism-Leninism in its castroite or any other variety.

The Marxist-Leninist line adopted by a few castroite groups in the early and middle 1960s had a significant element of Maoism mixed in. As was noted earlier, the Chinese and Cubans did not disagree openly over the best strategy and tactics for Latin America until the mid-1960s. The most pro-Chinese of all castroite groups—or the most castroite of all Maoist groups—was the Guatemalan 13 November Revolutionary Movement (MR-13). A number of castroite groups during the 1959–1976 period were open to what they considered truly revolutionary ideas from almost any part of the world. Very few seem to have felt outright disdain for learning from any other Marxist-Leninist experience than the Cuban, and none made such a fetish of it as Debray.

Castroite leaders named their organizations so as to convey a message about their movement and its objectives. They tried to reflect a national revolutionary stance unencumbered by apparently binding international associations. Thus, the vast majority of their names referred to revolution, national liberation, or revolutionary armed forces. They uniformly avoided the word "communist" in an effort to disassociate themselves from the established communist parties, which they more and more believed had ceased to be (if indeed they ever had been) truly revolutionary, and they avoided the designation "Marxist-Leninist," which by the mid-1960s had become the pro-Chinese trademark in the Sino-Soviet dispute. The most common names which emerged were the Movement of the Revolutionary Left (MIR), as in Chile, Peru, Venezuela, and Ecuador, and the National Liberation Army (ELN), as in Bolivia, Colombia, and Peru.[3]

In most countries castroite groups were small, seldom having more than an estimated several hundred active members. Rural guerrilla forces, such as the Colombian ELN and the Venezuelan FALN, were generally made up largely of peasants and "proletarianized intellectuals" (particularly students), with a smattering of workers. Urban organizations, most important among them the Uruguayan National Liberation Movement (MLN), the Tupamaros, or urban branches of predominantly rural groups, were composed primarily of radicalized members of the petit-bourgeoisie and proletariat. An important castroite leader in Chile openly acknowledged the predominance of student and petit-bourgeois elements in the MIR, but stated simply that revolutionary

---

[3] The MIR in Uruguay, but nowhere else, was openly pro-Chinese.

101

parties of Russia, China, and Cuba had at first been similarly composed.[4] Reflecting their continental support and aspirations, castroite groups in one country often had participants from fraternal organizations of other countries. The inter-American aspect of castroite membership was seen in the Bolivian ELN under Guevara and in the Venezuelan FALN.[5]

Not surprisingly, support for the guerrillas was stronger among intellectuals, particularly the university students, than in any other sector of society. Often this led to short-term recruits—the "weekend warriors" of Guatemala and Venezuela—though sometimes it produced fighters who enlisted for the long term. University campuses, at least those governed under a policy of university autonomy, sometimes provided guerrillas with a haven in the cities. Before December 1966, when Venezuelan President Raúl Leoni "neutralized" the Central University in Caracas, the seven-square-mile campus provided shelter, storehouses, and staging facilities for guerrillas and terrorists.

At times, castroite groups played a dominant role in university politics as well. During the mid-1960s, an alliance of the castroite MIR and the Venezuelan Communist Party (PCV) dominated politics at the Central University; after the split between the communists and the castroites in 1966–1967, the MIR continued to win the presidency of the Federation of University Centers at the University of the Andes in Méreda. In Chile, the MIR was active in all universities, though strongest at the University of Concepción where it was originally based.

Strategy and Tactics

By the mid-1960s, in contrast to the pro-Soviet and pro-Chinese parties, the castroite-nationalist groups generally fought for a joint national liberation and socialist revolution. The need to step up the revolutionary timetable was argued repeatedly by Che Guevara and Régis Debray, as explained earlier, and by the Latin American guerrillas themselves. Their conviction resulted from and led to a commitment to the castroite outlook on the road to power, on leadership, and on the composition of the united front of revolutionary forces.

---

[4] Miguel Enríquez, interview published in *Punto Final* (Santiago), 23 April 1968.
[5] On the ELN, see comments throughout Guevara's diary; on the FALN, see Patricio Garcia, "Chilenos combaten en la guerrilla venezolana," *Punto Final* (Santiago), supplement, 31 December 1968.

The castroite groups discussed in this chapter followed a road to power that was patterned in important respects on the path of the Cuban revolution as interpreted by Castro, Guevara, and Debray. Other castroite-oriented organizations, which followed chiefly urban or combined urban-rural roads, will be discussed in the following chapters.

The road to power emphasizing rural guerrilla warfare is the typically "castroite" road between 1959 and 1976, yet even this was far from static, as was shown in Chapter 2. It was the road followed by many of Latin America's best known guerrilla leaders and forces, including Douglas Bravo, Francisco Prada, Luben Petkoff, and the Venezuelan FALN; Moisés Moliero and the Venezuelan MIR; Luis Turcios, César Montes, and the Guatemalan FAR; Fabio Vázquez and the Colombian ELN; Luis de la Puente, Ricardo Gadea, and the Peruvian MIR; Che Guevara, the Peredo brothers, and the Bolivian ELN. These castroite guerrilla leaders, some of whom were killed during the 1960s and others of whom turned on Fidel Castro after the Soviet-Cuban rapprochement at the end of the decade, followed similar (though not the same) roads over the years. Most who survived into the late 1960s were critical of Régis Debray's formulation of the castroite road, as will be shown below. And yet, on balance, these guerrillas and their forces were castroite both because of their long-lasting respect for and contacts with the Cuban revolutionary leaders, and because of their basic attitudes toward revolution. A brief sketch of the history and positions of several of these castroite groups will make this clear.

Venezuela. Following its formation in the early 1960s, the National Liberation Front (FLN) and its military arm, the FALN, became the most important allied organizations in which the Venezuelan Communist Party (PCV) played a leading role. By 1966, however, the PCV association with the FLN-FALN was proving very troublesome. When some PCV officials began to propose a tactical retreat from guerrilla warfare, several guerrilla leaders turned against the party, which by exercising control through the FLN had been able to apply pressure on guerrillas with whom it disagreed. On 22 April 1965 five guerrilla leaders, including PCV politburo member Douglas Bravo, met secretly and set up a "Comando Unico" (often abbreviated CUFF) controlling both the FLN and the FALN, thereby putting the decision-making offices in the hands of the guerrillas themselves. According to documents issued at the time by the new command group, its officers were Bravo,

Gregorio Lunar Márquez, Elías Manuit Camero, Francisco Prada, Fabricio Ojeda, and four others who soon withdrew.[6] Thenceforth there existed two parallel FLN-FALN organizations. One, headed by Bravo (removed from the PCV politburo in May 1966 and expelled from the party in April 1967), was castroite and in rebellion against the PCV. The other, loyal to the PCV, was in overall command of increasingly less active forces entrusted to Pedro Medina Silva, one of the leading figures in the January 1966 Tricontinental Conference in Havana.

Relations between the PCV and the FALN (Bravo) became more and more hostile during 1966, with the hostility erupting before the general public in March 1967. Early in that month a former Venezuelan government official, the brother of the foreign minister, was kidnapped and murdered. On 6 March the Cuban paper *Granma* carried a statement by Elias Manuit, in which he, as president of the castroite FALN, admitted that his organization was responsible for the application of "revolutionary justice." Both the murder and the Manuit statement were condemned during the next few days by PCV leaders and by the loyalist FALN headed by Medina Silva.

On 13 March Fidel Castro made the dispute the subject of one of his longest speeches of the year. He quoted a number of documents issued by the contending groups, attacked the PCV idea of "democratic peace," and concluded that the Venezuelan communists had committed "treason" against the guerrillas. Thereafter the previously covert Cuban support for the FALN became overt and the dispute openly took on continental implications. The PCV conflict with the castroite FALN was made an example of what Castro (and Régis Debray) considered the betrayal of the guerrillas by a number of Latin American communist parties and thus their betrayal of the revolutions in their countries. Castro did not invite the PCV or the loyalist FALN to send delegates to the conference of the Latin American Solidarity Organization (OLAS) in Havana in August, while the castroite FALN and the MIR were each represented by at least four delegates. After the OLAS conference, Medina Silva issued a statement on behalf of the loyalist FALN condemning the OLAS and charging that the attending FALN delegation was a "usurper" that did not represent the real FALN.

The leaders of the castroite branch engaged in extensive self-criticism during 1966 and 1967 in an effort to understand and explain

---

[6] See *Confidencial* (Caracas), no. 32 (August 1966).

the failures of the guerrilla movement up to that time. The problems, according to a FALN statement issued in November 1967, were the following: "The military policy of the armed movement was based on false premises, which prevented the movement from taking advantage of the highly favorable conditions which were present in the first years of the war . . . operational activity . . . was subordinated to the political maneuvering." In a typical statement of castroite conflict with a pro-Soviet party, the FALN said that

> two diametrically opposed concepts met head on: the true revolutionary concept and the capitulationist one calling for the liquidation of the armed struggle. Throughout the struggle, errors were creating two different powers in the revolutionary camp. The real power was supported by the revolutionary policy of the armed urban and rural units and the rank and file of the parties, and the formal power was supported by the reactionary and capitulationist policy of the bureaucratic leadership of the parties. The resolving of the contradiction in favor of the former (with the formation of CUFF in 1966) made possible the application of a truly revolutionary policy politically and militarily, as well as organizationally and on a mass scale.

The tactical nature of the struggle was never determined clearly enough, leading to "ideological confusion which alternated between the adventurist coup mentality and electoral methods, between insurrectionalism and prolonged struggle." This, in turn, resulted in a serious "underestimation of guerrilla warfare and the armed apparatus in general." No serious campaign strategy existed and the party and mass structures failed to adapt themselves to the armed struggle. There was no true centralized headquarters.[7]

In December 1966 the FLN-FALN drew up the fundamental elements of its new military policy. CUFF gave its description of the "main enemy" that the Venezuelan people would face in their continuing struggle. This enemy was a "single force," even though it assumed "characteristics making it appear different from a political, military, economic and social point of view." Politically, in the long term, the enemy was "the whole governmental structure that supports the exploiting classes." In the short term, it was the Democratic Action (AD) government. The military enemy was the national armed forces

---

[7] CUFF statement quoted in *Tricontinental* (Havana), no. 6 (May-June 1968), pp. 14-16.

("the main shock troops of U.S. imperialism and the exploiting classes"), and the economic enemy was "Yankee imperialism's companies." [8]

Francisco Prada, a prominent FALN guerrilla leader, commented in an interview in mid-December 1968 that with the election of Rafael Caldera as president of Venezuela in late 1968, the Christian Democratic Party (COPEI) had become the main enemy. The fact that the Yankee monopolies and creole oligarchy had "changed their chief" was of secondary importance; the only road to liberation was still revolutionary war. The FALN, according to Prada, was continuing to build a "powerful people's army and an alliance of classes," a real National Liberation Front (FLN) that would bring together "in centers of iron discipline all Marxist-Leninists who participate in the liberation struggle." Strengthening the columns and guerrilla bases were the chief goals of the revolutionary movement.[9]

In an interview with Mexican newsman Mario Menéndez Rodríguez, Douglas Bravo indicated that the FALN was composed of four elements: the rural guerrilla forces, the urban guerrilla fighters, the patriotic officers in the garrisons, and the suburban guerrilla movement.[10] The leader of the FALN's urban guerrillas, Nery Carrillo, explained to Menéndez (in an interview in Caracas) that at that time the urban guerrillas were definitely subsidiary to the rural guerrillas. The urban guerrillas were important in part because they tied down substantial numbers of government forces in the city. According to Carrillo, the actions of the urban guerrillas had to be "quick, violent and very well synchronized." Ultimately, he added, the urban guerrillas would have to develop the popular insurrection in the city.[11]

According to Luben Petkoff, the FALN was originally made up largely of city dwellers, workers, students, and progressive intellectuals; by late 1966 it was 90 percent peasant.[12] Bravo emphasized in his talk with Menéndez that the program of the FALN was "vast and not

---

[8] Ibid., pp. 16-19.

[9] Francisco Prada interview, *Punto Final* (Santiago), supplement, 31 December 1968, p. 3.

[10] The interview, broadcast to Latin America in two sections on Havana radio on 24 and 31 December 1966, is part of a series of articles by Menéndez, editor of the Mexican magazine *Sucesos para todos*, which appeared in the 10, 17, 24, 31 December 1966 and 7 January 1967 issues of that publication. The articles on the FALN, and a later series on the Colombian ELN, contained many pictures and long interviews obtained during a prolonged sojourn with the guerrillas.

[11] See interview in ibid., 7 January 1967, pp. 17-20.

[12] Interview with Menéndez Rodríguez, broadcast on Havana radio, 23 January 1967.

sectarian," and remarked that the organization included men from a wide variety of parties (including the AD and COPEI). The leadership, however, was Marxist-Leninist. In his speech to the OLAS conference in August 1967, at which he served as one of four vice presidents, Prada stated unequivocally that "in Venezuela, the guerrilla struggle is based on Marxist-Leninist principles." [13]

Between 1968 and 1970, some of the best known FALN guerrillas broke with Bravo, either because they had lost faith in armed struggle or because they disagreed with his tactics. (Among them was Luben Petkoff, the brother of PCV (later MAS) leader, Teodoro Petkoff.) Francisco Prada was captured in 1971. During this period Bravo became openly critical of Fidel Castro for abandoning his international revolutionary obligations—specifically his support for the Venezuelan guerrillas.[14] Between 1970 and 1976 Bravo grew increasingly critical of the Soviet Union, openly sided with the Chinese in the Sino-Soviet dispute, and reportedly set up and led several small pro-Chinese guerrilla organizations.

Douglas Bravo and Francisco Prada were among the first and most severe critics of Régis Debray's *Revolution in the Revolution?* In his December 1968 interview, Prada (sometimes quoting Bravo) objected to Debray's formulations on the role of the party, the formation of the revolutionary front, and the role of urban guerrillas.[15] Bravo's 1970 critique of *Revolution in the Revolution?* is instructive both in providing information on Bravo's own policies (Bravo being for many years Latin America's most prominent castroite) and in providing an informed criticism of Debray from within the ranks of the castroite forces.[16]

Bravo approved of Debray's frontal attack on the "old dogmatism, schematism, and sectarianism" of most so-called revolutionary forces in Latin America. Unfortunately, however, Debray had fallen into the same trap himself; Venezuelan guerrillas knew from their own experience, and that of their fellows in other countries, that the French Marxist was frequently in error. And yet, Bravo noted, Debray's views were "completely shared by the Cuban comrades," and this could only in-

---

[13] Quoted from the complete official transcript of Prada's speech as released at the OLAS conference.

[14] See interview with Humberto Solioni, in *Marcha*, 15 May 1970.

[15] *Punto Final* (Santiago), supplement, 31 December 1968, p. 5.

[16] Bravo's interview, quoted in the next four paragraphs, is found in *Marcha*, 15 May 1970.

crease tensions between the Venezuelan guerrillas and the Cuban leadership. According to Bravo,

> the Cuban revolution occurred at a particular time, characterized by special circumstances. It was fundamentally an anti-dictatorial struggle in its first stage. Because of this, it had to have a completely different plan from the struggles that were to develop after the triumph of the Cuban Revolution in other countries of Latin America. From this point of view, the Cuban movement was able to bring together an immense bloc of men from the bourgeoisie, working class, peasants, and students, and pulled them all into the violence. In its second stage, beginning in 1960, the Cuban Revolution took on a new character, the socialist character. But the socialist character began after [the seizure of] power and that was, precisely, its fundamental difference from the liberation movements that are developing in Latin America. [The latter], from the moment they develop, will assume a national liberation and a socialist character and, in these circumstances, the alliances, blocs and classes are changed. This, then, is the element of the differences we have with the comrades of the Cuban Revolutionary leadership.

Bravo insisted that Debray's book was not based on the Latin American reality. Neither Latin American revolutionaries in general nor fighters in individual countries could draw important lessons from it since it "fell into another dogmatism, not formulating profound analyses but little recipes, interpretations which were, in large part, of a dogmatic variety."

More specifically, Bravo charged Debray with making myths of small groups of legendary men. He exaggerated actual conditions. He raised the problem of combat, of shooting, to the central position in every struggle,

> throwing aside, almost absurdly underestimating, the organization of the working class, the peasants, and the other classes which must necessarily carry out the historic role of destroying the oligarchy and imperialism in our countries. In the same way, Debray denies the role of the revolutionary party, of the Marxist-Leninist party as the most important instrument in the liberation struggle. And what is more, he denies the role of the liberation front, bringing out some correct arguments but reaching incorrect conclusions.

Thus, in *Revolution in the Revolution?,* Debray argues that the tactics of the Cuban revolution will create revolutions in all other Latin

American countries in just a few years. He believes that "the men from the mountains, disregarding the cities where the majority of the population is concentrated, disregarding other nuclei, would return triumphant in a few years and surround the cities." In sum, according to Bravo, "we can say that the entire tactic of Debrayism, or of the Cuban comrades who put it into practice in Latin America, is an incorrect tactic. It is a tactic of *focoismo,* the tactic of the shortcut, the tactic of underestimating the organization of the party, of the front, of the working class, and of the peasants."

And, finally, drawing a conclusion that some other guerrillas (among them César Montes in Guatemala) were unable to see, Bravo argued that, in truth, the tactic Debray described had not been followed in Cuba at all. It was "a distortion of what occurred in Cuba, a distortion which unquestionably resulted in defeats of great magnitude in Latin America, culminating in the destruction of the guerrilla nucleus in Bolivia and particularly in the death of Comandante Ernesto Guevara."

Another Venezuelan group, the Movement of the Revolutionary Left, was founded in 1960 by Domingo Alberto Rangel and other dissidents from President Betancourt's AD party. It supported armed struggle during most of the 1960s, its legal status (like that of the PCV) being "suspended" in 1962. For much of the 1960s, it was the main castroite group in Venezuela, sometimes competing and sometimes cooperating with the FALN. By the mid-1960s it was an avowedly Marxist-Leninist organization.[17]

Before 1964 the MIR had adopted no coherent tactic.[18] During that year it undertook serious study of revolutionary tactics for the country and concluded that at its present stage the revolutionary war was a war for national liberation from imperialism. In it, peaceful forms of struggle were subordinated to the nonpeaceful. The war would have to be protracted

> in order to wear down the relative strength of the enemy (imperialism and the dominant class) and build up the revolutionary forces. This would be possible only on the basis of a concrete development of the war, clarity regarding the strategic and tactical scope of various forms of armed struggle, building solid bases for the growth of the people's army, development of correct military and political tactics, not

---

[17] MIR, "¿Que es la propaganda?" *Confidencial* (Caracas), no. 9 (15 September 1964), pp. 2, 3.

[18] "Carta de Información No. 26, del MIR," ibid., no. 23 (22 June 1965).

commiting errors of principle, and winning the broad levels of the people for the war.[19]

The struggle should be directed against the principal enemy—civil-military "gorillaism," of which "Betancourtism" was merely one form. To direct the attacks against Betancourt alone would be to aid indirectly other "gorillas," some of whom were more dangerous than Betancourt himself, who seek to defeat the revolutionary movement. The two extremes to be opposed were conciliation (the principal danger), which sought to negotiate a return to legality, and leftism, which opposed all legal and mass struggles and would provoke artificial confrontations.[20]

In early 1968 an official of the Antonio José de Sucre Guerrilla Front (FGAJS, also called the Eastern Front), led by Carlos Betancourt, outlined the policies of his front in response to a questionnaire sent to MIR general headquarters by the Cuba-based journal *Tricontinental.* His comments on MIR attitudes toward carrying out the revolution were in many respects very close to those reported above, being based as they were on MIR resolutions of 1964 and 1965. According to this official:

> We are not waging just any kind of war, but are rather engaged in a war of national liberation fought by the workers and peasants with the aid of the proletarianized petty-bourgeoisie, under the specific conditions existing in our country. The nature of this war—a popular war of national liberation against imperialism—is not changed by the fact that today it appears in the form of a civil war. This only serves to show us that our basic task is to prepare and organize the masses for armed struggle, basing ourselves on these masses and identifying the liberation war with the class struggle of the workers and peasants, based on the fundamental contradiction existing within Venezuelan society today—the contradiction that exists between imperialism, the national bourgeoisie, and the landowners, on the one hand, and the entire Venezuelan nation, on the other hand. . . . Our strategy, which seeks a change in the correlation of forces—that is, it seeks to convert our relative weakness into an absolute fortress of strength—consists in using our military forces over diffuse fronts covering extensive geographical areas, taking advantage of the terrain's favorable characteristics in order to start the armed struggle of the masses there, where the enemy is politically

---

[19] "Carta de Información No. 12, del MIR," ibid., no. 11 (2 November 1964), pp. 11, 13.
[20] "Carta de Información No. 26, del MIR," ibid., no. 23 (22 June 1965).

and militarily the weakest. The idea of the Front was born of the need to link the guerrilla struggle of the peasant masses, and it arose mainly from the nature of the strategic objectives imposed on us by the present stage of the struggle.

This guerrilla leader further stated that the front was divided into two sets of detachments: "first, the zonal detachment, which operates in one of the Front's geographical areas and whose basic tasks are to organize and develop the work among the mass of peasants and to give military training to the peasants and the new combatants; the second, the mobile combat detachment, which operates throughout the Front's territory." The MIR recognized that it could not prevent national elections—the 1968 presidential elections were coming up—and concluded that "for us these elections—and the political crisis that is developing at the same time—are an episode in the long process of the people's revolutionary war which will produce more or less favorable results according to how we go about using them to advance our own strategic objectives." [21]

The Cuban government gave moral and material support to the MIR throughout the decade. In May 1967, Moisés Moliero landed on the Venezuelan coast as part of a Cuban-Venezuelan guerrilla force.[22] When the Leoni government responded by charging the Cubans with interference in Venezuelan affairs, the Central Committee of the Cuban Communist Party made its commitment of support to the revolutionary movements mentioned above: "We are accused of helping revolutionary movements, and we, quite so, are giving and will continue to give help to all revolutionary movements that struggle against imperialism in any part of the world, whenever they request it." [23]

It should be noted that during much of this period no party in Venezuela was more torn by internal dissension than the MIR. This dissension was the result of personal rivalries, of different views on the forms of armed and peaceful struggle, and of varying reactions to the pacification program and pardons introduced by President Caldera in March 1969. By the mid-1970s the MIR had gone full cycle; it had regained its legality and was represented in the national legislature.

[21] Luis Enrique Ball, interview in *Tricontinental* (Havana), no. 6 (May-June 1968), pp. 71, 72, 76.

[22] See *Izquierda*, May 1967.

[23] Central Committee statement in *Granma* (Havana), 21 May 1967; on the Venezuelan charge, see OAS Information Service News Release "backgrounder," "Foreign Ministers to Take Up Venezuelan Charges of Cuban Intervention," E-77/67 (12 September 1967).

Guatemala. The Rebel Armed Forces (FAR) was founded in December 1962 by members of three Guatemalan organizations: the Alejandro de León-13 November Revolutionary Movement (the MR-13), the "20 October" forces of the Guatemalan communists (the PGT), and the "12 April" student group. Its most important early leaders were Marco Antonio Yon Sosa and Luis Augusto Turcios Lima, founders of the MR-13 in early 1962, both of whom had been Guatemalan military officers trained by the United States government.[24] While the FAR carried out some actions during 1963 and 1964, tensions developed between the members of the original MR-13 and the PGT. The MR-13 believed the communists, with their United Resistance Front (FUR) and their support for a "national democratic" revolution, were not fully committed to the armed struggle; the PGT concluded that Yon Sosa and his followers were sectarians and under Trotskyite influence. Luis Turcios joined Yon Sosa in reestablishing the MR-13 as an independent organization by signing the "First Declaration of the Sierra de las Minas" in December 1964, but soon broke away to form the Edgar Ibarra Guerrilla Front (FGEI) and then to lead the old FAR forces in closer cooperation with the PGT. Turcios played an active part in the January 1966 Tricontinental Conference in Havana and died in an automobile crash in October 1966. He was succeeded by César Montes, his second in command. The FAR and MR-13 merged again in 1968 with Yon Sosa as supreme commander and Montes once again second in command. By early 1969 Yon Sosa and the MR-13 were again on their own and Montes had been demoted, the FAR being led by Pablo Monsanto and a national directorate.

The tensions over PGT influence on the FAR, which led to the withdrawal of the MR-13 in late 1964, were patched over in 1965. Troubles reemerged over the next few years, however, and by late 1967–early 1968 had resulted in a split within the PGT and a break between the communists and the FAR. In May 1965 the Central Committee of the PGT stated that it conceived of the FAR as "the organization responsible for directly carrying on armed struggle, under the control of the PGT and such non-Party revolutionaries as accept the fundamental ideas of Marxism-Leninism; not a parallel organization,

---

[24] Yon Sosa went to Fort Gulick in the Panama Canal Zone, and Turcios to Fort Benning, Georgia.

but an organization centered in the PGT." [25] But, in April–May 1967, César Montes told an Uruguayan reporter:

> The fact that some communists are in the FAR does not mean that our movement functions as the armed arm of any party. The FAR is not the armed arm of the PGT. Ours is a broad, patriotic movement with a very simple program: we Guatemalans want to be able to control ourselves without any foreign military, economic, or political intervention. We are creating the people's organization for the revolutionary war; within the guerrilla is the germ of the great people's army which ultimately will be able to offer a power alternative.[26]

After the reorganization of the FAR in 1965, the PGT began to promote young guerrilla leaders to important positions in the party. The PGT representative in Cuba during 1967, Oscar Palma, wrote in the Cuban Communist Party daily that his party had changed its structure, including its leadership, and was "abandoning old and narrow ideas, eradicating formalistic and bureaucratic methods, and bringing representatives of the young and vigorous generation of Marxist-Leninists into its Central Committee." [27] This, the party declared in March 1968, was in keeping with the concept of "integrated leadership" favored by the guerrillas.[28] Thus Debray understandably referred to a "renewed and rejuvenated" PGT when writing his *Revolution in the Revolution?* during 1966.[29] However, according to Montes—himself a member of the PGT politburo until the January 1968 break between the communists and the FAR—the "rejuvenation" of the Central Committee was merely a "maneuver to neutralize the most radical proposals and swamp the military leaders in an involved disciplinary setup." [30] The high degree to which strong supporters of guerrilla warfare had been integrated into the PGT leadership is indicated by the fact that when the FAR declared its independence, some 50 percent of the PGT Central Committee members and 40 percent of the politburo resigned from their positions in the party.[31] Many of

---

[25] Quoted in FAR declaration of 10 January 1968, in *Granma* (Havana), 25 February 1968.

[26] Montes interview with Eduardo Galeano, in *Guatemala: clave de latinoamérica* (Montevideo: Banda Oriental, 1967), pp. 20-21.

[27] *Granma* (Havana), Spanish ed., 6 February 1967.

[28] *Information Bulletin*, no. 122 (1968).

[29] Debray, *¿Revolución en la revolución?*, p. 34.

[30] Statement of 21 January 1968, in *Granma* (Havana), 3 March 1968.

[31] *Tricontinental Bulletin* (Havana), October 1968.

these remained or became leaders of the FAR, including Montes, secretariat member Gabriel Salazar and Central Committee members Camilo Sánchez and Pablo Monsanto.

The split between the PGT and the FAR, which actually occurred in late 1967 but was not formalized until January 1968, took on the same coloring as previous Latin American splits between pro-Soviet and castroite groups.[32] A FAR statement dated 1 January 1968 asserted that "the PGT's policy has always been to decide which is the main enemy, not in order to concentrate its struggle against this main enemy, but with the aim of making deals with lesser enemies; this was the policy which they pompously termed 'united-front work.' "[33] A statement dated 10 January condemned the PGT for its "stubborn insistence on 'other forms of struggle.' "[34] When FAR chief Montes announced his withdrawal from the communist party, he maintained that the dispute was between "two ideas, two attitudes toward war, toward the Revolution, toward the people, both determined by deep class roots and a historic moment," adding that "on the one side there is the revolutionary idea [of the FAR guerrillas] . . . a radical vision, revolutionary, audacious, young, dynamic. On the other side is the pseudorevolutionary idea [of the 'leading clique' of the PGT] . . . a submissive, opportunist, fainthearted, outmoded, passive vision." Thus he saw "two mutually exclusive tendencies in the revolutionary process" and a "struggle between healthy and malignant forces."[35]

The alternate roads proposed by the PGT and FAR in early 1968, immediately after their break, are evident in a March 1968 statement by the PGT Central Committee. According to this statement, the Guatemalan revolution at that time was an "agrarian, anti-imperialist and popular revolution," which would "pave the way for building socialism in the future."[36] Though it asserted that *the revolutionary war of the people is the road of the Guatemalan revolution,*" the statement argued that the main strategic problem of the present was a definition of this

[32] The PGT dated the split in its statement of March 1968, in *Information Bulletin,* no. 122 (1968).

[33] The 1 January statement is found in the journal *World Outlook* (New York), 8 March 1968.

[34] The 10 January statement is in *Granma* (Havana), 25 February 1968.

[35] The Montes statement is in ibid., 3 March 1968.

[36] The statement quoted in this paragraph is found in *Information Bulletin,* no. 122 (1968); emphasis in original.

road. With clear reference to the FAR, the March statement warned that

> the participation of the masses, their active involvement in the armed struggle, is vitally necessary for the revolution. . . . The guerrilla detachments alone, without their basic network and without the sympathy and support of the masses in general, can be easily defeated or stagnate and cease to exist. The guerrilla war should not be counterposed to the struggle of the masses, it should be the most progressive expression of the struggle. . . . The masses cannot be won over by the mere appearance of armed people.

The Central Committee then spelled out what was required of the party in order to back up the armed struggle:

> At the same time we should promote political struggle both among the masses, in order to win them over definitively, and in the solution of national problems, pinpointing and combating the vices of the regime and the system. We should promote class struggle in all fields—economic, political, and cultural—on the basis of a minimum program incorporating the struggle of the peasants for land and against evictions, the struggle against unemployment, for a general rise in the wages, against the high cost of living, against the crisis in the country, against the violation of the rights of man, for social freedom, in defense of sovereignty. We should support the concrete demands of the women, students and young people in general, support the popular forces in the conflicts that break out, and above all, mobilize all strata of the population, organize them and draw them into the struggle.

In an interview with the Chilean castroite journal *Punto Final,* PGT leaders pledged that with their military arm, the Revolutionary Armed Forces, the PGT would make "our already bloodstained Guatemala into another Vietnam." [37] The only objection the Rebel Armed Forces had to the PGT pledge to make Guatemala into "another Vietnam" was that they did not believe the communists were serious. In particular they condemned the PGT for devoting so much time and attention to nonarmed struggle. The FAR position came out clearly in a joint communiqué signed with the MR-13 after the death of Guevara in October 1967:

---

[37] *Punto Final* (Santiago), 10 September 1968. After the split between the Rebel Armed Forces and the PGT, the latter maintained its own FAR guerrilla force, the Revolutionary Armed Forces. Elsewhere in this study FAR refers only to the Rebel Armed Forces.

The death of Major Guevara, as we understand it, is, more than an irreparable loss to the continental movement, a battle cry, a declaration of war—as he himself stated—that must be heeded by all those of us who have taken up arms and are ready to convert these battle cries into clarion calls of victory. A battle cry that obliges us to define positions, to do away with all ambiguity, all vacillation. . . .

We believe that armed struggle is the only path by which to achieve the complete liberation and independence of our people, and that this armed struggle must be pursued unrelentingly, no matter what the circumstances, to its final consequences. . . .

We feel that the conception of protracted war must be continental in scope. . . .[38]

On 10 January the FAR proclaimed that "right now our guerrilla leaders are already the political leaders of the revolutionary struggle in our country. The time has come to change the motto of 'All must be prepared and willing to fight at any time' for the motto 'ALL MUST FIGHT NOW! ' "[39]

Guerrilla activities during the mid-1960s were chiefly rural, ranging from armed propaganda to clashes with government and military forces, kidnapping, and assassinations. Some urban terrorism was carried out, especially in Guatemala City. Between 1968 and 1970 kidnappings and assassinations were directed against foreign nationals as well as Guatemalans, prominent among the former being the murders of the ambassadors of the United States (1968) and West Germany (1970).[40] Well-defined FAR activities decreased during the 1970s because of a lack of effective leadership and forceful suppression of the FAR guerrillas by government and right-wing vigilante forces. Generally speaking, terrorism and counterterrorism continued from the right and the left.

The MR-13, when it reemerged as a separate organization in late 1964, was unequivocally pro-Chinese in the Sino-Soviet dispute and reflected strong elements of castroism, Maoism, Trotskyism (the Inter-

---

[38] Communiqué signed by Montes and Yon Sosa, dated October 1967; in *Tricontinental* (Havana), nos. 4-5 (January-April 1968).

[39] *Granma* (Havana), 25 February 1968; emphasis in original.

[40] FAR spokesmen said that John Gordon Mein was killed on 28 August 1968 when he refused to cooperate with his would-be kidnappers; Count Karl von Spreti was kidnapped on 31 March 1970 and killed on 5 April when the guerrillas did not get the ransom they demanded—payment of $700,000 and the release of twenty-two "political prisoners."

116

national Secretariat faction), and Yonism in its domestic policies. Internationally, the "First Declaration of the Sierra de las Minas" proclaimed the absolute support of the MR-13 for the twenty-five points of the Chinese Communist Party's "Proposal Concerning the General Line of the International Communist Movement" (14 June 1963): "the twenty-five points [is] a program and line based on the most authentic Marxist-Leninist principles. . . . This line and this program must be those of the socialist revolution." [41] The declaration repeatedly refers to China and Chinese policies in a positive manner, and on several occasions praises the "many militant communists of the PGT" who support the Chinese line.[42]

Domestically, the Chinese influence was not so clear-cut, though Juan Posadas, the head of the International Secretariat of the Fourth International, wrote in early 1966 that Yon Sosa's program was "the program of the Chinese." [43] Theoretical confusion abounded as a result of the diverse outside influences upon the MR-13 during its last five years of existence. (The MR-13 ceased to maintain a distinct identity after Yon Sosa was killed in a May 1970 encounter with Mexican troops on the Mexican-Guatemalan border.) The main influences were (1) Trotskyism, especially between 1964 and 1966, from several advisors who represented the Posadas branch of the Fourth International; (2) castroism, between 1964 and 1970, from Cuba and from the FAR; and (3) Maoism, throughout the period, from China, though apparently not as a result of direct Chinese initiatives.

A few examples of this cross-influence and confusion must suffice. On the stages of revolution, the 1964 declaration states that "Guatemala is ripe for a socialist revolution. This does not mean the immediate establishment of socialism but, as in the USSR under the leadership of Lenin in 1917, as in China, as in Cuba, to establish a Worker's State, worker's power, the dictatorship of the working class which builds socialism." [44] In reality the Soviet, Chinese, and Cuban governments that worked to establish socialism were quite different. Yon Sosa rejected the "false perspective of the so-called 'national democratic revolution' " within the PGT, as mentioned earlier. Yet the coalition

---

[41] *Primera Declaración de la Sierra de las Minas* (Montevideo: Comité Bancario de Lucha Antimperialista, 1965), p. 44.

[42] On the latter point, see ibid., pp. 26, 27, 29.

[43] J. Posadas, *La función de las guerrillas en la lucha por el poder obrero* (Lima: Voz Obrera, 1966), p. 28.

[44] *Primera Declaración de la Sierra*, p. 30.

government he rejected was essentially that employed by the Chinese after 1949, the new democratic government Chinese theoreticians regard as one of their most important contributions to Marxist-Leninist thought and practice, while the worker-peasant government Yon Sosa proposed was, at least theoretically, closest to the Cuban example. And, though the declaration emphasized the importance of Marxism-Leninism, it failed to emphasize the vanguard role of the Marxist-Leninist party. Again, this was more castroite than Chinese or Soviet. On the other hand, some of Yon Sosa's efforts over the years to establish base areas and carry out armed propaganda were more Maoist than castroite.

Colombia. The National Liberation Army (ELN) was formed in Santander Department in mid-1964. According to its founder and leader, Fabio Vázquez, it was conceived in a peasant hut and took to the guerrilla life, with a nucleus of eighteen peasant members, on 4 July 1964.[45] It carried out its first military action in January 1965. Toward the end of that year the ELN received a boost when it was joined by a young priest, Camilo Torres, who had developed a large following among Colombian students and others. Torres was killed in February 1966 and became the idol of many and the prototype, for some, of the "fighting Christian."[46] Among other important ELN leaders between the middle 1960s and early 1970s were two other Vázquez brothers, Antonio and Manuel, Víctor Medina Morón, Ricardo Lara, and a former Spanish priest, Domingo Laín. By the beginning of 1975, all were reportedly killed or captured, or had deserted except Fabio Vázquez, although the reporting of guerrilla losses in Colombia has been notoriously inaccurate for many years.

According to Fabio Vázquez, the ELN was formed as a political-military organization. "It is born of the peasant's need to solve his problems. The situation of misery, hunger, sickness, illiteracy, and repression suffered principally by our peasants forced them to launch a struggle against the oppressor system"; indeed, the group was described as "an army of peasants." The main ELN leader said in 1967 that

---

[45] Interview in *Sucesos para todos* (Mexico City), 1 July 1967, pp. 20, 22. Much of the material in this section is taken from a series of articles and interviews published by Mario Menéndez Rodríguez in the weekly *Sucesos para todos,* of which he was editor. See issues of 24 June, 1, 8, 15, and 22 July 1967.

[46] Representative of the expanding literature on Torres are Gerald Theisen, "The Case of Camilo Torres Restrepo," *Journal of Church and State,* Spring 1974, pp. 301-15; and John Gerassi, ed., *Revolutionary Priest: The Complete Writings and Messages of Camilo Torres* (New York: Random House, 1971).

though "a very high percentage" of its members were peasants, nevertheless, workers, students, and professionals also played a "very important role." This social makeup was a result (1) of the basic scene of struggle in the countryside, (2) of the immaturity of the Colombian proletariat, and (3) of the strength of the repressive forces. Thus, logically, the national liberation movement began in the mountains, was built up there, and would move in the end from the rural areas to the cities.[47]

Vázquez discussed the qualities and responsibilities of an ideal guerrilla leader in great detail. He must love the people and their cause; he must be remarkable for his honesty, sagacity, character, personality, spirit of sacrifice, bravery, and organizational ability; he must guarantee the continuity of the guerrilla force and must never go into the cities. Vázquez had nothing to say about commitment to Marxism-Leninism or the leader's role in a revolutionary party.[48] After commenting on the Venezuelan guerrilla struggle, and alluding to the "desertion" of the Venezuelan Communist Party, Vázquez offered a generalization typically castroite in substance on the development of the "true and worthy leaders of a people." He said:

> The people can be confused or deceived in choosing their leaders, but the process [of the armed struggle] unmasks the unworthy and elevates the worthy, those who do not loose faith, those who are not opportunists, and those who do not put secondary considerations, personal considerations, before the struggle; those who are true [revolutionaries], not those who have infiltrated movements in order to do them harm.[49]

The problem of communism and the revolutionary political party was discussed at some length by another ELN leader of the period, second-ranking Víctor Medina Morón. According to Medina, the ELN was branded "communist" to imply international connections to the guerrilla struggle, on which he commented: "It is not necessary to receive instructions from any other country to see clearly the struggle against the economic, political and military domination of the United States government; likewise, it is not necessary to profess Marxism in order to struggle against the gang of crooks who control the [Colombian] government." As to the need for a political party: "Today we think

---

[47] Fabio Vázquez interview, *Sucesos para todos,* 1 July 1967, pp. 20, 31, 33-34.
[48] Ibid., especially pp. 34, 37.
[49] Ibid., p. 41.

119

the Colombian people need a political-military organization that undoubtedly goes beyond the frontiers of what we traditionally consider a political party. This type of organization, which has its fundamental nucleus as an army of revolutionaries, is what we [in the ELN] are constructing." [50]

According to Fabio Vázquez, the political-military objectives of the ELN in 1967 and thereafter were

> the conquest of power for the popular classes, taking for its basic form of struggle the insurrectional way, because according to our concept of people's war—meaning by people's war that which is developed by the immense majority of the exploited against the great minority of exploiters—we think that when the legal channels of the political struggle are exhausted, the armed vanguard must come forth from the masses to guarantee the continuity of the struggle for political power.
>
> What is more, because of the wide knowledge mankind now has of the voracity, the unlimited cruelty of the reactionary oligarchy, in league with North American imperialism, we are sure they will not permit the people to rise to power by peaceful means. [51]

Vázquez concluded that the armed struggle, though it would be long and difficult, was the only road for the Colombians to follow. Thus the development of a guerrilla force was essential for the foundation of a National Liberation Army to fight for power with the oligarchy and North American imperialism in order to "take power and form a democratic and revolutionary government." Here it is clear that, just as the ELN does not insist on the leadership of a political party or the Marxist-Leninist ideology, it does call for peasant support for a socialist revolution. Manuel Vázquez, talking with Menéndez Rodríguez, argued that guerrilla warfare was the means by which to solve Colombia's problems, and that it was also the method all other Latin American peoples would have to use to win their liberty. He made a special point of emphasizing that even the Chilean people were no exception. Sooner or later, he concluded, all Latin America would be "one great guerrilla front." [52]

---

[50] Ibid., 15 July 1967, pp. 36, 37.
[51] This and the following brief quotation come from Fabio Vázquez, ibid., 1 July 1967, pp. 27-28.
[52] Manuel Vázquez, ibid., 8 July 1967, p. 31.

In 1967 ELN leaders were all unhesitating in their support for the Cuban revolution, though there were reports at the turn of the decade that Fabio Vázquez, like Douglas Bravo, was unhappy with Fidel Castro's decreasing support for Latin American guerrillas. The ELN suffered heavy losses during the early 1970s (particularly in 1974) as a result of government counterinsurgency actions and of internal dissension, though in early 1976 it continued to operate in several departments under the leadership of Fabio Vázquez.

Peru. The Movement of the Revolutionary Left (MIR) grew out of the APRA Rebelde, a splinter of the Aprista party of Víctor Raúl Haya de la Torre. Its origins and subsequent membership reflect its particular appeal to young intellectuals. The party's leader in recent years, Ricardo Gadea, brother of Che Guevara's first wife, said in 1972 that the MIR was not and did not propose to become a mass party, but a vanguard party representing the working class, rooted in the masses.[53]

During the early 1960s, some party leaders, particularly Luis de la Puente Uceda, became convinced that only armed struggle would bring national liberation to Peru, a position the party as a whole adopted in the mid-1960s. In one of his most detailed statements, de la Puente said:

> We think that, starting from certain minimum levels of party organization and prestige among the masses, we must devote ourselves to the work of insurrection convinced that during the preparatory stage in the guerrilla zones, and more intensively after the beginning of action, it will be possible to build the party and mobilize, organize, give consciousness to, and incorporate the masses into the armed struggle. This involves starting from the highest level of popular struggle, armed struggle, through which we shall be able to build a true revolutionary party and win over the masses.

De la Puente continued:

> (1) The objective and subjective conditions are present, and the latter, even if they are not fully ripe, will mature in the process of the struggle.
>
> (2) The exploited masses must immediately propose the seizure of power through armed struggle.
>
> (3) The strategy and tactics must in the first stage be those of guerrilla war, and later those of maneuver, or even positional warfare.

---

[53] Interview in *Caretas* (Lima), 22 May 1972.

(4) Given our condition as a mainly peasant country, and our geographic features, insurrection must start in the sierra or in the eastern Andean escarpments.

(5) Given the size of our country and its lack of geographical integration and transportation systems, its multiplicity of languages, races, and culture, it is advisable to organize several guerrilla centers to initiate and develop the struggle.

(6) The impact of guerrilla actions will serve to build and develop the party and to start mobilizing the masses, stimulating their consciousness, and incorporating them in the struggle, both in the countryside and in the city.

(7) Due to our condition as an underdeveloped country suffering from the combined oppression of latifundists, big bourgeoisie, and imperialists, it is essential to unite the exploited sectors: peasants, workers, petty bourgeoisie, within a united front led by the worker-peasant alliance represented by the revolutionary Marxist-Leninist party.

(8) The Peruvian revolution is part of the continental and world process, which demands progressive forms of integration in every aspect and stage, in order to defeat the oligarchy and imperialist forces which are working together all over the continent.[54]

In the armed struggle that began in mid-1965, some 125 guerrillas were killed, among them the two most important leaders, de la Puente and Guillermo Lobatón. Leadership of the organization was assumed by Ricardo Gadea, despite his imprisonment following the uprising. In 1967 Gadea counterposed the theory and practice of armed struggle to "the dogmas and conventions that Marxist thought has been accumulating during many years of reformism and scholasticism." [55]

The MIR did not give its support to the leftist military government of Juan Velasco that took over control in the late 1968 coup, though an MIR splinter—the Revolutionary Socialist League (LSR)—promptly did so. In a 26 July 1969 declaration, the MIR said that "as an institution the Armed Forces—taken as a whole—cannot progress to socialism. . . . By destroying the props of the capitalist society, the very bases of the armed forces are liquidated." The declaration main-

---

[54] De la Puente, "The Peruvian Revolution: Concepts and Perspectives," quoted in Richard Gott, *Guerrilla Movements in Latin America* (Garden City, N.Y.: Doubleday, 1971), pp. 349-50. The most Maoist aspect of this program is point seven. Also see de la Puente's statement of 7 February 1964, in Mercado, *Las guerrillas del Peru*, p. 84, for a united front proposal that is more Maoist than castroite.

[55] *Tricontinental* (Havana), nos. 4 and 5 (January-April 1968), p. 52.

tained that "revolutionary violence," that is, "armed power in the hands of the people," continued to be an "implicit necessity of (the) revolutionary process in moving to socialism." [56] This "castroite" opposition to the military government continued into 1976 despite the fact that Fidel Castro himself, and the Cuban government, adopted a friendly attitude toward the Velasco government shortly after it came to power.

A second and less important castroite group in Peru was the National Liberation Army (ELN), founded in 1962 by former members of the Peruvian Communist Party. It joined the guerrilla movement in 1965, though its activities and those of the MIR were not coordinated. Its main leader, Héctor Béjar, author of *Peru 1965: Notes on a Guerrilla Experience,* was held in prison from late 1965 until the military government's general political amnesty in December 1970.[57] Though the ELN continued to reject the military government, Béjar began working in the government-controlled National System of Support for Social Mobilization (SINAMOS) in 1972.

Bolivia. The National Liberation Army (ELN), formed in late 1966 by Cuban and Bolivian revolutionaries, received wide publicity in 1967 when it was under the leadership of Che Guevara. It reached its maximum size under Guevara in March 1967—fifty-one persons, including eighteen Cubans, twenty-nine Bolivians, three Peruvians, and one German. A month later there were forty-three ELN members, ten of whom with their leader Juan Acuna ("Joaquín") became separated from the main force under Guevara. Joaquín's force was wiped out by U.S.-trained Bolivian troops on 31 August and Guevara's suffered a similar fate on 8 October. Only five guerrillas survived to the end of the year—two Bolivians (including Guido "Inti" Peredo) and three Cubans (who escaped to Chile in February 1968 and arrived in Cuba on 6 March). The ELN was slowly reformed by Inti Peredo and remained under his leadership until his death in a shoot-out in La Paz in September 1969. Subsequently the guerrillas were led by lesser figures, including Jorge Ruiz Paz and Osvaldo "Chato" Peredo.[58]

---

[56] *Punto Final* (Santiago), 26 August 1969.

[57] The book won the Cuban Casa de las Américas essay prize in 1969; it was published in an English translation by the Monthly Review Press in 1970.

[58] Three Peredo brothers were active in the Bolivian ELN during the late 1960s and early 1970s just as three Vázquez brothers were prominent in the Colombian ELN. Roberto "Coco" Peredo was killed with Guevara in October 1967. He and Inti had been members of the Bolivian Communist Party for many years. A fourth, Antonio Peredo, was arrested in Cochabamba in late 1975 and charged with engaging in subversive activities.

Unlike most castroite groups, the ELN under Guevara did not issue many public statements outlining its objectives and strategy (perhaps because it was discovered by the government before it was ready to go into action), nor indeed was it known for many months that Guevara was in command of the group. The ELN road was stated concisely in a 1967 declaration "To the Miners of Bolivia," now known to have been written by Guevara:

> The mass struggle in the underdeveloped countries, with a large peasant population and extensive land area, must be undertaken by a small mobile vanguard, the guerrillas, established within the people. This organization will grow stronger at the cost of the enemy army and will serve as a catalyzing agent for the revolutionary fervor of the masses until a revolutionary situation is created in which state power will crumble under a single, effective blow, dealt at the right moment.[59]

Beyond this, ELN strategy came out in the actions of the guerrilla group under Guevara and in the diaries of Guevara and his Cuban comrades picked up by the Bolivian authorities in 1967.[60]

Members of the ELN during 1966 and 1967 were mostly Cuban and Bolivian nationals, though at various times fighters from several other countries were present as well. This was in keeping with Guevara's call in his 1967 "Message to the Tricontinental" for "true proletarian internationalism, with international proletarian armies." [61] It was thought desirable for the ELN to be international in membership since the war it sought to begin was more than national in scope. In the same 1967 message, Guevara spoke of creating a second or third Vietnam in Latin America, and in his "Necessary Introduction" to Guevara's diary, Fidel Castro wrote that

> Che did not conceive of the struggle in Bolivia as an isolated fact, but as part of a revolutionary liberation movement which would not delay in extending to other South American countries. It was his purpose to organize a movement devoid of sectarian spirit which would permit the incorporation of all those who wanted to fight for the liberation of Bolivia and the

[59] *Granma* (Havana), 14 July 1968; trans. in Bonachea and Valdes, *Che: Selected Works of Ernesto Guevara*, p. 186.
[60] For the texts of the diaries of Guevara, Harry Villegas ("Pombo"), Eliseo Reyes ("Rolando"), and Israel Reyes ("Braulio"), see James, ed., *The Complete Bolivian Diaries of Che Guevara and Other Captured Documents*.
[61] *Granma* (Havana), 23 April 1967.

rest of the peoples subjugated by imperialism in Latin America.[62]

But the ideas of a Vietnam in America and of a continental revolution were brought out most clearly in the diary of Harry Villegas ("Pombo"), one of the Cubans sent to Bolivia in 1966—ahead of Guevara—to lay groundwork for the operation. On 15 November 1966 Pombo wrote that Mario Monje, secretary-general of the pro-Soviet Communist Party of Bolivia had to understand that "the struggle in Bolivia will be long because the enemy will concentrate all its forces against it. Bolivia will sacrifice itself so that conditions (for revolution) can be created in neighboring countries. We have to make another Viet Nam out of America, with its center in Bolivia." [63]

The Bolivian operation was planned and led by Guevara and the Cubans, not by Bolivians, a fact brought out clearly in Guevara's diary and other documents. In his entry of 31 December 1966, Guevara reviewed a discussion held that day with Mario Monje:

The reception was cordial but tense. The question: Why are you here? was in the air. . . .

The conversation with Monje was initiated with generalities, but soon brought up the fundamental questions, summarized into three basic conditions:

(1) He would resign from the leadership of the party, but would succeed in obtaining at least its neutrality and would bring cadres for the struggle.

(2) The political and military leadership of the struggle would correspond to him as long as the revolution had a Bolivian environment.

(3) He would handle the relations with other South American parties, trying to bring them to a position of supporting the Liberation Movements (he gave Douglas Bravo as an example).

I answered that the first point was up to him as secretary of the party, although I considered his position erroneous. It was vacillating and expedient and served to protect the historical name of those who should be condemned because of their submissive position. Time will prove that I am right.

As to the third point, I had no objections to his attempting to do that but it was doomed to failure. Asking Codovila to support Douglas Bravo was the same as asking him to con-

---

[62] Fidel Castro, "Necessary Introduction," *The Diary of Che Guevara* (New York: Bantam Books, 1968), p. 14.

[63] Pombo's diary, in James, ed., *Complete Bolivian Diaries*, pp. 286-87.

125

done a revolt within the party. Time here will also be the judge.

As to the second point, I could not accept it in any way. I would be the military chief and would not accept ambiguities concerning this. Here the discussion turned into a stalemate and ended up in a vicious circle.[64]

According to Inti Peredo's account of Monje's visit, the PCB leader insisted that the Bolivian people would turn their backs on the guerrilla force—thus assuring its defeat—when they learned it was led by Guevara, a "foreigner." On this point Peredo commented: "Monje's words made us furious, above all when he branded Che a 'foreigner,' stupidly denying his rank as a continental revolutionary."[65] Fidel Castro put it even more bluntly when he wrote that Guevara was not willing to "hand over the command of the guerrilla nucleus—destined to carry out during its final development a fight of such ample dimensions in South America—to an inexperienced emptyhead with a narrow chauvinistic outlook."[66]

Shortly after Guevara's death, Inti Peredo—describing himself as the "accidental heir to the last and most valuable teachings of the greatest revolutionary genius of Latin America"—wrote to assure the world that "guerrilla warfare in Bolivia is not dead; it has just begun." In a statement dated July 1968, he criticized Bolivian leftists for giving only verbal support or no support at all to the guerrillas in 1966–1967. He called for a "broad anti-imperialist front" and outlined the way this front could be achieved:

> We are not against the people's struggles for the sake of obtaining reforms and other gains. But we feel sure these struggles will be much more fruitful and effective when they are waged against a government frightened and weakened by the actions of a guerrilla center.
>
> It is this guerrilla center that will prove to the people—with facts—that it is possible to face the power of imperialism

---

[64] *The Diary of Che Guevara,* pp. 43-44. Victorio Codovilla was the seventy-two-year-old (in 1966) head of the pro-Soviet Communist Party of Argentina. He and his party as a whole were unshakable foes of Guevara's tactics; the party, and particularly its youth branch, was even then being torn apart by dissidents calling for a more vigorous revolutionary policy than more conservative party members like Codovilla would accept.

[65] Peredo, *Mi campaña con el che,* p. 40.

[66] Castro, "Necessary Introduction," p. 15.

and its puppets, and that it is not only possible to face that power, but also that it is possible to win victory over it.[67]

The ELN, he wrote, would not be the "fighting arm" of any political party, and guerrilla warfare would not be an instrument of pressure for political struggle in the cities:

> The struggle waged in the cities must constitute a support for guerrilla action; therefore, the cities cannot lead the guerrillas. It is the guerrillas, as the armed vanguard group of the liberation movement, who should lead the movement. This comes about naturally. To try to do the opposite would be tantamount to rendering the guerrillas inoperative, bogging them down. In short, it would lead them to defeat.
>
> The struggle itself will bring forth its leaders. The true leaders of the people will be forged in the struggle, and no one who considers himself a true revolutionary should insist on leading or fear that his position will be taken from him.

Peredo concluded by repeating Guevara's call for a new Vietnam in Latin America, describing this as "an honor and a duty we will never refuse."

Immediately after an unsuccessful uprising in the Teoponte region north of La Paz, and after the military coup of 7 October 1970 which put leftist General Juan José Torres in power, the ELN General Headquarters issued a statement saying that individually some military men had "truly revolutionary" views, but that the military as an institution could not carry out genuine changes in the structure of Bolivia. The ELN then stated its own path:

> The ELN has not chosen its strategy of prolonged war because of any romantic notion, mechanical copy of other experiences or simple dogmatism. We believe that a genuine revolution presupposes the physical annihilation or expulsion from the country of the reactionary forces through armed struggle. This task can only be carried out by all the people, as a whole, when their level of awareness, organization and political and military experience qualify them to do so. The capacity of the popular masses to take power cannot arise overnight, as if by magic, nor can it be the fruit of spontaneity, as many of those who favor a putsch would believe. Our organization maintains that the only way to achieve this in the present historical circumstances is to begin a prolonged revolutionary war, in which the fighting vanguard, through its example, makes possible

---

[67] The quotations in this paragraph are from Inti Peredo, "Guerrilla Warfare in Bolivia Is Not Dead: It Has Just Begun," special supplement to *Tricontinental* (Havana), undated but published in 1968.

the growing awareness and incorporation into the struggle of ever broader sectors of the popular masses.[68]

After the rightist military coup of 22 August 1971, the ELN joined the ineffective Anti-imperialist Revolutionary Front (FRA), but suffered additional losses during 1972 and thereafter as a result of the government's armed actions. In February 1974 the ELN was one of four guerrilla organizations in southern South America to form the Revolutionary Coordinating Committee (the JCR, discussed below). An article in the JCR's journal, *Che Guevara,* published in November 1974, looked forward to a "prolonged war" in three stages: (1) a traditional guerrilla campaign, (2) an insurrection, and (3) a full-scale war against intervening imperialist armies. An attack was leveled against Bolivian "reformists" who rejected armed struggle in favor of "simple agitation" or a "pact with the bourgeoisie."

On 11 June 1975 the JCR press agency in Paris, APAL, announced that the ELN had formed the Bolivian Workers' Revolutionary Party (PRTB), which was expected to grow into the vanguard of the Bolivian revolution. The ELN would not disappear, but be the "armed fist" or "military force of the working class and Bolivian people" under the Marxist-Leninist leadership of the new party. According to an article in the 1 September 1975 issue of the PRTB's clandestine paper, *El Proletario,* this vanguard would raise the struggle of the Bolivian proletariat "to the level of a revolutionary war against the bourgeoisie and imperialism." The statement admitted that Che Guevara made "tactical errors" in 1966–1967, but reiterated its conviction that, as Guevara had said, revolution must be by armed struggle and be continental in scope. In mid-December 1975 the Bolivian government announced the arrest in the Siglo XX mining area of Antonio Peredo and a number of other Bolivians and foreigners said to have been the regional command of the PRTB.

Nicaragua. The Sandinist Front of National Liberation (FSLN) is a small castroite group that grew out of guerrilla struggles beginning in Nicaragua in 1958. The name was officially adopted in 1962.[69] In the

---

[68] Statement in *Tricontinental Bulletin* (Havana), no. 57 (December 1970), p. 45.

[69] According to FSLN founder Carlos Fonseca Amador, in *Direct from Cuba* (Havana), no. 29 (November 1970). The FSLN is named for Augusto César Sandino, a Nicaraguan general whose opposition to U.S. military occupation of Nicaragua (1927-1933), by means of guerrilla warfare, made him a symbol of anti-imperialist resistance.

words of the 1969 "Program of the Sandinist Front of National Liberation," the FSLN

> grew out of the Nicaraguan people's need for a *vanguard organization,* which through a direct struggle with its enemies, is capable of seizing *political power* and establishing a social system that will wipe out the exploitation and misery our country has suffered throughout its existence.
> The FSLN is a political-military organization whose objective is the seizure of *political power* through the destruction of the bureaucratic and military apparatus of the dictatorship and the establishment of a Revolutionary Government based on a worker-peasant alliance and the support of all the *anti-imperialist* patriotic forces of the country. [70]

The FSLN has always been small and of fluctuating membership—at its maximum probably not including more than 100 active fighters. Students have always played an important leadership role, while other intellectuals, peasants, and urban and rural workers have participated from time to time. Some members seem to be from the ranks of the country's communist party, the Socialist Party of Nicaragua (PSN), particularly from among those dissatisfied with PSN leadership and indecision on the question of armed struggle.

The FSLN was nearly eliminated in the mid-1960s and on several occasions thereafter. After serving several years in jail, guerrilla leader Carlos Fonseca Amador attended the 1967 OLAS conference in Havana and "declared war" on the Nicaraguan government. In August 1969 Fonseca was arrested in Costa Rica after fleeing across the border and in his absence FSLN leadership was assumed by a young worker, Efraín Sánchez Sancho. In October 1970 guerrillas hijacked a Costa Rican airliner and diverted it to Cuba; four U.S. passengers were held hostage and then released in exchange for Fonseca and three other Central American guerrillas. After his release, Fonseca travelled to Cuba and apparently remained there for most of the early 1970s, during which period the FSLN in Nicaragua engaged in only limited activities. In December 1974 the group suddenly gained international attention when it broke up a Christmas party in Managua, killed several persons, and kidnapped more than a dozen prominent political and business leaders. All were subsequently released in exchange for several impris-

---

[70] "Program," in *Tricontinental* (Havana), no. 17 (March-April 1970), p. 61; emphasis in original.

129

oned revolutionaries. The released prisoners and kidnappers were given safe conduct to Cuba.

Over the period of its existence, the FSLN carried out attacks on and assassinations of political and military officials and private citizens. These actions and sporadic kidnappings, robberies, and other activities won them little support from the Nicaraguan people in the city or the countryside, though popular support was surely discouraged by severe measures taken against FSLN members and even against suspected supporters of the organization.

Fonseca Amador stated in 1970 that the FSLN would "continue armed struggle in Nicaragua until the country is freed of imperialist exploitation and its sovereignty and freedom are rescued from the hands of the United States and its puppet Somoza." [71] The Executive Secretariat of the FSLN stated in 1970: "We are inferior [to the government] in material resources, but on the other hand we have an absolute political moral superiority that will permit us to fight for as many years as may be necessary to achieve the final triumph for our cause, which is that of the people." [72]

The Sandinist "Program," drawn up in 1969, says that following a "hard and prolonged people's war," the FSLN will establish a Revolutionary Government of the People, which will carry out extensive programs in all areas of national life. The measures to be adopted are presented under the general headings: the revolutionary government, dwelling on political issues; a basic and independent economy; agrarian revolution; labor legislation and social security; special plan for the Atlantic coast; liberation of women; administrative honesty; revolution in culture and education; respect for religious beliefs; independent foreign policy; abolition of the Chamorro-Bryan treaty; people's patriotic army; solidarity among peoples; Central American people's unity; and veneration of martyrs.[73]

Conclusions

By early 1976 the majority of the Latin American castroites discussed above, and many others not mentioned here, had been killed, captured,

---

[71] *Granma* (Havana), 1 November 1970.

[72] "FSLN: The People's War Continues," *Tricontinental Bulletin* (Havana), nos. 52-53 (July-August 1970), p. 34.

[73] Limited detail on the program is found in *Tricontinental* (Havana), March-April 1970, pp. 62-68.

or retired from the guerrilla life. To varying degrees the castroites were a contributing factor in domestic developments around Latin America and in the directions of U.S. Latin American policy. Policies of reform in some countries were inspired by dissatisfaction with the status quo, most vividly exemplified in the guerrilla struggles. The Alliance for Progress (and related programs) were also in part a response to castroite struggles—above all, in a broader perspective, to Cuban support for these struggles—and to the projected threat of widespread armed violence in the future. Taken on their own terms, however, the castroite activities were only partially successful. They did intensify contradictions and conflicts in some countries and cast a degree of doubt on the revolutionary credentials of a number of traditional revolutionary organizations. At the same time, they did not make the revolutions they sought. Rural-oriented castroite guerrillas carried out insignificant to moderately disruptive struggles in a number of countries, several dragging out for more than a decade. The persistence of Fabio Vázquez and Douglas Bravo, however, and their continued lack of success in launching revolutions in Colombia and Venezuela merely emphasize the overall ineffectiveness of the rural-oriented castroites. These groups often created a community of interests among a wide variety of reform-inclined groups who opposed violent change, as well as leading to the formation of right-wing vigilante bands.

The fact is that although poverty in most Latin American countries is apparent to all, national conditions and moods have rarely been conducive to rural castroite revolutionary movements. What the Marxist-Leninists call a mass "revolutionary consciousness" did not exist in Latin America during this period and was not created to a significant extent in any country but Chile during the early 1970s (which is discussed in Chapter 7) and perhaps in Argentina in the mid-1970s. Although not many Latin Americans are satisfied with conditions as they now are, a substantial number feel that adequate changes are on the way or at least possible through reform and evolutionary change. The millions who have little or nothing (sometimes not even hope) have not been won over by the vanguard actions of the guerrillas. The "small motor" simply has not set the "large motor" into motion. In general, the poorest peasants, the workers, and the unemployed do not trust the guerrillas; they certainly do not have enough confidence in them or their prospects for victory to make a commitment to guerrilla warfare that would bring the forces of the government and army down on their heads. This is the vicious circle that has upset castroite plans for years—mass commitment must (but will not) come before prospects can be considered good or victory possible. What is more, even those living in the most miserable conditions are not likely to deliberately seek a vast civil (or continental) war, immediately risking the lives of their families and friends, in pursuit of the imprecise promises of a few three-musketeer-type bravadoes (as the Maoists brand the castroites) who suddenly appear from the city and may just as suddenly return there.

The outstanding characteristics of the castroite line as it came from Cuba during the 1960s, and as it was to a considerable extent reflected by the Latin American guerrillas, were impatience, elitism, and intolerance. These qualities were born of youthful exuberance, feelings of depression and frustration, perhaps some inclinations toward "gangsterism," and conviction that political, economic, and social conditions could not be changed gradually—that the complete and sudden uprooting of the existing order was essential. (This final conviction was held by a substantial number of Latin Americans and others who nonetheless rejected or at least did not participate in the guerrilla vanguard.) Impatience prevented the castroites from undertaking the time-consuming process of building a mass base or carrying out the revolution by stages. Convinced that only their line was correct, the castroites were unwilling to establish contacts with most other groups; frequently, as a result of ideological and personal differences, major castroite groups (such as the Colombian ELN and the Venezuelan FALN and MIR) broke into two or more competing and occasionally warring factions.

6
Castroism: Urban Guerrilla Warfare

Urban guerrilla warfare and terrorism were employed in varying degrees during the period from 1959 to 1976 by some castroite groups known chiefly for their rural activities (and discussed in the preceding chapter), among them the Venezuelan FALN, the Guatemalan FAR, and the Bolivian ELN. The urban variant of guerrilla warfare was developed most fully, however, during the late 1960s and early 1970s, by groups in Uruguay, Brazil, Argentina, and Chile which were inspired and influenced by several "isms" according to differing national conditions and experiences. This chapter will be devoted mainly to the Uruguayan Tupamaros (MLN), the Brazilian National Liberation Action (ALN), and the Argentine People's Revolutionary Army (ERP), while the Chilean Movement of the Revolutionary Left (MIR) will be discussed separately in Chapter 7.[1]

Strategy and Tactics of the Urban Groups

Uruguay. For several years the most important and effective urban guerrilla organization in Latin America was the National Liberation Movement (MLN), the Tupamaros, in Uruguay.[2] The idea of the MLN

---

[1] A survey of the literature on the urban guerrilla is Charles A. Russell, James A. Miller, and Robert E. Hildner, "The Urban Guerrilla in Latin America: A Select Bibliography," *Latin American Research Review*, vol. 9, no. 1 (Spring 1974), pp. 37-79. The most important castroite-influenced urban guerrilla groups in Argentina, the Montoneros and the People's Liberation Army (ERP), grew out of (and after 1973 increasingly away from) Peronism and Trotskyism, respectively. On urban guerrillas in Argentina see Russell, Miller, and James F. Schenkel, "Urban Guerrillas in Argentina: A Select Bibliography," in ibid., vol. 9, no. 3 (Fall 1974), pp. 53-89.

[2] The name Tupamaro probably derives from Tupac Amaru, an Inca chieftain who led an unsuccessful rebellion against the Spanish in Peru in the 1780s.

arose among Uruguayan leftists, particularly among members of the Socialist Party, in the early 1960s. It was given its first organizational form (among rural sugar cane workers) by Socialist militant Raúl Sendic in 1962. The Tupamaros made their first raid in July 1963, stealing a quantity of arms from a rural rifle club. In part as a result of contacts with the anarcho-Marxist Abraham Guillén (see below), the group began to direct its attention toward the cities, since 70 percent of the population of Uruguay is urban and 45 percent is concentrated in Montevideo alone. Marked increases in the level of MLN activities were evident in 1965, 1969, and 1970. In October 1969 the Tupamaros briefly captured the town of Pando to mark the second anniversary of the death of Che Guevara. Attacks on law enforcement personnel during 1969 and 1970 seriously damaged the Robin Hood image the group had carefully cultivated during its early years.

The MLN attracted considerable international attention after mid-1970 by kidnapping foreign nationals serving in Uruguay, most important among them Brazilian diplomat Aloysio Dias Gomide (on 31 July 1970), U.S. security adviser Dan A. Mitrione (31 July 1970), U.S. agricultural expert Claude Fly (7 August 1970), and British Ambassador Geoffrey Jackson (8 January 1971).[3] After the seizure of Jackson, the Tupamaros turned their attention mainly toward kidnapping prominent Uruguayans.

The Tupamaros were long noted for the effectiveness of their organization and security, though the image of the group's invincibility was broken by numerous arrests in 1969. After the spectacular kidnappings of late July and early August 1970, the Uruguayan police arrested Sendic and several other top MLN leaders. Within two months, some 200 Tupamaros were reportedly in custody.[4] Between late May and early September 1971, impressive jailbreaks somewhat renewed

---

[3] Mitrione was "executed" while in captivity on 9 August; in 1973 the incident was made the subject of a controversial motion picture, "State of Siege"; for an almost exhaustive analysis of the film, see "The Unmaking of a 'Documentary'—Film vs. Fact," by Brookings Institution Senior Fellow Ernest W. Lefever, a paper published in *International Terrorism*, Hearings before the House Committee on Foreign Affairs, Subcommittee on Near East and South Asia (Washington, D.C.: U.S. Government Printing Office, 1974), pp. 207-19; also, Ratliff, review of "State of Siege," *Palo Alto Times*, 3 August 1973. Gomide was released on 21 February 1971, Fly on 2 March, and Jackson on 9 September. Fly has described his experience in *No Hope But God* (New York: Hawthorn Books, 1973), and Jackson his in *Surviving the Long Night* (New York: Vanguard Press, 1974).

[4] *New York Times*, 27 September 1970.

the Tupamaros' reputation; 38 women escaped on 30 July 1971 and 106 persons, including Raúl Sendic, fled through a tunnel on 6 September. During the national election in November, the Tupamaros were reportedly represented in the Broad Front by the 26 March Movement of Independents.[5] After the Broad Front lost the election, the MLN decided (in early 1972) to raise the level of the struggle by directly attacking the armed forces, with the apparently random killing of ordinary soldiers, a step that led to congressional support for a presidential declaration of "internal war." The declaration suspended some civil liberties and gave the military jurisdiction over acts of subversion. For the first time, the army joined the police in the suppression of the guerrillas, with two important results: (1) by the end of 1972 several thousand suspects had been arrested, more than 200 hideouts and storehouses had been found, several "people's prisons" had been uncovered, and the Tupamaros themselves acknowledged that they had suffered a serious setback in terms of personnel, supplies, and morale; and (2) the military took the first of what became a series of steps that within several years left formerly democratic Uruguay with a modified form of military-political dictatorship.[6] In August 1973 the MLN referred to the guerrillas' need to reorganize after a "temporary defeat" in 1972, blaming the turn of fortune on an underestimation of the enemy, too little reliance on "the people," and betrayals.[7] Although some individual Tupamaros, and the MLN experience as a whole, had some influence on guerrilla organizations in other countries in the years that followed, by early 1976 the guerrillas had ceased to play an important role in Uruguay's increasingly closed society.

The MLN is Marxist-Leninist in political ideology.[8] In a "Manifesto to Public Opinion," published in 1970, the group described itself as an "armed political organization of students, workers, employees, rural workers, intellectuals, and unemployed." [9] One MLN leader, identified only as "Urbano" in a long interview in 1970, drew particular attention to students who, like other sectors of the "radical middle class," constituted "an endless source of material for the MLN." He acknowledged that arrests during and after the July-August kidnappings,

---

[5] *Intercontinental Press* (New York), 13 December 1971.

[6] See Tupamaro interview in *Punto Final* (Santiago), 1 and 29 August 1972.

[7] See *Latin American Report* (San Francisco), August 1973.

[8] See *Juventud Rebelde* (Havana), 8 June 1970.

[9] *Granma* (Havana), 27 September 1970.

particularly the capture of "an important group of comrades" (including Sendic), had dealt the organization "a hard blow." In general, he noted that losses were "relatively high" in urban operations and indicated that "the replacement of infrastructure" was the greatest problem the Tupamaros faced.[10]

MLN domestic attitudes and policies developed over a number of years, particularly during the period of greatest MLN strength between 1968 and 1971. Urbano stated that the MLN chose armed struggle because "it was the only effective way to dethrone those who are determined to remain in power with weapons once they find this power threatened by the classes they oppress."[11] A Tupamaro interviewed by the Chilean castroite journal *Punto Final* said that the specific strategic line of the MLN, and of all "authentically revolutionary organizations," was

> to create an armed force with the greatest possible haste, with the capacity to take advantage of any propitious juncture created by the crisis or other factors. To create consciousness in the population, through actions of the armed group or other means, that without revolution there will be no change. To strengthen the trade unions and to radicalize their struggles, and connect them with the revolutionary movement. To produce material bases in order to be able to develop the urban struggle and the struggle in the countryside. To establish connections with other revolutionary movements of Latin America for continental action.[12]

The Tupamaros argued that the armed struggle accelerates and precipitates the mass movement, pointing to the examples of Cuba and China, and concluding: "At this point in history no one can argue against the premise that an armed group, no matter how small, has greater possibilities of successfully converting itself into a great, powerful army than a group that limits itself to issuing revolutionary 'positions.' " And further, "If there is no adequately prepared group, the revolutionary situations are wasted and not taken advantage of for revolution. . . . The armed group creates or helps to create the subjective conditions for

---

[10] Urbano, "Tupamaros: If There Isn't a Homeland for All, There Won't Be a Homeland for Anybody," *Tricontinental Bulletin* (Havana), no. 57 (December 1970) and no. 58 (January 1971); quotations from no. 58, p. 4; no. 57, p. 17, and no. 58, p. 10.

[11] Ibid., no. 58, p. 7.

[12] *Punto Final* (Santiago), 2 July 1968, supplement.

the revolution from the very moment that it begins to prepare itself, but above all, from the moment that it begins to act." [13]

Urbano explained that urban guerrilla warfare, rather than rural guerrilla warfare, was adopted in Uruguay because of the country's specific conditions. He noted that "the important thing, at this stage of the game, is the proof that the nucleus can come to life, survive, and develop in the city." Describing operations in the city, he asserted that "compartmentalization ('need to know') and discretion," as well as discernment and ingenuity, were crucial for the success of the urban guerrillas. Each column of guerrillas had its own action groups, logistics support, infrastructure, and contact groups which made possible "the simultaneous and autonomous operation of various columns." [14]

Urbano outlined the three (sometimes overlapping) kinds of actions carried out by the Tupamaros in late 1970. They were "tactical actions, aimed at obtaining supplies," "propaganda actions" which "by themselves define the movement's objectives and conduct," and "actions against the regime" which were "mainly aimed at undermining the foundations of the regime itself" and were particularly "directed against the forces of repression." Kidnappings, he said, were originally intended both to get money or secure the release of imprisoned comrades and to "undermine the foundations of the system." He explained that the kidnapped U.S. security adviser, Mitrione, who was "executed" on 9 August 1970, would have been released if the government had met the MLN's demand for release of 150 "political prisoners"; when the government refused, the "kidnapping-exchange method" had to be "carried to its logical consequences in order to save it as a tool." [15]

The Tupamaros generally sought to avoid the verbal conflicts which divided leftists in so many other countries. In December 1970 they announced their support for the Broad Front in the November 1971 national election, while at the same time restating their conviction that it was impossible to achieve revolution through elections. MLN support for the front was given "with the understanding that its principal task must be the mobilization of the working masses and that its labor among these masses does not begin nor end with the elections." [16]

---

[13] Translated in Carlos Nuñez, "The Tupamaros: Armed Vanguard in Uruguay," *Tricontinental* (Havana), no. 10 (January-February 1969), pp. 57, 56.

[14] *Tricontinental Bulletin* (Havana), no. 58, pp. 8-9, 11; no. 57, p. 17.

[15] Ibid., no. 58, pp. 3-4; no. 57, pp. 5-11.

[16] "MLN Position on the Broad Front," ibid., no. 62 (May 1971), p. 44; also see *Punto Final* (Santiago), 5 January 1971.

On 20 March 1971 the Tupamaros issued their "Program of the MLN Revolutionary Government." This first systematic statement of the policies an MLN government would seek to implement did not mean, according to the program, that the Tupamaros had ceased giving support to "any other transitional program that has the same ends, such as that proposd by the CNT [National Convention of Workers] and other people's forces." The MLN program commented specifically, and very briefly, on agrarian reform, industry, commerce, credit, urban reform, planning, foreign investments, wages, education, public health, old age and disability, justice, and the armed defense of the revolution.[17]

As early as 1968 the MLN stated that one of its chief objectives was "to establish connections with other revolutionary movements of Latin America for continental action."[18] According to Argentine security forces, the Tupamaros held a "roundtable" in May 1970—a follow-up to the OLAS conference of 1967—bringing together ten guerrilla groups that included, in addition to the Tupamaros, the Chilean MIR, the Bolivian ELN, the Argentine Montoneros, the Brazilian ALN, the Colombian ELN, and the Venezuelan FALN.[19] In early 1974, two years after it had been crippled domestically, the MLN joined the Bolivian ELN, the Chilean MIR, and the Argentine ERP in forming the Revolutionary Coordinating Committee (JCR).[20]

Brazil and Carlos Marighela. Urban guerrilla warfare carried out by revolutionary groups in Brazil occurred chiefly during the late 1960s and early 1970s. This section will touch on the two most important groups but be devoted primarily to Brazil's leading theorist and practitioner of urban guerrilla warfare, Carlos Marighela, whose *Minimanual of the Urban Guerrilla* became the most important writing on this form of revolutionary struggle to circulate in Latin America during the period from 1959 to 1976.

The National Liberation Action (ALN) was founded in São Paulo in 1968 by dissidents from the pro-Soviet Brazilian Communist Party

---

17 "Program of the MLN Revolutionary Government," *Tricontinental Bulletin* (Havana), no. 62, pp. 46-48.

18 *Punto Final* (Santiago), 2 July 1968, supplement; also see *Juventud Rebelde* (Havana), 8 June 1970, and *Tricontinental Bulletin* (Havana), no. 58, p. 14.

19 See Donald C. Hodges, *The Latin American Revolution* (New York: Morrow, 1974), pp. 159-60, 214-15. The Bolivian ELN publicly expressed its appreciation for MLN assistance shortly thereafter; see *Punto Final* (Santiago), 18 August 1970.

20 See Appendix D.

(PCB), the most important among them being Marighela, the founding coming after a 1967 split in the PCB.[21] By 1969 the ALN reportedly had branches in eighteen of twenty-two Brazilian states. The group carried out assorted acts of urban warfare, perhaps the most noteworthy of which was the kidnapping of the U.S. ambassador to Brazil on 4 September in cooperation with another small group, the Revolutionary Movement 8 (MR-8).[22] The ambassador was released in exchange for fifteen "political prisoners," most of whom went to Cuba. Marighela himself was killed on 4 November 1969. Joaquim Camara Ferreira, his successor, was dead by 23 October 1970 and the ALN, without its two major leaders, ceased to be the most active and important guerrilla group in the country. In early 1973 the ALN and several other guerrilla-oriented organizations issued a document which admitted that, having failed to win popular support, they had become "politically isolated."[23]

The Revolutionary People's Vanguard (VPR), also with some members from the PCB, was headed by Carlos Lamarca until his death on 17 September 1971. The group was most active and effective during 1970, when it kidnapped the Japanese consul general in São Paulo, the West German ambassador, and the Swiss ambassador, in March, June, and December, respectively. In exchange for these kidnapping victims, the VPR obtained the release of 115 "political prisoners." After Lamarca's death the VPR, while still operating in a number of Brazilian states, was considerably reduced in size and importance.

Carlos Marighela had been a prominent member of the Communist Party of Brazil (PCB) for several decades prior to his break in the mid-1960s. His dissatisfaction with the policies of the PCB is expressed clearly in his December 1966 letter of resignation from the party's executive committee. After reviewing the "illusions" of the PCB regarding the nonviolent road to socialism in Brazil, he wrote that

> for Brazil there is only one possible solution: armed struggle. We have to prepare for an armed rising by the people, with all that that implies. . . . What we must say now is that "the revolution will hasten to bring together and inform its scattered

---

[21] For a statement of the dissidents at the time of the break, see "Declaration by the Communist Group of São Paulo," in Carlos Marighela, *For the Liberation of Brazil*, trans. John Butt and Rosemary Sheed (London: Pelican, 1971), pp. 127-31.

[22] The MR-8 took its name from the date Che Guevara was captured in Bolivia, 8 October 1967. On the formation of the ALN, see *Punto Final* (Santiago), 28 January 1969.

[23] Document summarized in *Le Monde* (Paris), 15 February 1973.

forces," that "every step forward awakens the masses further, and that the programme of revolution draws them irresistibly on, for it alone expresses their true interests, their vital interests." [24]

This was not yet a call for guerrilla warfare in the cities, however; indeed, not many months previously he had written that "guerrilla warfare is not the right technique for urban areas." [25] In August 1967, a week after the end of the Latin American Solidarity Organization (OLAS) conference in Havana—which Marighela attended in defiance of PCB instructions—he wrote to Fidel Castro expressing his "complete agreement" with the resolutions adopted by the OLAS delegates and with the Cuban leader's comments in his closing speech, and concluded that "guerrilla warfare is the only means of uniting all the revolutionaries in Brazil, and bringing the people there to power." [26]

During 1968 and 1969, years marked by numerous armed actions by the ALN, Marighela elaborated on the objectives, strategy, and tactics of the guerrilla warfare for the benefit of Brazilians and other peoples, stressing for the first time that in Brazil it must begin in the cities. In an article intended for revolutionary comrades in Europe, completed in May 1969, Marighela put the ALN position thus:

> The outlook in Brazil is one of prolonged struggle in which there can be no short cuts or time-limits. We are beginning the revolutionary struggle with a slow but methodical urban guerrilla war directed against the interests of big foreign and Brazilian capitalists, causing uncertainty and insecurity among the ruling classes and wearing down and demoralizing the "gorillas' " military forces.
> From the urban front we shall go on to direct armed struggle against the *latifúndio* through rural guerrilla warfare. With the armed alliance of proletariat, peasantry and students in a decentralized and mobile guerrilla war, we shall extend our activities in all directions through the interior of Brazil and finally create a revolutionary army of national liberation to match the conventional army of the military dictatorship.[27]

Although known chiefly for his actions and writings on urban guerrilla warfare, discussed in some detail below, Marighela frequently tried to put urban and rural struggles into perspective for the revolu-

---

[24] Marighela, "Letter to the Executive Committee," in *Liberation of Brazil,* p. 187. He did not leave the party until late in the following year.

[25] See "Guerrilla Warfare and Its Use," in ibid., p. 179.

[26] "Letter to Fidel Castro," in ibid., pp. 124, 125.

[27] "On the Organizational Function of Revolutionary Violence," in ibid., p. 44.

tionary war as a whole. Early in 1969, in a broadcast from a captured radio station, he said that

> if rural guerrilla war is not launched out of the urban guerrilla movement and with a proper coordination of urban and rural struggle, the rural guerrilla movement will not survive. When we say that this year will be the year of rural guerrilla action we do so with good reason, because subversion in the urban areas has reached a certain level and the dictatorship is baffled by left-wing terrorism and the number of armed expropriations.[28]

And yet, as he wrote about the same time, "the whole urban struggle, whether on the guerrilla or mass-movement front, must always be seen as tactical struggle . . . the decisive struggle will be in the rural area." [29] Shortly after Marighela's death, the Cuban press published an article by Joaquim Camara Ferreira which said that in time armed struggle in the countryside would become the foundation of the liberation war.[30]

In June 1969 Marighela completed his *Minimanual of the Urban Guerrilla,* written chiefly to explain the conditions, characteristics, necessities, and methods of urban guerrilla warfare against the military government that replaced Brazilian President João Goulart in 1964. However, the book circulated widely outside Brazil as well, particularly through the promotion of the Cuban government, which published numerous editions in several languages around the turn of the decade.[31]

In his *Minimanual,* Marighela wrote that the central nucleus of the urban guerrilla movement—the best trained, most experienced, and most dedicated fighters—would be "indoctrinated and disciplined with a long-range strategic and tactical vision consistent with the application of Marxist theory, of Leninism, and of Castro-Guevara developments, applied to the specific conditions of the Brazilian situation." He described the objectives of the urban guerrilla as follows:

> Within the framework of the class struggle, as it inevitably and necessarily sharpens, the armed struggle of the urban guerrilla points toward two essential objectives:

---

[28] "On Rural Guerrilla Warfare," in ibid., p. 99.

[29] "Problems and Principles of Strategy," in ibid., p. 47; also see "Marighela Calls on the People to Join the Struggle" and "Call to the Brazilian People," in ibid., pp. 19-24, 119-23, respectively.

[30] *Granma* (Havana), 4 January 1970.

[31] In the following pages I use the edition translated in *Tricontinental* (Havana), no. 16 (January-February 1970); the work is also translated under the title "Handbook of Urban Guerrilla Warfare" in *Liberation of Brazil*, pp. 61-97.

(a) the physical liquidation of the chiefs and assistants of the armed forces and of the police;

(b) the expropriation of government resources and those belonging to the big capitalists, latifundists, and imperialists, with small expropriations used for the maintenance of individual urban guerrillas and large ones for the sustenance of the revolution itself.

The most common form of "expropriation" used to finance activities of the guerrillas was the "bank assault." The activity of sabotage was also said to have its own generally overlapping objectives—

to hurt, to damage, to make useless and to destroy vital enemy points such as the following:

(a) the economy of the country;
(b) agricultural or industrial production;
(c) transport and communication systems;
(d) the military and police systems and their establishments and deposits;
(e) the repressive military-police system;
(f) the firms and properties of North Americans in the country.[32]

Urban guerrillas, who formed "an armed alliance of workers and peasants, with students, intellectuals, and priests," had two "basic and indispensable obligatory qualities." First was "a politico-revolutionary motivation," flowing from personal experience and the aforementioned training in Marxism, Leninism, and Castro-Guevarism, and a conviction of "moral superiority," that comes from their certainty that in the struggle against the military government "to be an assailant or a terrorist is a quality that ennobles any honorable man." [33] Second was the necessary technical-revolutionary preparation. Since the "fundamental and decisive characteristic of the urban guerrilla is that he is a man who fights with arms," and since his "reason for existence . . . is to shoot," it follows that he must be trained in the use of revolvers, automatic weapons, shotguns, mortars, bazookas, bombs, Molotov cocktails, and his basic arm, the light machine gun. He must also be able to carry out the following actions among others: assaults, ambushes, expropriations, executions, kidnappings, sabotage, war of nerves, and terrorism, the latter "an arm the revolutionary can never relinquish," which must be carried out "with the greatest cold bloodedness, calm-

---

[32] *Tricontinental* (Havana), pp. 20, 37-39, 45.

[33] Ibid., pp. 55, 19, 16.

ness, and decision." The guerrilla must make use of the initial advantages available to him, such as surprise and mobility.[34]

Urban guerrillas are organized into small units that carry out local activities on their own initiative and actions of a strategic nature on orders from the general command. Their seven deadly sins are: inexperience, boasting, vanity (which involves neglecting rural guerrilla warfare), exaggerating their own strength, precipitous action, attacking the enemy when they are most angry, and improvisation.[35]

The urban guerrilla wholeheartedly attacks the "election farce and the so-called 'political solution' so appealing to the opportunists"; and in their presence he "must become more aggressive and violent, resorting without letup to sabotage, terrorism, expropriations, assaults, kidnappings, executions," and other such activities. In this and other ways it becomes apparent that "one of the permanent concerns of the urban guerrilla is his identification with popular causes to win public support." [36]

Argentina. The People's Revolutionary Army (ERP), the armed branch of the majority faction of the Trotskyist Revolutionary Workers' Party (PRT), was founded at the PRT's Fifth Congress (on 29 July 1970) in accordance with directives from the 1969 World Congress of the Fourth International (United Secretariat) held in Europe. The ERP, strongly influenced from the beginning by various forms of castroism, by left Peronists, by the anarcho-Marxism of Abraham Guillén, and by other revolutionary trends, remained formally affiliated with the Trotskyists until 1973.

According to the group's main leader, Mario Roberto Santucho, the ERP grew rapidly in size and in strict adherence to Marxism-Leninism on all political, ideological, and organizational issues.[37] An ERP leader interviewed by a Chilean journal in 1973 declared that "the road to workers' and people's power in Argentina is prolonged revolutionary war." The majority of the people, he added, particularly the vanguard, knew that elections would not lead to their liberation. Through a combination of legal and illegal activities, the ERP would seek to raise the consciousness of the people, realizing that as the

---

[34] Ibid., pp. 20, 23-25, 37, 47, 46, 30.

[35] Ibid., pp. 27-28, 53-54.

[36] Ibid., pp. 54, 53.

[37] "Interview with Mario Santucho," El Tupamaro (Montevideo), no. 3 (March 1974), translated in North American Congress on Latin America [hereafter NACLA], Argentina in the Hour of the Furnaces (Berkeley: NACLA, 1975), p. 101.

mobilization of the masses progressed the possibility of a military coup (which the ERP would resist) would increase. Finally, the ERP believed the Argentine revolution would be successful only if it were part of a continental revolution, a conclusion which, as he pointed out, put the ERP in full agreement with Che Guevara's strategic concept of the development of revolution—to "create two, three, many Vietnams and one of them—or several—in Latin America." [38]

ERP activities were from the beginning intended to take place in both city and countryside. In practice, they were chiefly urban until the formation of a major rural column in the northern province of Tucumán in 1975. The ERP has sought to develop a mass following by advancing a broad "democratic and anti-imperialist" program that calls for the establishment of a revolutionary people's government led by the working class, agrarian reform, the termination of all political and military pacts with the United States and of all agreements with organizations (such as the International Monetary Fund) that are "dominated by imperialist capital." [39] The unidentified ERP spokesman quoted earlier said that in order to develop a united front the ERP would "call on the entire left, all progressive and revolutionary workers' and people's organizations to close ranks, to support each other, and to present an organized common front to the political, ideological and military offensive of the bourgeoisie, in both its repressive and deceptive populist forms." [40]

Between 1970 and early 1976, the ERP regarded Peronism as a multi-class movement with some progressive sectors burdened by a bourgeois ideology. In May 1973 an ERP spokesman stated that

> since our founding we have continuously and constantly called for the operational unity of the armed revolutionary organizations, hoping to construct a solid, strong and unified People's Army in which Peronist and non-Peronist fighters will be united by the common methodology of prolonged revolutionary war, and a common ideal: the construction of socialism. [41]

In practice, as Santucho admitted in March 1974, relations with the armed Peronist movements, among them the Montoneros and the Revo-

---

[38] "Win or Die for Argentina," *Chile Hoy* (Santiago), 11-17 May 1973, translated in NACLA, *Argentina in the Hour of the Furnaces,* pp. 100-101.

[39] See, for example, *Cristianismo y revolución* (Buenos Aires), March 1971.

[40] "Win or Die for Argentina," p. 101.

[41] Ibid., p. 100.

lutionary Armed Forces (FAR), were irregular, "with frequent ups and downs." [42] Indeed, differences over relations with the Peronist left and the Peronist governments elected in 1973, among other issues, led to much dissension within the ERP and to the breaking off of several minority factions. When the ERP was outlawed, several weeks before Juan Perón's inauguration as president in mid-October 1973, Santucho declared that Perón was a counterrevolutionary in the service of capitalism. In the course of the next year most of the Peronist guerrilla left became increasingly critical of the government as well and, particularly after the succession of Isabel Perón in 1974, moved into active opposition. As the amorphous and poorly disciplined Peronist guerrillas took this turn against the government, more contacts with the ERP came about, in part through the Marxist-oriented FAR, which merged with the Montoneros in late 1973, and in part through one of the ERP's splinters—the 22 August group—which rejoined the parent party in 1974." [43]

Throughout the period from 1970 to early 1976, the ERP carried out a variety of operations, often modeled on those of the Uruguayan Tupamaros, ranging from robberies, kidnappings for ransom of prominent Argentine and foreign personages (particularly businessmen), and assassinations to open and large-scale armed confrontations with the military or police forces. Among their most widely publicized activities was the escape of twenty-eight guerrillas (not all from the ERP) from Rawson Prison in Patagonia on 15 August 1972, ten of whom (including Santucho) fled by hijacked plane to Chile, while the remainder were killed at the Trelew naval airbase by government authorities "while trying to escape."

Like the Tupamaros, the ERP in the beginning created a certain Robin Hood aura around its activities, as when the manager of the Swift meat packing plant in Rosario was kidnapped and released in 1971 in exchange for Swift's distribution of $57,000 worth of food and other supplies in Argentine slums. Later activities were more often military in character, often directed toward high-level military and police officials. During 1975 ERP activities were in large part concentrated in the rural areas of the northern province of Tucumán. The large-scale coordinated ERP attack on an army base and other targets in or near

---

[42] "Interview with Mario Santucho," p. 103.
[43] See Kenneth F. Johnson, "Guerrilla Politics in Argentina," *Conflict Studies* (London), October 1975.

Buenos Aires on 23–24 December 1975, during which some guerrillas sought refuge in a shantytown (where many civilians were killed in the shoot-out with military forces), demonstrated the distance the ERP had travelled from the "Robin Hood" days. The Argentine military overthrew the Perón government in March 1976, and the ERP was seriously weakened four months later when Santucho was killed in a shootout.

The Strategy of Abraham Guillén

Two veterans of the Spanish Civil War—Abraham Guillén and Alberto Bayo—served as teachers and theoreticians for guerrillas in Latin America. Bayo is the more widely known in the United States because of his role instructing Fidel Castro's expeditionary force while it was training in Mexico in 1955–1956. Once identified as "el maestro" by Che Guevara, Bayo was author of the short volume entitled *Ciento Cincuenta preguntas a un guerrillero*.[44] This brief manual, first published in Mexico in 1955, contains answers to 150 usually very specific questions on the organization and activities of a guerrilla force. It was reprinted by a variety of groups, sometimes under a name different from Bayo's, and circulated widely in and around the Caribbean, particularly in the early 1960s.[45]

Guillén is much the more serious thinker than Bayo, however, and exercised greater influence (both direct and indirect) on more guerrillas in Latin America. According to such diverse groups as the guerrillas themselves and national security forces, Guillén's *Estrategía de la guerrilla urbana* (1966, 1969) formulated much of the strategy and tactics of urban guerrilla warfare as applied in Argentina, Brazil, and Uruguay beginning in the middle 1960s.[46]

---

[44] See Hugh Thomas, *Cuba: The Pursuit of Freedom* (New York: Harper and Row, 1971), pp. 876-77, 882. According to Herbert Matthews, however, in his *Fidel Castro* (New York: Simon and Schuster, 1969), p. 89, Castro once denied "rather emphatically that he owed anything to Colonel Bayo in the way of guerrilla knowledge."

[45] One edition, put out by the Colombian Movimiento Obrero Estudiantil Campesino (MOEC) in 1960, was signed by Alejandro Gener B.

[46] Guillén himself claims considerable influence on the urban guerrillas in these three countries. Donald C. Hodges has translated a representative selection of Guillén's writings, including some previously unpublished manuscripts, and provided an introduction to Guillén's life and work. See Hodges, *Philosophy of the Urban Guerrilla: The Revolutionary Writings of Abraham Guillén* (New York: Morrow, 1973), especially pp. 2-18.

Of all advocates of guerrilla warfare in Latin America, Guillén has devoted the most time and energy to putting the strategy in broad perspective. Guillén is an eclectic, insisting that the writings and experiences of others should be studied and, when they are relevant to contemporary conditions, adapted and used, but never simply copied. He openly acknowledges that he has been inspired or influenced by such individuals as the Chinese military theorist Sun Tzu (ca. sixth century B.C.), the Greek commander Epaminondas (fourth century B.C.), and many more recent revolutionaries, including Marx, Bakunin, Lenin, Trotsky, and Mao Tse-tung, among others. By the late 1960s, he argued that the period of anarcho-Marxism had arrived.[47]

His published works, the first of which came out in the early 1950s, have provided an analysis of political, economic, and social conditions in Latin America as well as in many communist and so-called imperialist countries elsewhere in the world. These semi-scholarly writings, often repetitive and of uneven quality, have set the framework within which he justifies his insistence on continental revolutionary war as the only hope for Latin American liberation. His works on revolutionary war are not nearly so concise or narrowly technical as those of Bayo or Marighela, nor as dogmatically theoretical as Debray's *Revolution in the Revolution?*

Guillén first advocated a continental revolution in 1966, a year before Che Guevara's better-known call for such a strategy in his "Message to the Tricontinental." No country in Latin America would be able to achieve true liberation alone, according to Guillén, because all of them, with their economies based on one or just a few products, were economically dependent on the United States. An effort to create a revolution in only one country would be isolated (as in Cuba), asphyxiated (as in the Dominican Republic in 1965), debased economically (as in Bolivia in the 1950s and 1960s), or "bourgeoisified" (as in Mexico in recent decades).[48] Guillén argues that the United States, which has converted Latin America into its "commonwealth," has orchestrated an international strategy against revolution, and that this must be countered by a continental movement with revolutionary objectives.

---

[47] Abraham Guillén, *Desafío al pentágono* [hereafter *Desafío*] (Montevideo: Editorial Andes, 1969), p. 97.

[48] Abraham Guillén, *Estrategia de la guerrilla urbana* [hereafter *Estrategia*] (Montevideo: Liberación, 1969), pp. 57-58, 75. The first edition was published in 1966.

147

The efforts of repressive Latin American governments to form inter-American economic organizations will not lead to liberation for the masses and must be replaced by continental united front movements of the people.[49] The "Pentagon strategy" of the United States—described as the "strategy of the artichoke" since it involves the piece-by-piece dismantling of revolutionary forces—must be broken by guerrilla attacks on Yankee installations in many countries at one time.[50] In order to do this, Latin American revolutionaries must develop a scientific "operational strategy." This will be discussed in more detail below.[51]

A number of factors contribute to the cause of the revolutionaries, among them the revolutionary spirit of the times in general and the current conditions in Latin America. The masses are suppressed, as they are in many parts of the world, and thus united in misery and hopes for liberation, but in Latin America the masses are also united by their common heritage, religion, and (generally) language. Further, in Latin America there is a vast area within which the protracted revolution can be fought to the benefit of the revolutionaries.[52]

Revolutionary war, according to Guillén, "is an act of political violence taken when the political ends of the classes or peoples cannot be attained by peaceful means." Revolutionary war, he continues, "is total war: people and [liberation] army are united everywhere against domestic reaction and foreign invaders in a struggle without quarter which exacts the highest political tension."[53] Given the topography, economy, sociology, and politics of Latin America, the revolutionary war will have the following characteristics, among others: (1) a vast neocolonial area within which to harass and defeat the enemy; (2) the reactionary national armies whose operations are directed by the Pentagon; (3) the guerrilla forces; and (4) the favorably inclined population.[54]

The revolutionary war must be developed by an armed vanguard force of professional revolutionaries, who may be workers, students, or

---

[49] Ibid., pp. 57-58, 68-69.

[50] Guillén, Desafío, pp. 69, 100.

[51] Guillén, Estrategia, p. 185; Guillén, Desafío, p. 6.

[52] See Guillén, La rebelión del tercer mundo [hereafter Tercer Mundo] (Montevideo: Andes, 1969), p. 249; Guillén, Estrategia, p. 25; and Guillén, Desafío, p. 63.

[53] Guillén, Desafío, p. 55.

[54] Ibid., pp. 56-65.

members of some other class.[55] It must be a guerrilla force, which is at the same time the "liberation army and the armed party," composed of individuals who can combine the theory and practice of revolution.[56] Whatever class they come from, the members of the vanguard are important as individuals, for Guillén is convinced that man is superior to technology, agreeing with Mao Tse-tung's view expressed when he said the atomic bomb was a "paper tiger." [57]

The guerrilla party should not be "sectarian, dogmatic, or intolerant, but flexible, in a new style, not designated by any ism, operating politically in the name of the general interest in order to win over the entire oppressed population." [58] There should be room in the united front for everything from Marxism and libertarian socialism to "debourgeoisified" Christianity and "all progressive movements that have liberated themselves politically from Soviet bureaucracy, Yankee imperialism, and the native bourgeoisie." [59]

The revolutionary war must have mass support. Thus a broad united front must be built up against the landholding oligarchs, the comprador bourgeoisie, the reactionary military leadership, and other groups that work with the imperialists to oppress the masses—all of whom, when taken together, constitute between 10 and 15 percent of the Latin American population. The front will draw in (1) the peasants, (2) the industrial workers, (3) the students, intellectuals, technocrats, journalists, writers, and other representatives of the intelligentsia, (4) the middle classes, (5) the part of the Church oriented toward Christian socialism, (6) the part of the national bourgeoisie that wants to operate free from the imperialists, and (7) those members of the middle and lower levels of the military who want national political and economic independence.[60] This front, anchored in the alliance of the workers and peasants, must develop continental fronts

---

[55] "El pueblo en armas: estrategia revolucionaria," manuscript published in Hodges, *Philosophy of the Urban Guerrilla.* Also see Guillén, *Desafío,* p. 142; Guillén, *Estrategia,* p. 160. In the 1969 edition of *Estrategia,* Guillén leans toward a student vanguard in Latin America, the students described in one place as the "proletariat of tomorrow"; see pp. 141, 158.

[56] Guillén, *Desafío,* p. 73.

[57] Ibid., p. 56; Guillén, *Estrategia,* p. 21.

[58] Guillén, *Desafío,* p. 61.

[59] Ibid., p. 75.

[60] Guillén, *Estrategia,* p. 66; also see Guillén, *Desafío,* pp. 163-64; and Guillén, *Tercer Mundo,* p. 246.

of workers, youth, and peasants, as well as a Latin American Liberation Army.[61]

Such a widely based front could not be built on anything less than a broad program of a nonsectarian type. Thus, according to Guillén, the revolution must seek first to overthrow the oligarchs as well as ending imperialism and overthrowing its native allies and only then, at a second stage, begin to talk of and build socialism.[62] This is not to say that the vanguard should have no disguised political orientation. According to Guillén, revolutionary cadres should have socialist training, "but they should say nothing about socialism or related matters publicly." The struggle should be tied in to national conditions, not an existing ideology: "If Fidel had said in the Sierra Maestra that he was aiming at socialism, he would have lost the war." [63]

On the question whether the guerrilla war was to be in the city or the countryside, Guillén held several views between 1965 and the early 1970s. In his *Theory of Violence,* published in 1965, guerrilla war was considered almost entirely in a rural setting. He wrote, for example, that three "fundamental conditions" were necessary for the initiation of a revolutionary war: favorable population, a vulnerable enemy, and terrain of high mountains with woods.[64] That changed radically the following year with the publication of *Strategy of the Urban Guerrilla,* the first serious and detailed elaboration of the strategy and tactics of urban guerrilla warfare to be published in Latin America. In that volume he stressed that the "revolution's potential is where the population is," and thus the center of operations should be in the city if the greater part of the population is urban. Uruguay and Argentina, for example, "should undertake prolonged urban warfare based on many small military victories which together will render final victory." [65] In general, since the mid-1960s, Guillén has held that the struggle should take place in both city and countryside, the questions being which should be emphasized and (when the revolutionary forces are small in the beginning) which should come first.

61 Guillén, *Estrategia,* pp. 68-69, 84; Guillén, *Desafío,* pp. 121-24.

62 Guillén, *Desafío,* p. 163.

63 "El pueblo en armas," in Hodges, *Philosophy of the Urban Guerrilla,* p. 260.

64 *Teoría de la violencia* (Buenos Aires: Jamcana, 1965), p. 201.

65 Guillén, *Estrategia,* 1966 edition, quoted in Hodges, *Philosophy of the Urban Guerrilla,* pp. 238, 239, and *Estrategia,* 1969 edition, p. 79; also see Guillén's introduction to Che Guevara, *Guerra de guerrillas* (Montevideo: Provincias Unidas, 1968), p. 15; and Guillén, *Desafío,* pp. 64-65, 76.

Guillén does not find the vanguard he envisions in either the pro-Soviet communist parties or the Guevara-style castroite *focos*. The communists, he writes, have become "petty-bourgeois and nationalist," contributing nothing to the liberation of the peoples.[66] He is straightforward in his criticism of the *foco* approach as advocated by Debray and executed by Guevara in Bolivia in 1966–1967, a "rebel" approach in contrast to a truly revolutionary one. The rebels, in their voluntarist idealism, often mistake wishes for realities, go into action without thinking things through in advance, and launch insurrections without proper preparation. The revolutionaries, by contrast, analyze each situation before acting, carefully distinguish between allies and enemies, and build up a revolutionary organization on the basis of a clear program that will rally the oppressed and lead to the defeat of the oppressors.[67] Focoism, Guillén wrote in 1972, is actually "an insurrectional movement for piling up cadavers, for giving easy victories to the repressive generals trained by the Pentagon." [68]

Finally, Guillén makes it clear that in his judgment some of the best-known urban guerrillas have made serious mistakes. The "superb tactics" of the Uruguayan Tupamaros, for example, "have been nullified by a mediocre strategy and a questionable politics." [69] More specifically, Guillén wrote in 1972, the Tupamaros had made the following mistakes, mainly during the early 1970s: (1) they lost their mobility and security; (2) they failed to escalate their operations after early hit-and-run successes; (3) they resorted to unnecessary violence, such as the killing of ordinary soldiers, thus "descending to the same level as the reactionary army"; (4) they held hostages for extended periods of time in "people's prisons," focusing attention unnecessarily on their own "parallel system of repression"; (5) they allowed themselves to be forced into executing a hostage (Dan Mitrione) with adverse propaganda results; (6) they became overly professionalized, militarized, and isolated from the urban masses, remaining chiefly representatives of the rebellious petit-bourgeoisie; and (7) they "acted precipitately in attacking the newly elected government of President Bordaberry [thus provoking] the as yet untested government to declare a state of

---

[66] Guillén, *Desafío*, pp. 74-75.
[67] Ibid., p. 92.
[68] "El pueblo en armas," in Hodges, *Philosophy of the Urban Guerrilla*, p. 269.
[69] Ibid., p. 274; the following critique of the Tupamaros is taken from this source, pp. 263-77.

war," when it would have been far better to let the economic and social crisis discredit the new regime.

Conclusions

Abraham Guillén, in his *Strategy of the Urban Guerrilla* (1966), was the first to present a systematic and detailed argument for the extensive and prolonged use of urban guerrilla warfare in the major centers of Latin American population. His writings and other activities undoubtedly contributed substantially to the urban struggle that developed in Uruguay, Brazil, and Argentina during the late 1960s and early 1970s. Yet his contribution should be kept in perspective. Even before the Cuban Casa de las Américas published Debray's *Revolution in the Revolution?*, and before the death of Che Guevara in Bolivia, guerrillas and others in a number of countries had come to doubt—if they ever believed it—that rural guerrilla warfare was the essential road to the "liberation" of Latin America, as the Cubans and the Chinese seemed to be insisting. A decade after the publication of Guillén's book, it is possible to say that this form of struggle has had a significantly greater impact on the countries within which it has been waged than rural warfare, though that impact has by no means been consistently beneficial to the immediate interests of the working classes on whose behalf the guerrillas purport to be acting.

Urban guerrillas like Marighela called for the disruption or sabotage of the national economy and the existing order in general, theoretically to intensify the contradictions between the masses and what they considered the repressive minority of rulers, as a step toward the overthrow of the traditional system and its replacement by a revolutionary government. In practice this had not happened in any Central or South American country by the time of this writing (July 1976).

The urban guerrillas in Brazil did little more than win some international headlines for their kidnappings, contribute to the growth of right-wing counterterrorist organizations, produce a manual on guerrilla warfare, and get themselves killed. The Tupamaros in Uruguay had a far greater impact, both domestically and internationally. Reacting to a deepening national crisis which was not of their own making, they were unable to win significant popular support for their own remedies and in the end were the final major factor in the collapse of the Uruguayan democratic system and its replacement by a virtual military

152

dictatorship. The Tupamaros, during their heyday, made Uruguay a testing ground for urban guerrilla tactics, and some of the mistakes they made have been to varying degrees avoided in Chile and Argentina.

The Chilean MIR prior to September 1973 (discussed in detail in the next chapter) and the Argentine guerrillas (at least up to this writing) were much more effective revolutionary organizations. They sought with some success to avoid some of the problems Guillén noted in the Tupamaros (see above), among them violent actions that lost rather than gained public support. The Chilean and Argentine guerrillas won considerable sympathy and support among factory workers, and the MIR, more than the Argentine ERP or Montoneros, was influential among a significant minority of the peasants and others in the countryside. Yet the MIR was one of the main factors in the collapse of the Chilean democratic system and the Argentine guerrillas contributed substantially to the return of military rule in their country. Whereas the Chilean military virtually eliminated the MIR during the year after Allende's fall, the fortunes of the guerrillas in Argentina remain to be determined.

In general, many of the problems of the rural guerrillas reappeared in the changed setting. Like their rural counterparts, the urban guerrillas found it was often very difficult (1) to cooperate with other revolutionary organizations, (2) to work out effective policies on a regular basis, thereby leading to the steady growth and development of the guerrilla force, (3) to prevent the emergence of different views on strategic and tactical issues that in practice led to internal quarreling and even splintering of the organization, (4) to win the even passive support of substantial portions of the population, much less the active support of ever increasing numbers of individuals, and (5) to judge just how far they could push the existing power structure without unleashing a counterattack the guerrillas and their supporters were not yet prepared to meet.

Many of the lessons learned by the guerrillas were implicit in the program issued in February 1974 by the Revolutionary Coordinating Committee (JCR), an inter-American guerrilla organization founded by four of South America's most important guerrilla forces with extensive rural and urban experience: the Chilean MIR, the Uruguayan Tupamaros, the Bolivian ELN, and the Argentine People's Revolutionary Army (ERP).[70]

---

[70] See Appendix C.

This is a more sophisticated and in some respects more realistic statement than the "little recipes" of Debray. Though the statement is recognizably derived from early castroism and similar tendencies, the almost exclusively rural qualities of early guerrilla struggles have been tempered by years of theoretical discussion and bitter experience. (Indeed, the 1974 document is closer in many respects to the Maoism of the late 1960s than it is to the castroism of that period.) Several parts of the critique (such as the comments on bourgeois nationalism) are accepted to some degree by a number of Latin Americans who have no sympathy for guerrilla warfare or for the demand for leadership by a "Marxist-Leninist combat party of a proletarian character."

Still, the bulk of the critique is made up of gross exaggerations (for example, that there was an "uninterrupted succession of great popular struggles" in Latin America during the 1960s); simplistic distortions of history (for example, that "fascist regimes" were imposed, presumably in Uruguay and Chile, in fear of a "rising mass movement"); dogmatic assertions (for example, that real change can come in Latin America only under the leadership of a "Marxist-Leninist combat party of a proletarian character"); wishful thinking and demagoguery (for example, that the guerrillas will be able to "mobilize the entire people" and that the workers "will unleash the irresistible energies of the masses in all their intensity and thus win happiness for our peoples"); or outright warmongering (for example, that the oppression of "imperialism" is so terrible and firmly established as to require a "Vietnam War" sweeping across the continent to break its stranglehold).

7

Castroism and Communism in Chile

The positions and policies of castroism and communism discussed in the preceding chapters clashed in Chile as they did in several other countries. But Chile was unusual in that the conflicts extended beyond the pages of obscure theoretical journals and newspapers, and many of the parties involved had greater than marginal influence on the people in the country. The conflict between the pro-Soviet Communist Party (PCCh) and the castroite groups in Chile during the early 1970s played itself out in the presidential palace, the factories, and the countryside, profoundly influencing the policies of both the Popular Unity (UP) government and its many opponents, and shaping the lives of everyone living in the country.

Chile was one of the most complex and in many respects politically sophisticated countries in Latin America during the 1960s, immediately before the beginning of the Popular Unity period (1970–1973). The main trends of the 1960s provide a background for the events of the traumatic 1970s. Some of these trends were (1) the growth of industry and urban population with resulting social and economic dislocations; (2) increased (but not rapid) agrarian reform and the efforts, sometimes at best marginally successful, to raise the living standards of the country's poor; (3) legislation giving Chile control over its basic resources, particularly copper; (4) the growing strength of leftist parties, ranging from the Communist Party (PCCh) and Socialist Party (PSCh) on the Marxist-Leninist left to the more moderate Christian Democratic Party (PDC), and a corresponding decline in influence of traditional parties. Moving into the 1970s Chile had a generally effective constitution, congress, and court system, and a long and vigorous democratic tradition with an ever-expanding electorate. The nation had produced many outspoken and articulate leaders of contrasting and conflicting beliefs who called for all manner of policies, sometimes with unmistakably demagogic overtones.

Political, economic, and social tension, which had been building for many years, increased during the "Revolution in Liberty" conducted by PDC President Eduardo Frei between 1964 and 1970. What the Marxists called the class struggle, which was in reality not ever a struggle along strict class lines, developed much more rapidly, however, during the Popular Unity period under President Salvador Allende. More than ever before, the domestic situation in Chile was influenced by a variety of international factors, ranging from a general rise in Latin American nationalism to the policies of individual countries around the world.

During the Allende years there were four major political parties, with widely differing ideologies and constituencies, that could be counted on to win between 15 and 35 percent of the popular vote. These were the National Party (PN), the most conservative of the four, the left-reformist PDC, the PCCh, and the PSCh. Besides other minor parties there were ultra-right and ultra-left groups operating in large part on the fringes—or outside the limits—of the law and the democratic system.

The Communist Party of Chile played a leading role in founding the Popular Unity coalition of six leftist parties and movements at the end of 1969: the six were the PCCh, the PSCh, the Radical Party (PR), the Social Democratic Party (PSD), the Unitary Popular Action Movement (MAPU), which was a group of dissidents from the PDC, and the Independent Popular Alliance (AIP). Though the make-up of the UP shifted somewhat between 1969 and 1973, the PCCh and the PSCh remained its leading forces. The six UP parties and movements that won seats in the 1973 congressional elections, and regularly held cabinet ministries in the UP government, were the PCCh, PSCh, PR, MAPU, AIP, and Christian Left (IC), the latter formed by additional PDC and MAPU dissidents in 1971.

In general, President Allende, though a member of the Socialist Party, seems to have been in agreement with the basic line of the PCCh; he unquestionably received his strongest support from members of that party and its youth group. The castroite-leaning forces, on the other hand, were emphatically not in agreement with the communists and as time wore on became increasingly critical of President Allende. They comprised the bulk of the "ultra-left"—the term used by the PCCh as well as the opposition parties—and were concentrated in a half dozen groups, the most important being the Movement of the Revolutionary Left (MIR) and one wing of Allende's own Socialist Party. Though the MIR will be discussed in more detail than the PSCh because it represents a more typically castroite organization, the importance of the division within the Socialist Party can hardly be overestimated both for domestic policy and for foreign relations, as will be seen below.

The Communist Party

Background and Organization. During the late 1960s and early 1970s, the PCCh was the most important communist party in Latin America outside of Cuba. It grew from the fourth largest party in 1959 (behind the communist parties of Argentina, Brazil, and Venezuela) to the largest in 1973. At the end of 1969 the party claimed that its membership had doubled since 1965 to about 60,000; in 1973 it claimed some 200,000 members.[1] Even if the latter figure is inflated—which it almost certainly is—the PCCh probably had more members, and certainly more activists, than all other South American communist parties combined. In May 1971 a party leader gave the following breakdown on PCCh members: workers, 65.3 percent; peasants, 13.6 percent; white-collar, 8.9 percent; intellectuals and persons of middle-class background, 8.1 percent; and artisans, 4.1 percent. He further categorized the membership as follows: men, 70 percent; women, 30 percent; under thirty years of age, 30.6 percent; between thirty and forty, 29.1 percent; between forty and fifty, 20.7 percent; and over fifty, 19.6 percent. Shortly thereafter the secretary-general of the PCCh said that some 75 percent of party members came from the working class.[2]

The PCCh was run during the late 1960s and early 1970s by its secretary-general (Luis Corvalán), a political commission, a secretariat,

---

[1] Volodia Teitelboim claimed 200,000 in *Granma* (Havana), 14 January 1973; *World Marxist Review*, vol. 16, no. 7 (July 1973). These figures must be regarded with considerable skepticism, not only because some exaggeration is to be expected, but because party claims do not always seem consistent. For example, in early 1972 Luis Corvalán claimed "250,000 or so communists" (*El Siglo* [Santiago], 13 February), presumably including members of the communist youth, and Orlando Millas reported 120,000 three months later (ibid., 21 May).

[2] See Mario Zamorano, *World Marxist Review*, vol. 14, no. 9 (September 1971), and comments of Luis Corvalán in Eduardo Labarca, *Corvalán: 27 Horas* (Santiago: Quimantu, 1972), p. 79.

Table 2

PERCENTAGE OF VOTE FOR COMMUNIST PARTY OF CHILE

Year	Election	Percentage
1960	Municipal	9.5
1961	Congressional	11.7
1965	Congressional	12.2
1967	Municipal	15.1
1969	Congressional	15.7
1971	Municipal	17.0
1973	Congressional	17.1

and a central committee. The Central Committee was enlarged from fifty-five to seventy-five members in November 1969; the Political Commission was reduced from fifteen to nine members in March 1972; and the Secretariat was increased from six to seven members in March 1972. Among the party leaders, besides Corvalán, were Víctor Díaz, deputy secretary-general, Orlando Millas, Mario Zamorano, and Volodia Teitelboim. The party's 14th Congress was held in November 1969, immediately before the adoption of the Popular Unity program and the nomination of Salvador Allende; the 15th Congress, scheduled for November 1973, was postponed indefinitely after the September 1973 coup.

The Chilean communists have long been active in electoral politics. The PCCh helped form the Popular Action Front (FRAP) in 1956, two years before the party regained its legality (lost in 1948), and in 1957 won six congressional seats. During the period from 1959 to 1973, the PCCh slowly but steadily increased its percentage of the total vote in Chilean national legislative and municipal elections, as Table 2 indicates.

Throughout the years of the Popular Unity government, three cabinet positions were assigned at all times to members of the Communist Party, generally positions in the economic area. Those serving as ministers for varying periods of time between November 1970 and September 1973 were, as minister of labor, José Oyarce, Mireya Baltra, Luis Figueroa, and Jorge Godoy; as minister of the Treasury, Américo Zorilla and Orlando Millas; as economic minister, Millas and José Cademártori; as minister of justice, Sergio Insunza; and as minister of public works, Pascual Barraza. Orlando Millas was not the first of President Allende's ministers to be accused of violating the constitution, but he was the first communist to be so charged by Congress. These charges caused his resignation as minister of the Treasury (in December 1972) and minister of economy (July 1973); Figueroa was similarly forced to resign as minister of labor (June 1973).

The PCCh played an active role in working class affairs through the Single Center of Chilean Workers (CUTCh), the only important labor confederation in the country. At the time of its 6th Congress, in December 1971, it claimed 1 million members, though the figure is certainly inflated. The PCCh was the strongest single force in the CUTCh during these years though the extent of its leverage declined. In 1965 the PCCh held an absolute majority of seats in the Leadership Council, and the Socialist Party of Chile held the remainder. At the 5th Congress (November 1968) the council was expanded to include a few Christian Democrats and others though the PCCh retained fourteen out of twenty-seven positions and the PSCh retained seven. The 6th Congress enlarged the Leadership Council to fifty-four members and, after the rank and file balloting in May–June 1972, the positions were: PCCh eighteen, PSCh sixteen, PDC sixteen, and others four. Both the PSCh and the Christian Democrats protested the election, the latter claiming that irregularities had prevented it from winning, a conclusion reached by some independent observers as well.[3] Before the inauguration of Salvador Allende as president in November 1970, the CUTCh actively opposed most economic and labor policies of the Frei government. However, in accordance with an agreement signed at the end of 1970, the CUTCh cooperated in the formation and implementation of labor policy during the Popular Unity period. In 1972 the two top CUTCh officials (including three-time president Luis Figueroa) were appointed ministers in Allende's cabinet. CUTCh was outlawed in Chile in late 1973, but individual leaders in exile, particularly Luis Figueroa, travelled widely in Europe and elsewhere to develop opposition to the military government from international labor groups such as the Soviet-line World Federation of Trade Unions.

The Communist Youth (JCCh) in Chile was more active and successful than any of its counterparts in the hemisphere (except the youth organizations of Cuba and, perhaps, Venezuela). Whereas in 1964 all nine University Student Federations (FEU) were controlled by Christian

---

[3] For example, Juan de Onís, *New York Times Magazine*, 17 December 1972.

159

Democrats, in mid-1970, just before Salvador Allende became president of Chile, the Popular Unity parties were dominant in seven. The JCCh, with some 20,000 members at the time, held the presidency in the FEU of four universities, including the University of Chile in Santiago, and led secondary school unions and the youth departments of the CUTCh and "Ranquil," the latter a peasant and Indian confederation. The JCCh, which claimed that its membership had risen to 75,000 in 1973, was the most effective youth group supporting and defending candidate and President Allende between 1970 and 1973. Besides working within the universities, the JCCh carried out nationwide activities through its Ramona Parra Brigades, the Youth Commands of the UP, and other organizations. The JCCh was active in Chilean electoral politics during the 1970s—four of its members were elected to the national Chamber of Deputies in March 1973, including JCCh Secretary-General Gladys Marin. Although the JCCh waged an unceasing campaign against the "ultra-leftists" in Chilean politics, some young communists, particularly those in the Ramona Parra Brigades, were involved in street fights, seizures of private property, and clandestine activities such as the penetration of the military. After the fall of the Allende government, some JCCh members appear to have adopted (at least theoretically) a more militant posture.

What were the general lines of communist policy leading into and during the Popular Unity period? And what were some of the specific issues which caused significant dissension between the PCCh (more often than not in cooperation with President Allende) and the "ultra-left"—between the communists and the castroite forces both within and outside of the Popular Unity alliance?

Strategy and Tactics. Late in 1969, the PCCh set down its objectives for the coming period in the documents and speeches of its 14th Congress. According to the political resolution of the Congress, "the most revolutionary task in Chile today is to fight for the abolition of imperialism and the power of the monopolist and landed oligarchy, for socialism will have no perspective unless this task is accomplished." [4] In his report to the Congress, Luis Corvalán said the "reformist" Christian Democratic government of President Eduardo Frei, which had one more year in office, was "at the service of the powerful against the people."

---

[4] Published in *El Siglo* (Santiago), 30 November 1969; abridged translation in *Information Bulletin*, nos. 1-2 (1970).

Although he described Christian Democracy as "going downhill," he noted that "reformism maintains strong positions in some sectors of the people, and may make its way in others, including circles that formerly rejected it. It tends to reappear with fresh impetus under other names, other titles, and other leaders in civilian dress or in uniform." [5]

At the plenary meeting of the party in April 1969, Corvalán stated that in 1964 the FRAP had "offered the country a socialist-communist government" for which it was not yet ready. The nation still was not prepared for such a government in 1969, he commented, and proposed that the PCCh should sponsor a "popular movement and a government with a broader social and political base." [6]

Thus in November 1969 Corvalán hailed the arrival of the Popular Unity movement—which the PCCh had played a leading role in forming—the goal of which was to carry out the "combative struggle of the masses of the people for their immediate demands, against the reactionary policy of the government, to clear the way for their own victorious road." Quoting a party manifesto of December 1968, Corvalán told the delegates at the congress that the PCCh advocated a "multiparty government of the people" in Chile:

> Chile needs an anti-imperialist and anti-oligarchical people's government that has the support of the national majority, constituted by all the parties and currents that agree to a program of revolutionary transformations. In it must be the workers, the peasants, the employees, the women, the young people, the small and middle businessmen, not only through the parties that speak for them but also through representatives of their mass organizations in the corresponding institutions and echelons of the administration of the state.

Such a government, he continued, would allow "the existence of opposition within the framework of the laws of the country," and these laws would "be inspired, of course, by the interests of the people and not of the privileged." He concluded, quoting from the call for the congress:

> We communists believe that in a regime of a government of the people and, later, under the conditions of socialism, all the people's movements will maintain their own identities, all religious beliefs will be respected, and there will therefore exist ideological and political pluralism, without prejudice against each movement's promotion of its own ideas. [7]

[5] *El Siglo* (Santiago), 24 November 1969.
[6] Ibid., 14 April 1969.
[7] Ibid., 24 November 1969.

One editorial by the PCCh stated that the signing of the "Basic Program of Popular Unity" in December 1969 marked a "new and higher stage in the political development" of the country.[8] Another argued that the political picture had changed in Chile, that not since 1938 had such a broad section of political forces and social sectors worked together. Party leaders repeatedly stated that a multi-party government was a special characteristic of the advance toward socialism, and even of the consolidation of socialism, in Chile.[9]

The "Basic Program of Popular Unity," signed after a meeting of the six participating organizations, was promptly published in the PCCh organ, *El Siglo*.[10] This document, which the PCCh adopted as its own immediate program, rejected the "reformism" of the Frei government, pledged to rid the country of the influences of "monopolistic capitalism" and "imperialist exploitation," and promised to "begin the construction of socialism in Chile." It called for an "assembly of the people" to replace the existing two houses of the congress and for "democratization" of the political process on all levels. Other objectives included (1) the nationalization of basic resources controlled by foreign capital and domestic monopolies, while leaving the vast majority of enterprises entirely or partly under private ownership; (2) the acceleration of agrarian reform, with special emphasis on the development of peasant cooperatives; and (3) greatly increased state control over social, cultural, and educational programs. The program stated that the "popular government" would be "multi-partied" and include all "revolutionary" parties, movements, and trends; it would "respect the rights of opposition that is exercised within legal bounds." [11] This program, according to Luis Corvalán, was meant to "liberate Chile from imperialist domination, to destroy the power centers of the oligarchy, to take the coun-

---

[8] See *Principios* (Santiago), June-September 1970.

[9] See comments of Orlando Millas, in ibid., and of Luis Corvalán, *El Siglo* (Santiago), 2 December 1970.

[10] 23 December 1969; English version in *Tricontinental* (Havana), March-April 1971.

[11] The foreign policy objectives outlined in the basic program included complete political and economic independence for Chile, maintenance of relations with all countries irrespective of their ideological and political positions, friendship and solidarity with independent or colonial peoples ("especially those developing their struggles for liberation and independence"), and promotion of "strong Latin American and anti-imperialist feelings by means of a people's international policy." The program described Cuba as the "advanced post of the revolution and the construction of socialism on the Latin American continent."

try out of underdevelopment, to build an independent and modern economy, to create a new condition of justice and a more advanced democracy, and to begin the construction of socialism." [12]

Both before and after the September 1970 presidential election, the PCCh warned against what it considered open and concealed enemies, from the declared reactionaries to those who disguised themselves with ultra-leftist garb (see below). At the end of the year, Corvalán wrote that the people had to be converted into a "truly invincible force" in order to ward off reactionary and imperialist threats: "The people of Chile and their government, on the one hand, and imperialism and the oligarchy, on the other, are entering a period of successive confrontations." He concluded that

> the possibility that the people will be forced into some kind of armed confrontation in the future cannot be discounted. In this connection, the principal task for the present consists in continuing to isolate the enemies of change, to tie their hands, to put them in straitjackets, in order to spare the country the civil war into which they would like to drag it.[13]

In an "Appeal to All Chileans," published in October 1971, the PCCh National Conference directed particular praise to the nationalization of the major U.S. copper companies and the telephone company (ITT), the "abolishment of textile monopolies," the "institution of state control of the banks," and the accelerated agrarian reform.[14] According to Corvalán, a year later, nationalization had dealt a blow to the "whole system of imperialist domination"; agrarian reform had put an end to the "omnipotence of the latifundist"; and state control over important aspects of the economy had "substantially undermined but not completely broken" the "economic might of the financial oligarchy." UP (and PCCh) objectives were still to "break reactionary resistance, extend the state sector, push ahead in agrarian reform, make all state-owned enterprises pay their way, raise production and productivity, develop economic planning, take the offensive against inflation, assure supplies of the

---

[12] *El Siglo* (Santiago), 2 December 1970.

[13] Ibid. The article was translated in *World Marxist Review*, vol. 13, no. 12 (December 1970), pp. 5-12, and, in shortened form, in *Pravda* (Moscow), on 1 December. The reference to "straitjackets" and several other statements drew widespread criticism from non-UP forces in Chile.

[14] *El Siglo* (Santiago), 4 October 1971. See *Information Bulletin*, nos. 21-22 (1971) and *El Siglo* (Santiago), 4 September 1971.

things the country needs, improve job discipline," combat bureaucracy, and extend education, housing, and public health.[15]

The outstanding feature of the Popular Unity reforms, said Corvalán, was that they were being implemented "in accordance with the constitution and on the basis of the principles of law and order which have been formed in the course of Chile's history." "Much that has been achieved is irreversible," Corvalán continued; the remaining task was one of making "the whole process of the country's development irreversible, of consolidating it, and taking it further." [16]

Addressing the June 1971 plenum of the PCCh Central Committee, Volodia Teitelboim gave the party's backing to President Allende's May Day call: "The great battle for Chile, now and henceforward, is production." [17] In the "Appeal to All Chileans" of 1971 the PCCh called for a number of specific activities in the immediate future:

(1) greater output at enterprises, mines, in agriculture and improvement of the services;
(2) immediately rendering effective participation of the working people in management of all enterprises in the state and mixed sectors, economy, public services and government offices;
(3) organization of supply commissions in which housewives, trade unions, maternal centers, block committees and shop keepers from every village and block would fight speculators and ensure regular supply of the prime necessities;
(4) the creation of centers for implementation of the agrarian reform on all confiscated estates to give effect to the transfer of land to the peasants;
(5) preparation for the Sixth Congress of the United Trade Union Center of the Working People of Chile [CUTCh] as a true expression of the unitarian will of the working people;
(6) increased vigilance of the masses and committees for the protection of enterprises and public service offices;
(7) abolition of bureaucracy and achieving effective and true solutions of every concrete problem.[18]

A secret report of the PCCh Political Commission, prepared immediately after the UP electoral defeats in January 1972, was published in

---

[15] *World Marxist Review*, vol. 15, no. 11 (November 1972); and Orlando Millas, *El Siglo* (Santiago), 5 June 1972.

[16] *Pravda* (Moscow), 2 January 1972.

[17] *El Siglo* (Santiago), 25 June 1971.

[18] *Information Bulletin*, nos. 21-22 (1971).

an opposition paper in early February. It mentioned the need to open discussions with the Christian Democratic Party (PDC) and the weakening of UP policies as a result of dissension within the PSCh and harassment by the "ultra-left." The political commission suggested that the party should promote collective support for President Allende by all UP parties. One of the most serious problems was in the countryside. The PCCh noted that though the UP had "expropriated farms to turn over to the peasants at a rate five-times faster than previous governments," the UP was "not becoming stronger in the countryside." UP agrarian policy was inconsistent and bursting with subjectivism from the "ultra-left." [19]

The primary domestic enemies of the Popular Unity during 1973 were on the right, the "mummies" (*momios*) and reactionaries associated with the National Party, the "fascists" of the Fatherland and Freedom group, and the right-wing of the PDC. According to the PCCh, the members of these parties, in varying degrees, sought to discredit the UP government by creating economic chaos in the country with such devices as strikes, induced inflation, and the black market. Their ultimate objective, in the view of the PCCh, was to regain power from "the people" (as represented by the UP) by whatever means were necessary, including civil war or military coup. In the process, it was said, these groups freely broke the constitution and laws, relying in large part on what the PCCh regarded as a reactionary and obsolete legislature, court system, and comptroller general. The reactionaries engaged in all manner of slander, provocation, and sedition, particularly through their mouthpiece *El Mercurio*. The most extreme elements carried out terrorist activities and warned UP members that "Jakarta" was approaching— referring to the extermination of several hundred thousand communists and other leftists in Indonesia in 1965.

To defeat these forces, the PCCh publicly called for greater unity within the UP and better relations with some other groups, such as the left-wing Christian Democrats, outside the governing alliance. The party sought first to improve relations within the ruling coalition. The UP parties had agreed on a common program in 1969 and had updated it in early 1973, but they often disagreed on the strategy and tactics to be followed in carrying out the program. Early in the year a major dispute over the social, mixed, and private areas of the economy centered around a bill submitted by PCCh Economic Minister Orlando Millas. The bill

---

[19] *El Mercurio* (Santiago), 3 February 1972.

was considered a sellout by the PSCh and other smaller groups within and to the left of the UP and resulted in a series of public statements back and forth.[20] PCCh-PSCh relations were strained on other issues as well, as were PCCh relations with the MAPU and IC groups, these disputes paralleling PCCh conflicts with the MIR and other groups outside the UP coalition.

In the months prior to 4 March 1973, the party directed its attention to defeating opposition candidates in the congressional elections, arguing that "the hypocrites and liars, the pharisees, the merchants of infamy, must be swept out of the National Congress." [21] After the election, the PCCh argued that President Allende, the UP, and the Chilean people had won a great victory. The PCCh-controlled *Puro Chile* headlined the triumph: "El Pueblo: 43%. Los Momios: 55%." [22]

The call for the 15th Party Congress, drawn up at the plenary meeting in late March, listed the primary post-election concerns of the party. These were the prevention of a civil war; the effort to win over the majority of the people from all sections of the population; the solution of national problems through mass struggle and an offensive in the social, economic, political and ideological fields; the strengthening of UP unity; the unification of economic management and increased emphasis on the battle for production; the expanded role of the popular government and mass organizations; the creation of a new culture; and international solidarity of all revolutionary peoples.[23]

Post-Coup Analyses. Whereas the PCCh acknowledged some mistakes and shortcomings of the UP government, in public it maintained that the primary reasons for Chile's troubles in 1973 were long-standing economic and political exploitation and recent subversive activities by domestic reactionaries and foreign imperialists. The PCCh repeatedly charged the United States government and U.S. businesses with hostile

---

[20] For example, see the exchange of open letters between Corvalán and PSCh Secretary-General Carlos Altamirano in *El Siglo* (Santiago), 8 February and 15 February 1973. Also see below.

[21] "Manifesto," *El Siglo* (Santiago), 21 January 1973, and *Principios* (Santiago), January-February 1973, translated in *Information Bulletin,* no. 3 (1973).

[22] *Puro Chile* (Santiago), 6 March 1973; see Robert Moss, *Chile's Marxist Experiment* (New York: Halsted Press, 1973), Chapter 8; also see Corvalán, *Para que nuestra revolución siga avanzando* (Santiago, 1973); and Corvalán speech in *Principios* (Santiago), March-April 1973.

[23] *El Siglo* (Santiago), 13 May 1973.

and subversive actions toward the UP government. During 1972 and 1973 criticism of ITT was as frequent as criticism of the CIA.

In 1974 PCCh leaders in Chile and in exile began serious preparation of the strategy and tactics to be followed by Chilean revolutionaries in the post-coup period. Plans for the present and future were, predictably, developed in large part on the basis of lessons learned from the Popular Unity years. In the most extensive analysis published during 1974, René Castillo acknowledged that the majority of the Chilean people were not prepared for defense of the Allende government in September 1973. Acceptance of the military government had begun to disintegrate within six months, however, and the anti-imperialist and anti-oligarchic front of earlier years had now taken on the form of an anti-fascist front. The participation of the PCCh and PSCh remained essential to the unity of the working class, the UP forces, and the politically minded sectors generally. The democratically inclined Christian Democrats (those who were not followers of former President Eduardo Frei) must be brought into the front along with unaffiliated left organizations. Building the front would not be easy. Common viewpoints would have to be identified and practical solutions found for a variety of problems. Disagreements would be a logical development but they must not become antagonistic. Efforts must be made to split the military forces by urging "patriotic" elements to join the ranks of the people. Finally, the working class must follow an independent and principled policy avoiding the pitfalls of left and right opportunism.[24]

Articles published after the coup clearly indicate that the PCCh believes the Chilean left must learn from the failures of the Allende years. Castillo mentioned the obvious resistance put up by "foreign capital and the local oligarchy," but emphasized the many ways in which the left not only failed to isolate the reactionaries but even played into their hands: (1) The UP was too slow in eliminating old state institutions, even when the reactionaries were misusing those institutions to rebuild their positions; the parties did not fully understand nor deal with the problems in the essential terms of class struggle. (2) The UP was unable, in part because of missed opportunities, to gain a dominant position in the press, radio, television, cinema, and schools, by means of which it could have made a deep political and ideological impact on the masses. (3) The UP was unable to resolve many economic problems which, over time, were aggravated by the reactionaries. (4) The UP was

---

[24] *Information Bulletin* (Prague), no. 19 (1974).

167

unable to unite the majority of the people behind it and to isolate the main enemies. (5) "The Popular Unity parties and movement believe that the defeat [of the Popular Unity government] was due mainly to the absence of a united leadership pursuing a principled policy and avoiding the pitfalls of 'left' and right opportunist deviations." One of the most pronounced features of right deviation was "economism" among the more politically backward workers—that is, the willingness to settle for economic gains short of revolution. (6) There were manifestations of bureaucracy. Finally, Castillo concluded,

> the September coup was possible because imperialism and internal reaction had built up a broad anti-government front. This was its class composition: the monopoly bourgeoisie and agrarian oligarchy made up its core and it included the vast majority of the middle and petty bourgeoisie, most of the middle strata, the backward elements of other social groups. . . . We assess our defeat primarily as a political one and only after that as a military one. The isolation of the working class from its allies enabled the reactionaries to launch their coup. Isolation ruled out the possibility of the working class and the people taking up arms.[25]

The Communist Party insisted that the 1970–1973 experience did not prove that victory in the socialist revolution would have to come by armed struggle, as claimed by the "reactionaries and the representatives of petty-bourgeois revolutionism who echo them." Though nonarmed victory would now be more difficult, the party refused to insist during 1974 on any single road to power. It did argue that the anti-fascist front rejected individual terror, adventurism, and conspiracy. When the people returned to power they would adopt a new constitution and new laws, establish new government departments and institutions. "The new anti-fascist state will guarantee a multi-party structure and the normal activity of all democratic parties." It would carry out a "fundamental reform of the armed forces and the carabineer corps." Essentially the same line was maintained into 1976.[26]

Between the fall of Allende and early 1976 the PCCh was active in the Anti-fascist Alliance, made up chiefly of UP parties and members

25 René Castillo, *World Marxist Review*, vol. 17, no. 7 (July 1974).

26 Ibid., vol. 17, no. 8 (August 1974); also see ibid., March and September 1974. Later statements of the PCCh position are found in *Information Bulletin* (Prague), supplement to no. 2 (1975); and *Information Bulletin*, no. 17 (1975). Also see Viktor Shragin, *Chile, Corvalán, Struggle* (Moscow: Political Literature Publishing House, 1975).

in exile. The alliance, which held several well publicized meetings each year in European cities, devoted much of its attention to promoting opposition to the Chilean government among the governments and peoples of Europe and the United States.[27]

Movement of the Revolutionary Left

Background and Organizations. The Movement of the Revolutionary Left (MIR) in Chile was formed in 1965 mainly by dissident members of the Socialist Party (particularly young persons from the Concepción region), with some like-minded non-PSCh revolutionaries as well. In December 1967, after some leadership changes, it adopted a more militant line than it had previously held, in the spirit both of the OLAS conference held during July–August of that year in Havana and of Che Guevara's undertaking in Bolivia.[28] Armed actions by the MIR led to a crackdown on the group by the Frei government during 1969 and most members spent much of the next two years in hiding or in jail. After Salvador Allende's inauguration as president of Chile in November 1970, all "political" charges made against members of the group during the preceding years were dropped, many individuals were released from custody, and the MIR surfaced once again. Between November 1970 and September 1973 the MIR played an active and influential role in the Chilean political scene on and beyond the left-most fringes of the Popular Unity government, which it never joined organizationally and which it frequently criticized. Despite friction with the government during much of Allende's term of office, members of the MIR and other ultra-left groups made up the president's private security guard, the Grupo de Amigos Personales (GAP).

In both its early and its later years, the MIR was particularly active among university students, its center of operations being the University of Concepción. The MIR controlled the University Student Federation

---

[27] Typical statements of Alliance objectives are found in *L'Unita* (Rome), 13 February 1974, and *Information Bulletin*, no. 16 (1975). A statement attributed to the reformed UP coalition in Chile is found in *L'Unita* (Rome), 15 June 1974.

[28] On the socialist origins, see Fernando Casanueva V. and Manuel Fernández C., *El Partido Socialista y la lucha de clases en Chile* (Santiago: Quimantu, 1973), p. 213. For the change in line compare the post-1967 policies outlined below with the earlier line in "De la crisis de la 'Revolución en libertad' surgia la revolución socialista; Tesis Nacional aprobada en el II Congreso del M.I.R.—Noviembre de 1966," in the journal *Estrategia* (Santiago), January 1967, pp. 1-24.

(FEC) at Concepción during the late 1960s and early 1970s through its front, the University Movement of the Left (MUI), until it lost a bitterly contested election to a Popular Unity slate in January 1972. The much less successful Revolutionary Students' Front (FER) at the University of Chile in Santiago was also controlled by the MIR. Within the universities, as elsewhere, the MIR was almost as critical of the Communist Party and its youth organization as it was of its declared enemies on the right.

During the Popular Unity period, the MIR was active in (and generally controlled) a variety of other numerically small but active fronts and movements outside the university. The most important of these organizations were the Revolutionary Workers' Front (FTR), the Movement of the Revolutionary Poor (MPR), and the Revolutionary Peasant Movement (MCR), which carried out their various activities building a "mass base" among the people—the workers, the poor, and the peasants—in the city and countryside.

The strength of the Revolutionary Workers' Front was not found in the formal structure of the CUTCh. The FTR candidate for CUTCh president in the May–June 1972 election, Alejandro Alarcón, received only 10,000 of some 560,000 votes cast. Rather, it was developed and concentrated first in isolated unions, then more generally in the workers councils and communal commandos in the industrial belts (cordones industriales) that were organized in factory zones surrounding Santiago. Communist influence in these areas was eroded by the MIR and other ultra-leftists (particularly those in the PSCh) throughout the Allende period. During the last year ultra-left influence increased dramatically, particularly after the October 1972 strike. By mid-1973 the ultra-left policy of developing an "alternate power" to the government (see below) was well under way.

The Movement of the Revolutionary Poor was an outgrowth of the "First National Congress of the Homeless Poor" (pobladores sin casa), held in the La Granja district of Santiago less than a month before Allende's inauguration as president. Its main leader was Víctor Toro, one of the few members of the proletariat ever to rise to an important position in the MIR. Walled or fenced-in campamentos were set up in various parts of Santiago with such descriptive names as "Nueva La Habana" and "Ho Chi Minh." Entrance to these squatter settlements was limited and strict discipline was generally maintained. Illegal land seizures in the countryside were sometimes launched by commando

170

squads from these *campamentos*.[29] Though the settlements received some government aid, the communities were self-governing and were very seldom approached by the national police.

The Revolutionary Peasant Movement, the rural equivalent of the urban MPR, was the most important of several ultra-left groups responsible for organizing hundreds of extralegal land seizures beginning before Allende's election and continuing into September 1973. MCR leaders had no patience with the legal agrarian reform President Allende spoke about—nor did many government agrarian reform officials in the outlying areas. *Tomas* (illegal seizures) were carried out on many medium-sized and small landholdings, including the holdings of some who had only recently received their land in an earlier stage of the reform movement. The MCR was particularly active among the Mapuche Indians in Cautín Province, but led hundreds of *tomas* in other provinces as well. The best known MCR leaders were "Comandante Pepe" and "Comandante Nelson." Seizures were increasingly made in cooperation with members of the MAPU and PSCh, organizations within the Popular Unity coalition, and with other small non-UP groups or individuals.

After the September 1973 coup, the MIR virtually disappeared for many months and, though a few leaders were captured or killed, the organization seemed to have remained intact. A bank robbery at the end of September 1974, however, resulted in the police discovery of an important MIR hideout on 5 October and the death of Miguel Enríquez, MIR secretary-general during the entire Allende period. Over the next eighteen months several of Enríquez's immediate successors—among them Andrés Pascal Allende, the former president's nephew—took refuge in foreign embassies and in exile. By early 1976 most MIR leaders and members generally had been killed, captured, or withdrawn in one way or another from violent struggle within Chile's borders. The MIR seemed in complete disarray though its potential for eventual reconsolidation should not be discounted.

Strategy and Tactics. The MIR's frequently stated objectives were the overthrow of Chile's political, economic, and social system—which it charged with serving only the interests of the capitalists and "imperialists"—and its replacement by a socialist state that served the workers.

---

[29] See February 1972 interview with Compañera Natalia, vice-president of the "Che Guevara" settlement, in Robert Moss, *Chile's Marxist Experiment,* p. 115.

The controversial position of the MIR in the Chilean left did not derive from this long-term goal, however, but from its idea of the proper road to its achievement.

On the first anniversary of Che Guevara's death, the MIR National Secretariat called for immediate preparation for armed struggle in Chile. An editorial in the party paper pointed out what it called the "fundamental lessons" of Che Guevara's revolutionary activities for all Latin America: "The struggle for the Latin American revolution will be a protracted guerrilla war in which many will fall by the way, among whom Che was undoubtedly the greatest, but neither the first nor the last." [30] Luciano Cruz wrote in mid-1969 that the MIR used the "greatest care in building up the political and organizational apparatus upon which the armed struggle would rest." And he added: "We have learned from history. We have decided to follow the example of Lenin, Fidel, and Che. Thus let us put it succinctly: we are going to proclaim the armed revolution." [31] Miguel Enríquez wrote several months later that the MIR had conducted "agitation, propaganda, and political activities among the students, townspeople, farmhands, Indians, and worker fronts, in addition to all the tasks that a revolutionary organization should carry out." The only activity in which it did not participate, he said, was the "electoral circus." [32]

A long statement by the National Secretariat of the MIR, dated April–May 1970, on the subject of the forthcoming presidential election described the electoral process as "nothing more than a mechanism of self-preservation for the ruling class, a more refined and subtle method than brute coercion." The MIR argued that elections were "not a road toward the conquest of power," and predicted that even if the "difficult popular electoral victory were to occur, the ruling classes [would] not hesitate to carry out a military coup." While regarding the UP program as "essentially leftist reformist," the MIR nonetheless pledged: "[In the event of a military coup] we will not hesitate to place our growing armed apparatus, our forces, and all we have at the service of the defense of the workers' and peasants' conquest." Its own fundamental task during 1970 would be to carry out "armed revolutionary actions and militant mobilizations of the masses" in order to maintain and extend the high

[30] *El Rebelde* (Santiago), October 1968.
[31] *Punto Final* (Santiago), 1 July 1969.
[32] Ibid., 9 September 1969.

172

level of social struggle in the country.[33] This line brought the MIR into constant conflict with the Communist Party of Chile.

In October 1970 the National Secretariat of the MIR released a document on the results of the election which acknowledged that the MIR had overestimated the rightist response to a leftist victory and underestimated the ability of the UP to defend its success at the polls. While maintaining that the election had merely postponed armed struggle, the MIR pledged to defend Allende's government and to intensify mass mobilization. It warned that once the "euphoria of the triumph" had passed, the UP would have to "satisfy the desires of the masses concretely and in a short time." The strategy of the bourgeoisie and "imperialism" would be to discredit the UP by keeping it from carrying out its programs, thus opening the way for a reactionary takeover with some degree of popular support.[34]

After violent clashes between the MIR and the JCCh during late 1970 led to the death of one MIR militant, a truce was reached with the UP generally, lasting through the April 1971 municipal elections which the MIR supported. But by mid-1971 the MIR was again charging that the UP was failing to make a revolution in Chile.[35] On 1 November Miguel Enríquez accused the UP of moving too slowly in its agrarian and other programs, of neglecting—and at times even thwarting—the mobilization of the masses, and of losing strength and support while the opposition groups were "confusing some sectors of the popular masses" and generally consolidating their forces.[36]

After the Popular Unity loss in the January 1972 by-elections, the tension within the coalition became more and more serious as the differences among opposition forces were increasingly set aside. According to the MIR, President Allende asked the "big question" in his state of the nation speech on 21 May: Would the existing institutions be able to "open up the way for a transition to socialism?" The president and the communists led the UP members who generally answered in the affirmative; the MIR led an ever more militant number who answered in the negative. The difference was made tangible only two months later.

In July 1972, in defiance of the communists and President Allende, the MIR joined the majority of the Concepción branches of the Popular

---

[33] Ibid., 12 May 1970, supplement.
[34] Ibid., 13 October 1970, supplement.
[35] See the exchange between Nelsón Gutiérrez and Salvador Allende, in ibid., 8 June 1971.
[36] *Intercontinental Press* (New York), 10 January 1972.

Unity in forming a "People's Assembly" which was to supersede the "reactionary" National Congress. Allende denounced the action as a "divisionist maneuver" which strengthened the opponents of the UP, and all the main headquarters of the UP parties in Santiago repudiated it, though not without some dissenting voices. This event was a turning point in the history of the Popular Unity government. More clearly than ever before, the ultra-left idea of class struggle stood in contrast to the idea of the communists and the president; the MIR and its revolutionary comrades had created (at least temporarily) an alternative power base to that of the "bourgeois" state structure. During the next fourteen months the effort to develop a permanent and more broadly based "alternate power" became the all-absorbing, open, and partially realized objective of the *miristas,* many socialists, most of the radicalized Christians (MAPU and IC), and some lesser groups. The very activities that consolidated the forces of the opposition—such as the October 1972 strike and the disputed control over nationalized or threatened domestic industries—also consolidated and radicalized the ultra-left, leaving Allende and the communists increasingly isolated and weakened in the middle.

The MIR broadened its attacks on President Allende and some of his ministers, above all on the communist economic minister, Orlando Millas, both for their alleged concessions to the enemies and for some of their criticisms of the MIR. They were particularly incensed when the secretary-general of government said the MIR and FTR, which were accused of carrying out actions intended to "create a climate of agitation and call into question the stability of the government," had been "infiltrated by the Fatherland and Freedom and ultra-rightists." [37] A month before the coup the headline of an *El Rebelde* editorial proclaimed: "The Government has capitulated: the masses will only be able to rely on their own forces." [38]

The MIR repeatedly published "programs" during 1973. When on 27 February *El Rebelde* concluded that the reformists had "hit bottom," the paper called for national reliance on the "power of the people," the workers' and peasants' councils and teams, and a revolutionary program. The main objectives in a typical program were extensive nationalization of enterprises of all sorts and the establishment of workers' management;

---

[37] *El Rebelde* (Santiago), 18-24 April 1973.
[38] Ibid., 14-20 August 1973.

expropriation of estates over forty hectares in size without indemnification; control over distribution and supply of goods by workers and the people through the Supply and Price Boards (Juntas de Abastecimientos y Precios, or JAP) and similar organizations; unilateral suspension of payments on the external debt to "U.S. imperialism," and other actions in defense of national interests in the face of "imperialist aggression." Crucial to revolutionary change was the rejection of faith in "peaceful" revolution within the present "bourgeois" system. Indeed, the people had to set up an autonomous and parallel power. This power would give the UP government a strong proletarian and popular basis when the government carried out revolutionary activities, but would be capable of opposing the government when "anti-popular" actions were taken. This policy was implemented throughout the country in workers' and peasants' councils and commandos but was carried out most dramatically in the industrial belts which surrounded the capital city.[39]

The idea and development of "alternate power" advanced rapidly during late 1972 and 1973 under the slogan "Push Ahead without Compromise" *(Avanzar sin Transar).* The "people's power" movements and organizations in city and countryside, communal commandos *(comandos comunales),* were developed in theory and practice—the former in party meetings, published statements, and political forums, and the latter in the organizational activities in the industrial belts, squatter settlements, and peasant communities.[40]

Six weeks before the military coup a major article in the castroite *Punto Final* on the communal commandos noted that whereas some groups insisted that the organs of people's power should be "subordinated organizationally to the actions of the government, the MIR has reiterated the historical necessity for their independence," since they have as their "fundamental objective the erection of an alternative power to the bourgeois state which would permit them to destroy the latter and create a new state. Thus, to subordinate the action of the commandos

---

[39] See ibid., 27 February-5 March; "Manifiesto del MIR," ibid., 19-26 June, supplement; ibid., 11-16 July.

[40] Two major political forums were held in late 1972. The first brought together top-level spokesmen from the Communist Party, Socialist Party, MIR, MAPU, and IC; see their comments in *Punto Final* (Santiago), 5 December 1972, supplement, pp. 21-48. The Communist Party did not show up for the second—perhaps it was not invited—which included representatives from the MIR, PSCh, IC, MAPU, and Christians for Socialism; see comments in ibid., 16 January 1973, supplement, pp. 1-22. Also see "Los Trabajadores y el poder popular," ibid., 8 May 1973, supplement, pp. 2-16.

to the institutional apparatus and bureaucratic functionaries, even though the government is in the hands of the Left, would mean to weaken their character and totally annul their strategic projection." [41] The correct popular power alternative would be a social-revolutionary alliance of the peasants, poor, lowest levels of the petit-bourgeoisie, under the leadership of the working class, in the form of an autonomous organization. The first step toward incorporating the workers and others was made at the Cordón Industrial Cerrillos on 23 May, reportedly at the initiation of the workers themselves.

After the military coup, the MIR continued to advocate a more militant road to socialism than the PCCh and some other leftist groups. In mid-1974, the MIR Political Commission sent Edgardo Enríquez, brother of the secretary-general, abroad to explain MIR tactics to the world. At an interview in Cuba in late June he said the military government could be overthrown only by a "long and difficult people's war, full of sacrifices." The MIR was engaged in "preparing the conditions for starting this war." The immediate objectives of the organization were (1) setting up a political front for popular resistance, including the UP parties, progressive Christian Democrats, and the *miristas* themselves; (2) "setting up a movement of people's resistance as a mass organization and a base for the political front, with the participation of all those workers who are not affiliated with any political party and want to fight"; and (3) "setting up the first embryonic units of the People's Revolutionary Army, the military organization of the resistance" which should enlist all persons willing to fight militarily against the regime.[42] Several days later the Paris daily *Le Monde* reported on an interview with Enríquez in which the MIR leader acknowledged that resistance to the junta up to that time seemed modest. "But there will soon be spectacular and effective action." Enríquez added that the main purpose of the united front, whatever it might be called, was "quickly to reach the stage of armed propaganda and then the armed struggle in the cities and the countryside." [43] The bank robbery at the end of September was probably considered one of the first "spectacular and effective actions."

---

[41] See "Comandos Comunales: Organos de Poder del Pueblo," ibid., 31 July 1973, supplement, p. 3. Also see comment by Víctor Toro in *El Rebelde* (Santiago), 27 February 1973.

[42] *Granma* (Havana), 7 July 1974.

[43] *Le Monde* (Paris), 7 July 1974, quoted in *Intercontinental Press* (New York), 22 July.

The Socialist Party

The Socialist Party of Chile was in no way a tightly knit group comparable to the MIR. Rather, it was a seriously disunited party broken into two main factions: (1) those, like Salvador Allende, who sought revolutionary change, but in a measured way, essentially along the lines of the Communist Party, and (2) the "castroite" faction which gained ascendancy within the party under Secretary-General Carlos Altamirano shortly after Allende's inauguration, and which often gave only grudging support, or offered unmistakable opposition, to the Popular Unity president and the coalition's program.

Although Senator Altamirano and his followers in the PSCh occasionally differed on tactical issues with the MIR, they agreed with the *miristas* on most of the issues raised in this chapter. They clearly drew the line between the castroite and communist positions on "consolidation" (a favorite PCCh word), the social areas of the economy, and mass mobilization. "Consolidate what?" asked Manuel Cabieses on the cover of his fortnightly castroite journal *Punto Final* in mid-1972. Cabieses, a regular contributor to the Socialist Party daily *Ultima Hora,* maintained that the economic revisionism of Orlando Millas of the PCCh resulted at least in part from Millas's misreading of Soviet history. The PCCh suggested a new economic policy of sorts without realizing that Lenin had resorted to such a line only after the full conquest of power by the proletariat. No NEP would work in Chile as long as the reactionaries held positions of power.[44] The castroite Socialists, like the MIR, regularly called for the continued and rapid expansion of the revolutionary process, without pauses to consolidate, concessions to the opposition, or curtailment of mass mobilizations from below. What was more, many Socialists encouraged and participated in *tomas,* in such activities as the Concepción People's Assembly, and in political work among workers, peasants, and members of the military which went beyond—and was often in conflict with—the official Popular Unity lines.

On several occasions in early 1973, Senator Altamirano offered similar and consistent interpretations of the October 1972 strike, the Millas bill on the economy, the incorporation of military officers in the cabinet, and the long-delayed granting of a price increase for the Papelera (the country's only major private supplier of newsprint, thus regarded

---

[44] Manuel Cabieses, "Las tareas de los revolucionarios en la etapa actual," *Punto Final* (Santiago), 20 June 1972, supplement, esp. p. 3.

by the opposition as an essential aspect of a free press) which had almost been forced into bankruptcy by mounting inflation and government price fixing. Though a member of congress himself, Altamirano considered that body antiquated and anachronistic—a "paper tiger" when it came to revolutionary action.[45] During the Allende period, and particularly in 1973, Altamirano continued to denounce the congress, the courts, and the comptroller general as reactionary and stated that the Supreme Court and the majority of the congressmen had stepped outside the Chilean constitution. Early in 1973 he concluded that since "the bourgeoisie abandons its legality whenever it is convenient to do so, there can be no reason for a revolutionary to fear or respect it."[46]

The importance of the castroite Socialists and the extraordinary impact they had at crucial points in the Popular Unity period are illustrated by their role in setting the direction of relations between the United States and the Chilean government in 1971. During much of his first year in office, President Allende seems to have believed that an immediate direct confrontation with the United States (government or business) was not in the best interests of the Popular Unity program or of his own long-term revolutionary objectives. While the official U.S. position toward Chile in early 1971 was "correct but minimal," U.S. Ambassador Edward Korry in Santiago, with what he considered the interests of the United States in mind, also began to work on a policy of accommodation with the Chilean government. As Ambassador Korry explained in a September 1974 interview: "This process began very tentatively but it suddenly began to jell in January, February of 1971, and it really started to take off in April and early May, and suddenly it was stopped. Now, we learned, and it was confirmed to us by Dr. Allende's closest advisors, that the reason he stopped was that a veto was interposed by the then head of the Socialist Party, Senator Altamirano." Korry backed up his story by an explanation of the sudden collapse of a carefully negotiated settlement between the Allende government and the Cerro copper company in mid-1971. In his September 1974 interview, Korry commented:

> It took five months to negotiate this thing, and I was the middleman, and the agreement was reached. Allende per-

---

[45] See Altamirano's 1968 article, "El Parlamento, 'Tigre de Papel,'" in Julio César Jobet and Alejandro Chelén, *Pensamiento Teórico y Político del Partido Socialista de Chile* (Santiago: Quimantu, 1972), pp. 307-27.

[46] "Entrevista con Carlos Altamirano," *Punto Final* (Santiago), 13 February 1973, supplement, p. 4.

sonally expressed his happiness that we had done this, to me. [Four of the five Chilean negotiators] gave a party for Mr. Gordon Murphy, the chairman of the board of Cerro, the night before this was to be signed on nationwide television. Well, 30 minutes before it was due to be signed, Mr. Allende said he was terribly sorry, there'd have to be a postponement. He explained to me he had "a little trouble in my chicken coop." . . . He asked me for two weeks to sort it out and told me to assure Washington that he would do this. I said, "Mr. President, it is your country. I can't give you two minutes, two weeks, two years. It is entirely your decision. I know the rooster who is loose in your chicken coop." [47]

President Allende's apparent inability to follow through on agreements such as this one turned the tide in what was at best an extremely touchy and tentative effort to avoid confrontation between Chile and the U.S. [48]

Communist-Castroite Relations

More specifically, it may be asked, what were the relations between the communists and the castroites in Chile, and what effect did they have on the events of 1970–1973? Luis Corvalán told delegates to the 14th PCCh Congress in November 1969 that ultra-leftist groups weakened the "people's movement" and were "characterized by their impatience, by unsteadiness in the struggle, by repeated turning from one extreme position to another, by lack of confidence in the masses, by lack of calmness in struggle, and by lack of organization spirit, discipline, and strength." Addressing the same congress, Jorge Insunza applied the words of Karl Marx: "Their activities consist precisely of trying to anticipate the revolutionary process, to carry it on to a crisis artificially, and to improvise a revolution without the conditions for a revolution being present. For them, the only condition for revolution is sufficient organization of their conspiracy." [49] During the 1970 campaign the PCCh characterized

---

[47] From transcript of "Chile and the CIA," a "Firing Line" interview with Edward M. Korry taped on 20 September 1974, published by the Southern Educational Communications Association, 1974, pp. 6, 8.

[48] On the problem of U.S. government and business relations with the Allende government, see articles by Paul Sigmund and others in Francisco Orrego Vicuña, ed., *Chile: The Balanced View* (Santiago: Gabriela Mistral, 1975); and David Holden, "Allende and the Myth Makers," *Encounter* (London), January 1974, pp. 12-24.

[49] See *El Siglo* (Santiago), 24 November and 27 November 1969.

members of the MIR as "terrorists, adventurers, renegades, and declassed elements." [50]

When members of the Communist Youth killed an MIR militant at the University of Concepción a month after President Allende's inauguration, however, most Chilean leftists concluded that their disputes only weakened the cause of the people, and relations began to improve, at least on the surface, for the time being. On 13 December 1970 Luis Corvalán said: "We believe that a kind of understanding is coming between the UP and the MIR, naturally including the communists, since the MIR is closing ranks around the government headed by Comrade Salvador Allende." [51] But this period of conciliation did not last.

In June 1971 Volodia Teitelboim said that Marx and Lenin, in their times, had "analyzed, fought, and unmasked" the ultra-left, "whose schizophrenia is mixed with crime and extremism." According to Teitelboim, "their adventurous and suicidal action is removed from all reality and helps to orchestrate the campaigns of right-wing sedition." [52] In 1972 PCCh leaders sometimes maintained that the "ultra-left" received far too much attention in the news media, as Luis Corvalán said in his press conference on 26 May, but in fact the "ultra-left" was condemned, often at great length, in virtually every PCCh speech and statement on domestic affairs. Jorge Texier elaborated the PCCh critique of the MIR at mid-year:

> The ultra-leftists' "revolutionary" activity manifested itself above all in the countryside. They incited the peasants to seize land and interfered with the procedure of the agrarian reform specified by the Popular Unity, and this tended to turn what was an anti-oligarchic measure into an unwarranted attack on small and medium landholders and to mislead the politically ignorant peasants. The government's intentions were misrepresented, the reactionary press and opposition parties gained arguments in their favor and indeed extended their social base in some rural areas. [53]

Volodia Teitelboim told a meeting of party militants in early August that every victory for the people was followed by a provocative act by the MIR that enabled the right to go on the offensive. Indeed, he

---

[50] *World Marxist Review,* vol. 13, no. 8 (August 1970).

[51] *El Siglo* (Santiago), 15 December 1970.

[52] Ibid., 26 June 1971.

[53] *World Marxist Review,* vol. 15, no. 7 (July 1972); also see Texier article in *Principios* (Santiago), May-June 1972.

charged that there were contacts which brought a "link-up of attitudes" between the ultra-left and the ultra-right.[54] On the day of President Allende's second state of the nation address in May 1972, just after the first of several UP crises involving castroites in the MIR, the Socialist Party, and other groups, the PCCh lined the streets of downtown Santiago with party militants displaying banners that proclaimed: "With President Allende and the Program of the Popular Unity we defeat the provocations of the ultra-right and the ultra-left." [55] During 1973 communist criticism charged the MIR with trying to set up a government that was parallel to and competing with the UP government led by President Allende, thereby splitting the UP alliance and working class.[56]

For several months after the September 1973 coup, the PCCh refused to undertake serious public analyses of leftist shortcomings during the years of Allende's presidency, arguing that such analyses would "prejudice the popular parties' unity" during the post-coup period when unity was essential.[57] During 1974, however, the analyses began to appear and the criticism of the castroite elements in Chilean politics came out, if anything, stronger than before the coup. In a major two-part article published in the *World Marxist Review,* cited earlier, René Castillo wrote that the Popular Unity parties and movements thought the defeat of the Popular Unity government was the result mainly of the absence of a united leadership pursuing a principled policy and avoiding the pitfalls of opportunist deviations on the left and the right. One especially important factor that worked against united leadership was the "ceaseless subversion of the ultra-left elements," which did "grave damage to the popular movement." The ultra-left groups provoked clashes with potential allies and drove them into the enemy camp; they rejected all compromise and alliances; they rejected any work with progressive Christian Democrats or patriotic members of the military. Ideologically, their dogmatism found expression in virtual disregard of the gains of popular rule. Thus, Castillo wrote, "the Chilean experience has reaffirmed that ultra-leftism is a boon for imperialism and reaction." [58]

[54] *El Siglo* (Santiago), 6 August 1972; also see ibid., editorial, 19 May 1972; and the PCCh Political Commission internal document published in *El Mercurio* (Santiago), 3 February 1972.

[55] Observation of the author.

[56] See, for example, Corvalán's letter to PSCh Secretary-General Carlos Altamirano, *El Siglo* (Santiago), 8 February 1973.

[57] See *Information Bulletin,* no. 20 (1973).

[58] *World Marxist Review,* vol. 17, no. 7 (July 1974).

Of course, the feeling was mutual. As was shown above, the MIR leaders firmly denied the possibility of revolutionary change by means of the "bourgeois" state system; thus they regarded the UP program, and Communist Party policies in general, as simple reformism. Specific issues may be clarified here by a look at several confrontations between the PCCh and the MIR.

(1) On 16 January 1972 the Popular Unity lost by-elections for two congressional seats (involving several provinces) to candidates of the united opposition, the results showing a decline in UP voting strength varying from 3 to 10 percent between April 1971 and January 1972. An internal document of the PCCh Political Commission stated that "the elections have confirmed a deterioration in the positions of the government." The activities of the "ultra-left" were "without a doubt" one of the factors in the deterioration since the opposition (always called "the enemy") had been able to "give the impression of an identity between the outrages of the ultra-left and the actions of the government." The UP position in the countryside had been particularly weakened by ultra-left influence. Thus, the PCCh concluded that it was necessary to step up "the battle against ultra-left positions," which indeed the party did after the election. Finally, the communists expressed serious concern over the consolidation of the National Party-Christian Democratic Party alliance. The PCCh Political Commission called for dialogue with receptive Christian Democrats in an effort to isolate the main enemy, noting "the fact that the Christian Democrats and the Right, Tomic and Alessandri, were not united in the presidential election was not 'an error of calculation by the enemy' but the result of a political action by the popular forces." [59]

The MIR retaliated with a declaration by its national secretariat. According to the declaration, a renewed PCCh offensive against the MIR forced a public response, which the *miristas* said they would rather have avoided. The electoral results were "serious reverses," but "not a defeat of the workers." Rather, they were "the defeat of the political strategy applied over the past year [by the UP], a strategy that is fundamentally that of the PCCh." The public had become confused, said the MIR, by the ideological uncertainty the UP expressed toward the Christian Democrats, by the UP's refusal unequivocally to declare the PDC a party representing the interests of imperialism, the landlords, and

---

[59] See "Apreciación Comunista del Momento Político," *El Mercurio* (Santiago), 3 February 1972.

the fascists. Thus when the UP itself (up until just before election time) called the Christian Democrats "progressive and allies" it was not surprising that the PDC received votes from all sectors.[60]

On agrarian policy the MIR argued that the PCCh had incorrectly analyzed the class structure of the countryside and had become a pillar of support for the "big managerial-agricultural bourgeoisie" which it disguised under the name of "middle landlords and rich farmers." The most serious shortcoming of the "anti-peasant" policy of the PCCh was its failure to take account of the fact that the confrontation in the countryside was between the "big agricultural bourgeoisie" on the one hand and the rural proletariat and poor peasants on the other. PCCh policy coincided with "the policy that imperialism has been promoting in Latin America" since 1959. MIR policy, on the contrary, was aimed at mobilizing the masses in order to destroy the social, economic, and political power base of the big bourgeoisie by legal and extralegal means.[61] Faulty PCCh (and UP) analyses resulted in an indecisive agrarian policy and left the poor in the countryside "to fight for themselves." The MIR's Revolutionary Peasant Movement stepped in when the UP refused to lead. This pusillanimous UP policy created the conditions within which "some peasants, in their spontaneous struggle, wrongly attacked small proprietors. The MCR and the MIR never led mobilizations against small proprietors, against those we only seek to protect. On the contrary, if the MCR and the MIR had not assumed leadership of these spontaneous struggles undertaken by the peasantry, the class struggle in the countryside would have descended into anarchy." [62] The MIR concluded: "The peasant movement will continue to resort to extralegal struggle, to land seizures [tomas], as the only road in view of the refusal of the PCCh and the Popular Unity to establish a correct agrarian policy." [63]

(2) In October 1972 there occurred a costly nationwide strike by businessmen, professionals, truckers, and others. Allende's government, with the strong support of the PCCh, agreed to the formation of a new cabinet including three officers from the military. In the meantime, many businesses and factories had been taken over by workers acting

---

[60] "El MIR Responde à los ataques del Partido Comunista," *El Rebelde* (Santiago), 1 February 1972.

[61] *La Política del MIR en el Campo* (Santiago: El Rebelde, 1972), most of which is translated in *Intercontinental Press* (New York), 17 April and 1 May 1972.

[62] "El MIR Responde," *El Rebelde* (Santiago), 1 February 1972.

[63] *La Política del MIR en el Campo*, p. 38.

on their own or under the leadership of MIR, PSCh, and other militants. The MIR regarded the military-coalition cabinet as a sellout by the reformists, a roadblock in the way of the people and of the achievement of popular over bourgeois power. The only revolutionary response to this new government setup was to increase the mass mobilizations and struggles.[64]

(3) In late February 1973 the MIR National Secretariat issued a response to what were called "serious imputations, injurious allusions, and customary deformations of our policies and intentions" by the PCCh.[65] Seven of the MIR's points were these:

First, MIR support for "autonomous people's power" was opposed by the PCCh because the PCCh expected a long period of struggle for reforms within the capitalist system, within the state of bourgeois law, by parliamentary action, in order to arrive gradually at socialism—what the MIR called the "reformism of the past." The MIR, however, argued that an alternative power to the bourgeoisie and the existing government was essential. Whether the alternative power would be opposed to the existing government would depend upon the policies the existing government followed with regard to the innumerable immediate and long-term interests and needs of the masses.

Second, the MIR rejected the bill on the three areas of the economy introduced by communist Minister of the Economy Orlando Millas, considering it a major and inexcusable concession to the proprietary instincts of the bourgeoisie.

Third, the PCCh was wrong in its overall attitudes toward economic tasks and class struggle. Greater revolutionary power would not come from increasing production, but by leading the workers in a takeover of the economy.

Fourth, before November 1972, the MIR regarded the Allende government as one that was "predominantly left reformist, which broadened democratic liberties in Chile and instituted a limited reform plan for the benefit of the working class." It accomplished some things despite its vacillations and lack of confidence in the masses. The post-November government was an alliance of petit-bourgeois reformism and sectors of labor reformism with high officials of the armed forces. The

---

[64] MIR National Secretariat statement, dated 8 November 1972, reported by *Prensa Latina,* 8 November.

[65] The following seven points are taken from "El MIR Responde al Partido Comunista," *Punto Final* (Santiago), 27 February 1973, supplement, pp. 1-8.

center of action of the government was no longer the workers' parties; the Allende/armed forces alliance predominated, supported by the communists.

A true Government of the Workers, as a forerunner to the conquest of power and establishment of a proletarian state, can only be established as a result of the broad mobilization of the masses and their organization in autonomous forms of power. A true Government of the Workers is that which effectively supports the struggle of the masses and assures its stability not in the bourgeois state and its body of officials, but in the mobilized masses, aware and organized in their own class institutions—the Communal commandos and councils and other organizations of workers and people's power, and in the democratization of the armed forces.

Fifth, the PCCh was wrong to make avoidance of "civil war" or a "blood bath" the central issue in the March 1973 congressional elections. Rather, the emphasis should have been on "how the vanguard can assure through correct leadership that the proletariat and the masses can win in the various encounters of the class struggle and even in a civil war of the bourgeoisie if such is launched as a response by a class with its privileges and interests threatened."

Sixth, the MIR was seeking revolutionary unity in the only way possible—by unmasking the reformism and conciliation of the PCCh and some others in the UP.

Seventh, the MIR rejected PCCh efforts to develop a policy which would give a major role in the alliance to the national bourgeoisie.

Conclusions

Disputes between communists and castroites in many countries came to little more than a tempest in a teapot—not so in Chile between 1970 and 1973. The lack of unity among the leftist parties, the result above all of the differences between Allende and the communists on the one hand and the castroites on the other, was the most important of several factors contributing to the downfall of the Popular Unity government.

In September 1970 Salvador Allende narrowly defeated the candidates of the National Party and the Christian Democratic Party, receiving some 36.6 percent of the total vote, and falling considerably below the absolute majority required for direct election to the presidency. Consequently, in accordance with the Chilean constitution, the final decision was made between the two leading candidates—Allende and Jorge Alessandri (who received 34.98 percent)—by the Congress. Since the Popular Unity controlled only 80 of 200 seats in Congress, Allende had to win the support of many Christian Democrats to secure his election by the Congress. Traditionally, the legislature had selected the frontrunner in the popular election, and Allende predictably insisted that this traditional practice should be honored as always. Though most Christian Democrats wanted to follow the precedent, or felt obliged to do so, many were deeply apprehensive about the Popular Unity's long-term intentions. After extensive discussion between UP and PDC legislators, Allende's agreement to support a Statute of Constitutional Guarantees designed to guarantee the freedom of Chilean citizens and the withdrawal of Alessandri, the Congress voted for the UP candidate on 24 October. Allende was inaugurated early the next month.

Neither Allende nor the Popular Unity ever had the support of the majority of the Chilean people, though UP candidates won 49.73 percent in the March 1971 municipal elections. If Allende had ever thought he had majority support, even on a single major issue—such as the replacement of the two-house congress by a single People's Assembly—he would have called for a national plebiscite. He frequently stated that he intended to do so.[66] But no plebiscite was ever held. During most periods UP support ranged between 36 and 42 percent of the population, a fairly good backing for an ordinary president, but not enough for one trying to carry out such a program of revolutionary change.

Allende might have made up for his lack of majority popular support in several ways: (1) by uniting all socialist-oriented groups around the Popular Unity program; (2) by slowing down the rate of change, recruiting additional support from the center-left spectrum in Chilean politics; or (3) by greatly accelerating the overthrow of the "bourgeois state." During his thirty-four months in office Allende almost always tried to follow the first line, showed periodic receptivity toward the second line, and made some concessions to the third line. Any of these followed with consistency might have been preferable to what actually transpired for the Popular Unity government or Chileans generally.

---

[66] Three months after his inauguration, Allende told Régis Debray: "We present a bill and it turns out the Congress rejects it; we hold a plebiscite. I will give you an example. We propose that there no longer be a bicameral congress and it is rejected by Congress; we go to a referendum and we win. And so the end of the two chambers and we have to go to the one house we have proposed." In "Allende habla con Debray," *Punto Final* (Santiago), 16 March 1971, p. 39.

186

If revolutionary changes had been made in a more orderly fashion and consolidated, roughly as Allende and the Communist Party of Chile proposed instituting the Popular Unity program, the revolution might well have been irreversible by the time of the 1976 presidential election. Opposition unity would not have been so strong under less obviously and immediately threatening conditions, and greater respect for law and traditional government practice (themselves weakening opposition unity) would probably have made military participation in political affairs unnecessary (it was in fact begun by the president himself) and would have provided no clear-cut incentive or justification for a military coup. This line would have sought—and indications are that it would have achieved—a modus vivendi with the United States. But this line presupposed a degree of leftist unity that was highly unlikely—indeed, out of the question—from the beginning. The castroite groups were convinced that domestic and international forces would, through one tactic or another, on one pretext or another, sidetrack or overthrow this revolutionary gradualism.

The line of opening to the center-left in an effort to draw in the left wing of the Christian Democratic Party was explored with greater or lesser urgency from the time of the Popular Unity defeats in the January 1972 by-elections. This policy never really got off the ground; if it had, the original Popular Unity alliance, and President Allende's own party, would almost certainly have split down the middle. The result might not have been much more popular support; it would certainly have radically increased the ultra-leftist opposition to Allende's programs.

The castroite line, which had a certain appeal to Allende at times, was probably never a viable alternative during the Popular Unity period, as Allende, the communists, and many others on the left insisted. Yet it was demanded by an outspoken and effective element in the Chilean scene which insisted, with increasing urgency, that the revolution had to become radicalized quickly or it would be lost. Miguel Enríquez put it in simple and easily recognizable castroite terms at a press conference on 22 May 1972 when he said there were two lines on the Chilean left— the reformist and the revolutionary, the former identifiable chiefly with the Communist Party of Chile and the latter with the MIR. But very little that happened in Chile between 1970 and 1973 was that simple and no one realized this more clearly than President Allende. His concessions to the castroite line alienated the Communist Party of Chile, his main source of support, increased the hostility of the opposition parties, and raised the threat of a military coup.[67]

As time went on, the castroite and communist lines pulled ever farther apart—not so much in theory as in practice. The theoretical implications of the castroite approach had been present from the beginning, and regularly condemned by the communists, even though the complex ideas on such concepts as the communal commandos and alternative power were developed in the course of the struggle. It was the development of the castroite line in practice which widened the breach, offering a direct threat to all so-called "bourgeois" sectors of society and a challenge to some of the workers' parties and the Popular Unity government as well. Competing lines within the left, with all their ramifications, played a major role in creating problems for the Allende government—political, economic, constitutional, international—and then made these problems increasingly difficult to resolve. In the end this shattering lack of uniformity and consistency among leftist parties and individuals—indeed, at times, in the president himself—was perhaps more than any other factor responsible for the fall of the Allende government and the failure of the Popular Unity experiment.[68]

---

[67] After Allende's death, Debray wrote that some day everything would have to be told about what Allende did to "get the continental armed revolution which so fascinated him, even if his spirit rejected it, out of its rut." Though it demonstrated what Debray called a "glorious incoherence," Allende considered it a question of personal honor to help any Latin American guerrilla who sought his assistance. *Le Nouvel Observateur* (Paris), 17 September 1973.

[68] On the Allende years, see Moss, *Chile's Marxist Experiment,* and articles collected in Orrego, ed., *Chile: The Balanced View.*

Conclusions

Castroites and communists in Latin America during the period from 1959 to 1976 consistently agreed only on the most basic of long-term objectives, such as the need to eliminate U.S. influence in the area and to carry out a socialist revolution. Analyses of domestic conditions varied greatly, as did judgments on popular receptivity toward substantive political, economic, and social change and on the most effective ways to cultivate a revolutionary consciousness among the masses. Fundamental differences of opinion existed on the following points, among others: (1) the desirability of united fronts that would incorporate members of the nationalistic bourgeoisie or the military; (2) the value and methods of infiltrating and influencing the military, political parties, student organizations, labor unions, and the like; (3) the possibility of revolutionary change (even the early stages of such change) within the existing institutional framework; and (4) the need for armed or nonarmed revolutionary struggle based in the city, in the countryside, or in both. As a result of conflicting views on these and other issues, many organizations doubted or openly denied the revolutionary credentials of their Marxist-Leninist rivals. Indeed, they often would not even concede the common ground on the most basic of objectives mentioned above—many repeatedly accused their rivals of selling out to the establishment, to the revisionists, to the petit-bourgeoisie, or to some other non-socialist ideological or political force.

Marxist-Leninists often disagreed as much with each other as with their common enemies when it came to determining the most suitable political tactics for any specific national situation. The three basic forms of revolutionary struggle were (1) the so-called peaceful or nonarmed road, which chiefly involved electoral participation (when possible) and activities among workers and students; (2) the violent or armed road, characterized particularly by guerrilla warfare in the countryside or the city (or, in a few cases, both); and (3) a combination of significant aspects of armed and nonarmed struggle.[1] The armed and nonarmed roads were followed most frequently, in some instances with significant influence in individual countries, though without ever culminating in the establishment of socialism. The third road was generally only a subject of debate between communist and castroite groups, since in practice few groups could carry out significant armed actions while participating actively in open and nonarmed political activities. Indeed, while several pro-Soviet parties (most important among them the Communist Party of Colombia) proclaimed the third road, only the castroite-nationalist MIR in Chile, during the explosive Popular Unity period (1970–1973), was ever in a position to place serious emphasis on both roads at once. Keeping a finger in every pie—or keeping all options open—was most nearly possible during certain periods for international powers, particularly the Soviet Union, whose long-term interests were little affected by the complex play of forces, the day-to-day ups and downs, in individual Latin American countries.

It is more realistic (and more to the point) to recognize how difficult it was for these parties and organizations to follow the armed and nonarmed roads at the same time. The complex and frustrating problems of playing a significant (much less a vanguard) role in the struggle to transform traditional political, social, and economic conditions and institutions—hotly debated by most other revolutionaries and reformers as well—frequently turned up conflicting analyses that produced conflict between rival Marxist-Leninists, reaching its peaks of intensity and publicity when the international powers were most actively involved. Most of those involved stated (and no doubt believed) that a lack of unity had a crippling effect on the liberation struggle, though most also insisted, directly or indirectly, that unity had to come on their own terms or be a "sellout."

---

[1] The "peaceful" road involved violence at times when government authorities broke up strikes and demonstrations or when Marxist-Leninists confronted each other. One instance of the latter occurred on 2 December 1970 in Concepción, Chile, when members of the Communist Youth (JCCh) Ramona Parra Brigades and the Movement of the Revolutionary Left (MIR) clashed during university council elections, leaving one member of the MIR dead.

It is difficult to say precisely what impact the various Marxist-Leninist groups had in most nations. The pro-Soviet parties were sometimes important in leftist political affairs in Chile, Uruguay, Venezuela, and several other countries, though this often had little to do with their communist ideology and programs. They generally rode piggyback on international trends, particularly developments in the Western Hemisphere, and on the conditions and issues brought into being at least as much by other groups in their countries as by their own activities. Indeed, the successes of the pro-Soviet parties may in fact have been their contributions to creating conditions of dissatisfaction within existing structures without overexposing their own participation in the process. The declaration of twenty-four Latin American communist parties issued in June 1975 expressed (in typically propagandistic terms) the dissatisfaction with traditional ways felt by many Latin Americans in the mid-1970s, and conveyed communist satisfaction with the situation. The document asserted that the communist parties should play a "decisive historical role" in the further development of the struggle, but recognized that such a role was not guaranteed "by virtue of the social forces they represent and the exact theory that guides them." It would come only through exemplary leadership and actions.[2]

The castroites, many of whom were fired by deeply felt idealism, frustration, or urge for adventure, also contributed in some degree to the growing disillusionment with the traditional order. And yet their violent activities generally failed to rally significant support from any strata of society—with the occasional exception of the workers and middle-class intellectuals—generally drawing instead indifference or an emphatic rejection from the vast majority of the population. In the end, most of their guerrilla struggles, carried out in isolated mountain areas, were either crushed or dragged on inconclusively for extended periods of time, some groups degenerating into squabbling factions fighting as much among themselves as against either their Marxist-Leninist rivals or the declared enemies.

Among the largely or entirely urban guerrillas most successful in drawing significant support for a time from a variety of social and economic groups were the Chilean MIR, the Uruguayan Tupamaros, and possibly some of the guerrillas in Argentina. However, while the guerrillas in Venezuela (urban and rural) may have strengthened democracy in that country in the early 1960s, the Tupamaros and most other urban

---

[2] Published in *Granma* (Havana), 22 June 1975; see Appendix D below.

guerrillas ultimately had the opposite effect, contributing to the partial or total collapse of democratic government, as in Uruguay, Chile, and Argentina between 1972 and early 1976.

Among the organizations on the Marxist-Leninist left, the castroite groups contributed most to the polarization of forces and to the increase in what they and the communists describe as "fascism" in political parties and the military. Most castroites frankly regarded this "intensification of the class struggle" as desirable, indeed essential, for raising the political consciousness of the masses. As the castroite groups saw it, the repression of military governments was bound to drive the masses into rebellion and spark the mass-based revolution.

Although significant differences remained among Latin American Marxist-Leninists in early 1976, a degree of theoretical convergence had occurred and interparty strife was at its lowest point in a decade. While most pro-Soviet parties continued to promote the nonarmed road, after major setbacks in Uruguay and Chile during the early 1970s, they were more outspoken than ever before in their calls for armed defense of revolutionary advances when attacked by imperialist and reactionary interests. In most countries the pro-Chinese organizations were increasingly inconsequential, leaving behind them theoretical lessons from Mao rather than positive historical examples of their own. Castroite groups, most of which look more to each other than to Cuba for moral and material support, have professed and occasionally demonstrated increasing awareness of the need for patient propaganda work among the people (as long proposed by the pro-Chinese and some others) if mass support is to be won and the revolutionary struggle to be successful. Though their strategy still rests chiefly on armed struggle, castroites generally have come to recognize (at least theoretically) the need to follow both armed and nonarmed roads, in the city as well as in the countryside.

This relatively quiescent state of affairs among Latin American Marxist-Leninists is in part an outgrowth of shifting relationships among the three communist powers themselves, as well as changes in the international setting generally. In early 1976 Marxist-Leninist groups were not so often pushed into competition with each other by aggressive policies of the Soviet Union, China, or Cuba, as they had been earlier. Also, no major competition among the followers of the various Marxist-Leninist roads is currently being played out in Latin America. Most of the important Marxist-Leninist organizations of the combative years have been at least temporarily reduced to relative insignificance by military forces in or behind the seats of power, or by the broader turn of events.

And yet the probability of significant national and possibly international disruption in the future by self-professed Marxist-Leninist groups is ever present. Political, economic, and social conditions are improving very slowly, if at all, in many countries. Unless evidence of significant progress toward resolving some of the formidable problems is clearly established, present frustrations will increase and the stage will be set for the resurgence of these or other groups of similar inspiration, not to mention non-Marxist-Leninist groups as well. Paradoxically, a significant measure of progress may itself encourage demands for further changes that will themselves provide new opportunities for the organizations discussed in this volume and their successors. The probability of a resurgence of activity by Marxist-Leninists in Latin America will be increased markedly if major communist powers again decide that such a state of affairs would be in their interests. The undisguised Cuban and Soviet participation in the Angolan civil war during late 1975 and early 1976 caused many Latin Americans to fear increased international involvement in Latin America in the years ahead.

As of early 1976, many Latin American Marxist-Leninists seem to have learned some lessons from the intense factional struggles and bitter defeats of the recent past. It is possible that they will cooperate more— or at least fight less—in the years to come than they have in the past. On the other hand, factionalism is a feature of Latin American politics generally, as well as of communist groups in recent years, and it is possible that as truly important revolutionary situations emerge in the future, the Marxist-Leninists will again find themselves as much in competition with each other as with their proclaimed common enemies.

Appendix A

CONFERENCE OF
LATIN AMERICAN COMMUNIST PARTIES,
HAVANA, NOVEMBER 1964

In November 1964 the communist parties of Latin America held a major conference in Havana, attended by observers from the Communist Party of the Soviet Union but not from the Communist Party of China. Among the main issues discussed were: (1) the most productive strategy and tactics for revolution in Latin America midway through the decade, with special attention devoted to setbacks suffered in the early 1960s, (2) the relationship between Fidel Castro's government in Cuba and the pro-Soviet international communist movement, and (3) the threat to the international communist movement posed by the Sino-Soviet dispute. The conference and its resolutions put the Cuban government on the Soviet side in the conflict with China for the first time, though for a while Castro continued to profess neutrality. The conference also appeared to represent a reaffirmation of Moscow's authority over the communist movement in Latin America, after some compromises with the revolutionary leadership in Cuba. For a short time the meeting seemed to portend greater coordination and cooperation among Latin American communists and between these parties and Cuba.

No documents of the conference were ever published, but an official communiqué was released two months after the event. The complete text of that communiqué follows.[1]

A conference of the Communist Parties of Latin America, attended by representatives of all the parties, was held near the end of 1964. The conference took place in an atmosphere of fraternal cooperation and in a spirit of frank understanding and comprehensiveness with respect to

---

[1] "Comunicado de la conferencia de los partidos comunistas de América Latina," *Cuba Socialista* (Havana), vol. 5, no. 42 (February 1965), pp. 140-42; translated by the author.

common problems. There was a useful exchange of experiences acquired in the struggle of all the peoples of the continent against imperialism, and for national liberation, peace, democracy, and socialism.

The conference devoted special attention to questions of solidarity with the Cuban people and their government. In its resolutions, the conference stressed the need to promote solidarity with Cuba throughout the continent and to make the effort more resolute and better coordinated. In developing this solidarity movement, organizations, individuals, and parties not only fulfill an international and Latin American duty but also at the same time defend the interests, liberties, dignity, and future of their own peoples.

Among the tasks confronting the solidarity movement, special attention was devoted to the demand for the reestablishment of diplomatic and commercial relations with Cuba; the struggle against the economic blockade, and for the development of trade; the denunciation of preparations for aggression and of activities of the counterrevolutionaries and other agents of the CIA; the timely rebuff to the defamatory campaign organized and directed by North American imperialism against the people of Cuba and their government; and the organization of an extensive propaganda campaign on the achievements of the Cuban revolution in all spheres—economic, social, and cultural.

The conference made the following recommendations with regard to the support of the struggles of other peoples of Latin America against imperialism:

(1) To promote the creation of solidarity movements or juntas, giving a permanent character to the campaigns against repression so that these campaigns will not be limited to sporadic manifestations or isolated declarations.

(2) To give active support to those who are currently being subjected to cruel repressions as, for instance, the Venezuelan, Colombian, Guatemalan, Honduran, Paraguayan, and Haitian fighters.

(3) To push forward the struggle against colonialism on the continent, giving resolute support to the cause of independence for Puerto Rico and British Guiana; for the automony of Martinique, Guadeloupe, and French Guiana; for the return of the Malvinas [Falkland] Islands to Argentina; and for the national aspirations of the British and Dutch colonies in the Caribbean.

(4) To organize on a continental scale the active solidarity of all the Latin American peoples with the liberation struggle of the people of Venezuela.

(5) To intensify solidarity with the anti-imperialist struggle being waged under difficult conditions by the Panamanian people.

(6) To advance intense campaigns for the liberty of imprisoned Communist leaders, among them: Jesús Faría, Gustavo Machado, and

Pompeyo Márquez, in Venezuela; Pedro Saad, in Ecuador; Jacques Stephen Alexis, in Haiti; Antonio Maidana, in Paraguay; Mario Alves, Iván Ribeiro, and Astrogildo Pereira, in Brazil, as well as freedom for all persecuted patriots, labor fighters, and democrats.

(7) To develop the spirit of solidarity within the Latin American proletariat by promoting labor protests in all enterprises and bringing these to the attention of World Federation of Trade Unions and all the independent united workers centers in Latin America.

The conference also emphasized the need for promoting rapprochement between the various parties, the exchange of their experiences, and better mutual understanding.

The conference attentively considered the subject of the differences which have arisen within the international Communist movement and, with these in mind, adopted a resolution whose major points are as follows:

For the unity of the international Communist movement. The Communist parties of Latin America, whose representatives gathered for an exchange of experiences, reaffirm their determination to fight actively for the unity of the international Communist movement, a unity based on the principles of Marxism-Leninism and on the programmatic declarations of 1957 and 1960.

The parties consider said unity the fundamental guarantee of the success of our struggle against imperialism, for the national and social liberation of all peoples, and for world peace and for the building of socialism and communism.

In this regard, we are profoundly disturbed by the situation in the international communist movement, in which are manifested sharp contradictions that have engendered the danger of a split, exposing us to our enemies and encouraging their aggressiveness.

The parties consider it imperative to exert every effort toward smoothing the road to unity, to facilitate understanding in the socialist camp, and to avoid anything that increases the danger of a division, impedes fraternal and constructive dialogue, or makes more difficult actions by the fraternal parties in a single front with a view to overcoming present differences and concentrating all energies against the imperialists and other reactionary forces.

It is necessary to stress our common viewpoints that are the expression of our shared ideology, Marxism-Leninism, and to do everything necessary in order to make the firmest unity of principles prevail.

Consequently, considering the harm that has come upon the international communist movement from the course the controversy has taken, the conference calls for the immediate end to all public polemics and stresses the need to find adequate means whereby the problems can be resolved in the spirit of fraternity which should govern the relations among the Marxist-Leninist parties.

At the same time, the conference considers the unity of each party a necessary condition for carrying forward the revolutionary process in each country. Therefore, all factional activity—whatever its nature and origin—must be categorically repudiated.

The conference believes that firm steps must be taken to assure the unity of the international communist movement and, to this end, bi-lateral and multi-lateral meetings and conferences that may be necessary for all the Marxist-Leninist parties must be sponsored.

Appendix B

LATIN AMERICAN SOLIDARITY ORGANIZATION CONFERENCE, JULY–AUGUST 1967

The Latin American Solidarity Organization (Organización Latinoamericana de Solidaridad, or OLAS) was created in Havana on 16 January 1966 by the twenty-seven delegations that participated in the recently concluded Afro-Asian-Latin American People's Solidarity Organization (AALAPSO, or Tricontinental) conference.[1] The organizational meeting was presided over by Pedro Medina Silva, a leader of the Venezuelan Armed Forces of National Liberation (FALN), who served as vicepresident for Latin America at the Tricontinental conference, and by seven of the eight members of the politburo of the Cuban Communist Party, including Fidel Castro. Prominent members of other Latin American delegations included Mario Monje (Bolivia); Salvador Allende, chairman, Clodomiro Almeyda, and Luis Figueroa (Chile); Diego Montaña Cuéllar (chairman, Colombia); Luis Turcios (chairman, Guatemala); Cheddi Jagan (chairman, Guyana); Jorge Turner, chairman, and Floyd Britton (Panama); and Moisés Moliero (Venezuela).

The delegates at the organizational meeting agreed to the formation of national committees and an organizing committee made up of delegates from Brazil, Colombia, Cuba, Guyana, Guatemala, Mexico, Peru, Uruguay, and Venezuela. The organizing committee was divided into

---

[1] Delegations participated from Argentina (seven members), Bolivia (three), Brazil (seven), Colombia (six), Costa Rica (three), Cuba (forty-one), Chile (nine), Ecuador (two), El Salvador (two), Guadeloupe (four), Guatemala (five), Guyana (three), Haiti (five), Honduras (three), French Guiana (three), Jamaica (two), Martinique (two), Mexico (six), Nicaragua (three), Panama (four), Paraguay (five), Peru (eight), Puerto Rico (four), Dominican Republic (five), Trinidad-Tobago (two), Uruguay (six), and Venezuela (fifteen).

"Olas" means "waves" in Spanish. Fidel Castro told the delegates to the conference: "OLAS is the wave of the future, symbol of the revolutionary waves sweeping a continent." *Granma* (Havana), 20 August 1967.

two subcommittees, one in charge of organizing and conducting the preconvention business of the conference scheduled for 1967, and one responsible for publicizing the opening conference and publishing the bulletin *OLAS*. The only two permanent positions on the organizing committee, those of the secretary-general and the press secretary, were filled, respectively, by Haydée Santamaría, a member of the Central Committee of the Cuban Communist Party, and Miguel Brugueras of the Cuban press agency Prensa Latina. In addition to the abovementioned activities, the committee was responsible for issuing all invitations to the 1967 conference. In January 1967 it sent a detailed questionnaire to all national committees, 25 international organizations, and 197 Latin American institutions. The information gathered in these questionnaires about political, social, and economic conditions in Latin America was compiled in fourteen volumes by six special commissions made up of more than 1,000 analysts and their assistants. The organizing committee retained its leadership role until the election of the OLAS president at a meeting of delegation presidents early in the 1967 conference.

The First Conference of the Latin American Solidarity Organization was held in Havana between 31 July and 10 August 1967. According to the official list of participants there were 158 registered delegates in attendance: from Argentina (six persons), Bolivia (four), Brazil (four), Colombia (five), Costa Rica (nine), Cuba (twelve), Chile (eight), Ecuador (four), El Salvador (eight), Guadeloupe (four), Guatemala (four) French Guiana (four), Guyana (two), Haiti (four), Honduras (six), Martinique (four), Mexico (six), Nicaragua (six), Panama (six), Paraguay (seven), Peru (eight), Puerto Rico (three), Dominican Republic (six), Surinam (three), Trinidad-Tobago (four), Uruguay (ten), and Venezuela (eleven), as well as one honorary delegate from the United States. Among the delegates were: Carlos Altamirano, Clodomiro Almeyda, and Volodia Teitelboim (Chile); Néstor Valle, chairman, and Oscar Palma (Guatemala); Floyd Britton (Panama); Juan Mari Bras (Puerto Rico); Rodney Arismendi, chairman, Ariel Collazo, and José Díaz (Uruguay); Francisco Prada (Venezuela); and Stokely Carmichael (United States). Other individuals at the conference included 38 observers from international organizations (AALAPSO, the International Union of Students, the Confederation of Latin Americans in the German Democratic Republic, the Permanent Congress of Trade Union Unity of Latin American Workers, the Continental Organization of Latin American Students, the World Federation of Democratic Youth, the World Federation of Trade Unions, the Women's International Democratic Federation, the World Council of Peace, the Tricontinental Committee for Support to the People of Vietnam, the International War Crimes Tribunal, the International Organization of Journalists, and the Japanese Council against the Atomic and Hydrogen Bombs). Some 25 observers were present from the socialist countries (North Vietnam, North Korea, Bulgaria, Czechoslovakia, Hungary, Mongolia, Poland, East Germany, Rumania, and the Union of Soviet Socialist Republics), and seven from the National Liberation Front of South Vietnam. The Soviet Union sent only two accredited observers and, though there are indications that they were invited to attend, the People's Republic of China and Albania sent none. Yugoslavia was apparently the only communist country to be purposely excluded. Special foreign guests totaled 38; among them were Carlos Marighela (Brazil), Roque Dalton (El Salvador), and Elizabeth Burgos, subsequently the wife of Régis Debray (Venezuela). The foreign press was represented by 157 persons from 38 countries, including 8 from the Soviet Union and 2 from the People's Republic of China.

Most of the delegates were ultra-leftists and guerrilla fighters, typified by Venezuelan FALN leader Francisco Prada. Some pro-Soviet communists and their followers were present, though they seem to have been dominant in only a few delegations, most important among them the Uruguayan. A few pro-Chinese delegates attended, though not as official representatives of pro-Chinese parties. The fact that most of the delegates were little known in their own countries was noted by Marcel Niedergang in *Le Monde* on 2 August, and by the Yugoslav press agency Tanjug, which asserted on 1 August: "Many delegations consist of quite unknown personalities, representing groups and organizations which have no influence in their own countries." [2]

Three of the four vice-presidents at the conference were castroite in orientation: Francisco Prada (Venezuela), Néstor Valle (Guatemala), and Gerardo Sánchez (Dominican Republic). The fourth vice-president was Rodney Arismendi, the secretary-general of the Communist Party of Uruguay, the only pro-Soviet communist given a high position. Arismendi was also the only pro-Soviet communist to come close to a full endorsement of the guerrilla-oriented line of the conference, and is

[2] Chilean Senator (subsequently President) Salvador Allende did not attend the conference, though he was on the Chilean organizing committee set up in June 1967 after much dispute between the Communist and Socialist parties.

generally believed to have worked constantly behind the scenes to smooth over differences between Cuba and the Soviet Union.

The purposes of the Latin American Solidarity Organization, as stated in Article 1 of the statutes adopted by the OLAS conference in August 1967, were:

(a) To develop and promote the unity of the anti-imperialist movement and organizations in each one of the Latin American countries.

(b) To develop and promote the unity of the anti-imperialist movements and organizations of all the peoples of the continent.

(c) To support, by all means within their power, the peoples of Latin America that struggle against imperialism and colonialism, especially those who are engaged in armed struggle.

(d) To coordinate the struggle against U.S. imperialism to achieve a united answer of the Latin American peoples to its continental strategy.

(e) To promote the solidarity of the Latin American peoples with the national liberation movements of Asia, and Africa, and with the progressive movements all over the world.[3]

According to the statutes, OLAS is composed of three bodies: the Conference, the Permanent Committee, and the National Committees. The Conference, described as "the deliberating body and highest authority of the Organization," is comprised of the national committees of member countries and was scheduled to meet every two years. (No second conference was held during the 1967–1976 period.)

The Permanent Committee was "the executive body and the highest authority between the Conferences." It was based in Havana and made up of representatives from one-third of the member countries. Its function was to work for the purposes of OLAS as described in Article 1 of the statutes (quoted above). It was charged with coordinating and guiding the activities of the National Committees and with controlling their composition. It was responsible for convoking the Conference every two years and had the power to call special continental meetings when it considered them necessary.

---

[3] This and all other quotations in this section are, unless otherwise noted, from the official English-language translations mimeographed during the conference, dated July-August 1967. There are minor differences in some of the translations which appeared in weekly English editions of *Granma* (Havana).

The National Committees, according to the OLAS statutes, represented the "most active, anti-imperialist and deep-rooted people's groups in each one of the Latin American countries." Political organizations that filled certain requirements had the right to be members of the National Committees. They had to "be anti-imperialist, representative, and unitary," "accept the General Declaration of the Tricontinental Conference and the General Declaration of the First Conference of OLAS," and "accept the Statutes of the Latin American Solidarity Organization." The statutes stated further that in "those countries where revolutionary armed struggle is developing, all organizations and movements that effectively support or participate in this struggle shall be considered anti-imperialist." In particular cases, mass organizations could become part of the National Committees, but only if they fulfilled additional requirements. Any National Committee might recommend that changes be made in its own membership, but all final decisions had to be made by the Permanent Committee in Havana. The National Committees were expected to work for the achievement of OLAS goals through unifying and coordinating revolutionary forces in their countries.

The official agenda of the conference was divided into four main sections, the first three of which were in turn broken down into thirteen subsections. The four main sections were:

(1) The anti-imperialist revolutionary struggle in Latin America.

(2) Position and common action against the political-military intervention and the economical and ideological penetration of imperialism in Latin America.

(3) The solidarity of the Latin American peoples with the struggles for national liberation.

(4) Statutes of the Organization of Latin American Solidarity (OLAS).

Four working committees were set up to discuss and issue statements on the four central topics. Though all meetings were held in secret some delegates told news reporters most of what went on. Making reference to these delegates, Fidel Castro commented on 10 August: "There were indiscretions, and nearly all the things discussed are known more or less." [4]

Speeches at the conference were given by three different groups of participants: the Cuban hosts, delegates to the conference, and observers and special guests from socialist countries and international organizations.

---

[4] Ibid., 20 August 1967.

Cuban President Osvaldo Dorticós addressed the opening session of the conference on the evening of 31 July. He discussed what he called "an imperialist world strategy against the peoples and the liberation movements, a strategy which daily acquires greater ferocity." The Latin American people, he asserted, were confronted with two alternatives: "to reply with arms to the challenge of imperialist violence or to renounce all hopes of liberation." [5] Armando Hart, organizing secretary of the Cuban Communist Party, serving as chairman of the Cuban delegation, presented a concise castroite analysis of the main objectives of the conference, namely, how to draw up a "common strategy for the struggle against Yankee imperialism and against the bourgeois oligarchies and wealthy landowners that have allied themselves with the interests of the United States Government." [6] Fidel Castro's speech at the closing session on 10 August was summarized in the text (pp. 44-45).

Prominent among those at the conference who spoke in support of the castroite line were Francisco Prada of Venezuela, Fabio Vázquez of Colombia (who sent a taped message), and the delegations from the Dominican Republic, Ecuador, Guatemala, and Peru. Among the least enthusiastic were Volodia Teitelboim of the Communist Party of Chile and the delegation from Costa Rica.

Stokely Carmichael, the "honorary delegate" from the United States, received more attention, especially from the foreign press, than anyone at the conference besides Fidel Castro himself. In one of the longest speeches delivered at the conference, Carmichael stated on 2 August that "the American city is, in essence, populated by people of the third world" and that the urban guerrilla warfare U.S. Negroes needed to wage in order to win their "liberation" was merely one part of the international struggle between the "third world" and "Yankee imperialism." At a press conference held shortly after the eruption of violence in Detroit and other U.S. cities, he asserted that these U.S. Negro "rebellions" should be linked up with the outside world because "when the [U.S.] has 50 Vietnams inside the United States, and 50 Vietnams outside the United States, that will mean the death of imperialism." [7]

Most of the speeches by observers from other countries and international organizations were shorter and less militant, in accordance with their pro-Soviet positions in the communist world. Notable exceptions

[5] Ibid., 6 August 1967.
[6] Ibid., 13 August 1967.
[7] Ibid., Spanish ed., 3 August 1967.

were those of the Vietnamese, Korean, and Syrian delegations, as well as the address of the representative of the AALAPSO Executive Secretariat. The first plenary meeting was held on 1 August and proclaimed "in honor of the people of Vietnam." The privilege of speaking first was granted to the chairman of the eight-member delegation from North Vietnam, and of speaking second to the chairman of the seven-member delegation from the National Liberation Front of South Vietnam. Messages were read from North Vietnamese President Ho Chi Minh and North Korean President Kim Il-sung, among others.

The long report submitted by the Cuban delegation clearly reflected the tone and content of the discussions held and resolutions passed by the OLAS delegates. It sought to show that "the duty of every revolutionary is to make the revolution" (as Fidel Castro had said in his 1962 "Second Declaration of Havana"), above all by guerrilla warfare. It discussed Marx, Lenin, and the international nature of revolution. Great stress was put on the history of "colonialism" and "imperialism" in Latin America, and on Latin American revolutionaries, beginning with Simón Bolívar and passing through José Martí to Che Guevara.

Emphasis on the specifically Latin American nature of the "anti-imperialist struggle," often overriding the Marxist-Leninist element, was evident on many occasions throughout the conference. Cuban President Dorticós gave his opening address before a large picture of Bolívar, and Fidel Castro in closing the conference spoke before one of Guevara. Latin American speakers, beginning with Dorticós frequently mentioned Bolívar, San Martín, Martí, and other nineteenth century heroes, and many of the resolutions quoted these men and recounted their achievements.

The conference passed resolutions condemning U.S. and OAS activities in Latin America; declaring support for guerrillas in Latin America, Negroes in the United States, the peoples of Asia, Africa, and the Arab world, and the AALAPSO; and hailing the fiftieth anniversary of the October Revolution in the Soviet Union. Che Guevara was proclaimed an honorary citizen of Latin America.[8]

The main aim of the conference, according to the General Declaration, had been "to tighten the ties of militant solidarity among anti-imperialist fighters of Latin America and to work out the fundamental lines for the development of the continental revolution." The declaration

---

[8] For a summary of the resolutions of the four working committees, see ibid., 27 August 1967.

ended with a twenty-point review of the essentially castroite line adopted by the conference in which the delegates proclaimed:

(1) That making the Revolution constitutes a right and a duty of the peoples of Latin America.

(2) That the Revolution in Latin America has its deepest historical roots in the liberation movement against European colonialism of the nineteenth century and against imperialism of this century. The epic of the peoples of America and the great class battles that our peoples have carried out against imperialism in earlier decades constitute the source of historical inspiration of the Latin American revolutionary movement. . . .

(3) That the essential content of the Revolution in Latin America is to be found in its confrontation with imperialism and the bourgeois and landowner oligarchies. Consequently, the character of the Revolution is the struggle for national independence, emancipation from the oligarchies, and the socialist road for its complete economic and social development.

(4) That the principles of Marxism-Leninism guide the revolutionary movement of Latin America.

(5) That armed revolutionary struggle constitutes the fundamental course of the Revolution in Latin America.

(6) That all other forms of struggle must serve to advance and not to retard the development of this fundamental course, which is armed struggle.

(7) That, for the majority of the countries of the continent, the problems of organizing, initiating, developing and crowning the armed struggle at present constitutes the immediate and fundamental task of the revolutionary movement.

(8) That those countries in which this task has not yet been undertaken nevertheless *will regard it as an inevitable sequence* in the development of revolutionary struggle in their countries.

(9) That the historic responsibility of furthering revolution in each of these countries belongs to the people and to their revolutionary vanguards in each society.

(10) That the guerrilla is the nucleus of the liberation armies, and guerrilla warfare constitutes the most effective method of initiating and developing the revolutionary struggle in most of our countries.

(11) That the leadership of the Revolution demands, as an organizational principle, the existence of a unified politico-military command, as a guarantee of success.

(12) That the most effective solidarity that the revolutionary movements may practice among themselves, is the furthering and the culmination of their own struggle in their respective countries.

(13) That the solidarity with Cuba and the collaboration and cooperation with the armed revolutionary movement is an undeferrable international duty of every anti-imperialist organization of the continent.

(14) The Cuban Revolution, as a symbol of triumph of the armed revolutionary movement, constitutes the vanguard of the Latin American anti-imperialist movement. The peoples that develop the armed struggle, as they advance along this road, put themselves in the vanguard.

(15) That the peoples who have been directly subjected by colonialism of the European countries, in order to achieve their liberation, must have an immediate and basic objective: that of struggling for independence and uniting with the general struggle of the continent as the only means of avoiding being absorbed into U.S. neocolonialism.

(16) That the Second Declaration of Havana, that expresses the beautiful and glorious revolutionary tradition of the past 150 years of American history, constitutes a document outlining the program of the Latin American Revolution which has been confirmed, deepened, enriched and made more radical by the peoples of this continent during the last five years.

(17) That the peoples of Latin America have no differences with any other peoples in the world and extend their hand of friendship also to the peoples of the United States, whom they exhort to undertake the struggle against the repressive policy carried out by imperialist monopolies.

(18) That the Latin American struggle strengthens its ties of solidarity with the peoples of Asia and Africa, and those of the socialist countries, the workers of the capitalist nations and especially with the Negro population of the United States which suffers class exploitation, poverty, unemployment, racial discrimination and the denial of their most elementary human rights, and which constitutes an important force within the revolutionary struggle.

(19) That the heroic struggle waged by the people of Viet Nam gives invaluable aid to all revolutionary peoples who are

fighting imperialism, and constitutes an inspiring example to the peoples of Latin America.

(20) That we have approved the Statutes and created the Permanent Committee, in Havana, of the Organization of Latin American Solidarity, which constitutes an inspiring example to the Latin American peoples.[9]

The conference took two days longer than had been expected, apparently because the castroite and pro-Soviet members of the working committees could not agree on the wording of some resolutions. In the end the Cuban viewpoint was reflected on American and international issues, though some slight concessions were made to avoid an open conflict with the Soviet Union. One dispute came over an attack on the pro-Soviet Communist Party of Venezuela (PCV) in the "Resolution on Solidarity with Venezuela." With the passage of this resolution by a vote of fifteen to three (El Salvador, Bolivia, and Uruguay opposed), and nine not voting, OLAS condemned the "bungling and opportunistic position of the rightist leadership of the PCV, which, in abandoning the road of armed struggle, betrays the revolutionary principles and serves the interests of imperialism and the oligarchies and all their policy of oppression." [10] The bitterest dispute was that over the resolution to condemn "certain Socialist countries" for giving credits and technical aid to "oligarchic" governments in countries such as Brazil, Chile, and Colombia. This resolution, aimed at the Soviet Union and several of its East European allies, was passed by the same number of votes (Costa Rica, El Salvador, and Uruguay reportedly in opposition), but was never published.[11]

---

9 Official conference document; emphasis in original.
10 Translated from the Spanish edition of the official conference document.
11 See *New York Times*, 10 August, and *Le Monde* (Paris), 11 August 1967.

Appendix C
THE FOUNDING OF THE REVOLUTIONARY COORDINATING COMMITTEE, FEBRUARY 1974

It is the road of Vietnam; it is the road the people must follow; it is the road that America will follow, with the special characteristic that the armed groups may form something like coordinating committees [juntas de coordinación] *to make more difficult the repressive task of the Yanqui imperialism and to facilitate our own cause.*

Che Guevara, "Message to the Tricontinental"

The Revolutionary Coordinating Committee (Junta de Coordinación Revolucionario, or JCR), made up of the Chilean Movement of the Revolutionary Left (Movimiento de Izquierda Revolucionaria, or MIR), the Uruguayan National Liberation Movement (Movimiento de Liberación Nacional, or MLN), which is to say the Tupamaros, the Bolivian National Liberation Army (Ejército de Liberación Nacional, or ELN), and the Argentine People's Revolutionary Army (Ejército Revolucionario del Pueblo, or ERP), announced its formation on 13 February 1974 in Buenos Aires. At that time the JCR released the following "joint declaration" which the Mexican leftist magazine *Por Que?* (20 June 1974) described as "the most important political document that has been published in Latin America since the 'Second Declaration of Havana'" twelve years earlier.[1]

The National Liberation Movement (Tupamaros) of Uruguay, the Movement of the Revolutionary Left (MIR) of Chile, the National Liberation Army (ELN) of Bolivia, and the People's Revolutionary Army (ERP) of Argentina sign this declaration to make known to the workers, the poor peasants, the poor in the cities, the students and

[1] Complete text of JCR document translated by the author from *Por Que?* (Mexico City), 20 June 1974.

intellectuals, the aborigines, and the millions of exploited workers of our long-suffering Latin American homeland, their decision to unite in a Revolutionary Coordinating Committee.

This important step is the result of a felt need, of the need to pull together our peoples in the area of organization, to unite the revolutionary forces against the imperialist enemy, to carry out with greater effectiveness the political and ideological struggle against bourgeois nationalism and reformism.

This important step is the realization of one of the principal strategic ideas of Comandante Che Guevara, hero, symbol, and precursor of the continental socialist revolution. It is also a significant step toward reviving the fractured tradition of our peoples who were able to come together like brothers and fight as one man against the oppressors of the past century, the Spanish colonialists.

Our struggle is anti-imperialist. The peoples of the world live under the permanent threat of the most aggressive and rapacious imperialism that has ever existed. They have seen, and not with indifference, the genocide organized and directed by Yankee imperialism against the heroic Vietnamese people. In this unequal war, whose flames have not yet been extinguished, the warlike and treacherous character of the imperialism of the North has been fully demonstrated. But this war has also shown once again the weakness of its system, in spite of all its military power, against a people resolved to fight and determined to be free at any price.

Since the last century the Latin American peoples have borne the antiquated colonial or neocolonial yoke of the imperialists; they have suffered successive military interventions and unjust wars fomented and executed by the North American army and multinational monopolies.

These include the despoliation of Mexico, the occupation of Puerto Rico, the interventions in Santo Domingo and Playa Girón, and many other bellicose acts that our America does not forget and will never forgive. And there is Shell, Esso, Standard Oil, United Fruit, ITT, the money of Mr. Rockefeller and Mr. Ford. And the CIA, which with "Papy" Shelton, Mitrione, and Siracusa, left an indelible mark on the enslaving and oppressive policies of the United States against the people's movement in Latin America.

Latin America marches toward socialism. The First of January 1959, with the triumph of the Cuban Revolution, began the final march of the Latin American peoples toward socialism, toward true national independence, toward the collective well-being of the peoples. It is the just and open rebellion of the exploited people of Latin America against a barbaric colonial capitalist system imposed since the end of the last century by Yankee and European imperialism, which with force, deception, and corruption, seized our continent. The cowardly creole bourgeoisie and their armies did not know how to honor the revolutionary liberationist legacy of the glorious anti-colonial struggle of our people which, led by heroes like Bolívar, San Martín, Artigas, and many others, won independence, equality, and liberty.

The ruling classes, defending their petty group interests, joined forces with the imperialists, collaborated with them, facilitating their economic penetration, progressively handing over control of our economies to the insatiable voracity of foreign capital. Economic domination led to political and cultural control and subordination. So began the neocolonial capitalist system which for a hundred years has been exploiting, oppressing, and deforming the working classes of our continent.

From the beginning of the century the working class began to rise up against the system, unfurling the then-little-known banner of socialism, united indissolubly with the banner of national independence, striving to awaken the peasants, the students, all the healthy and revolutionary of our peoples. Anarchism, socialism, communism as organized movements of the working class led in the mobilization of the broad masses with energy and heroism and were indelible milestones in the revolutionary struggle. The legendary Nicaraguan leader, Augusto César Sandino, metalworker, led one of the most heroic of these battles in his own small country when his guerrilla army checked and defeated the interventionist North American troops in 1932. In the decade of the 1930s a formidable surge of the masses developed throughout the continent which checked the neocolonial domination built up by Yankee imperialism, the No. 1 enemy of all the peoples of the world.

But this formidable revolutionary mobilization of the masses was not crowned with victory. The active counterrevolutionary intervention, political and military, direct and indirect, by Yankee imperialism, taken with the deficiencies of anarchism, socialist currents, and the communist parties, were the causes of a temporary defeat. The majority of the communist parties, the most conscious, consistent, and organized groups of this period, fell into reformism. Some of them, like the heroic and battle-hardened Salvadorian Communist Party, suffered defeats with scores and even thousands of martyrs. For this reason, the impetuous surge of the masses was deflected from its revolutionary road and fell under the influence and direction of bourgeois nationalism, a dead-end for the revolution, a clever and demagogic means utilized by the ruling classes to prolong the life of the neocolonial capitalist system through deception.

After the formidable triumph of the Cuban people—under the skillful and far-sighted leadership of Fidel Castro and a group of Marxist-Leninist leaders—managed to defeat the army of Batista and establish on the island of Cuba, within the very beard of the imperialists, the first socialist state of Latin America, the people of the continent were strengthened in their revolutionary faith and initiated a new and profound general mobilization.

211

With steps forward and errors, our peoples and their vanguards hurled themselves resolutely into the struggle against imperialism and for socialism. The decade of the 1960s saw an uninterrupted succession of great popular struggles, violent guerrilla combats, and powerful mass insurrections. The April War, the general uprising of the Dominican people, required the direct intervention of Yankee imperialism which had to send 30,000 soldiers in order to choke out this magnificent insurrection with a massacre.

The legendary figure of Comandante Ernesto Guevara personified and symbolized this entire period of struggle just as his exemplary life and his clear Marxist-Leninist strategic conceptions illuminated the new revolutionary surge of our peoples which grew day by day in power and solidarity, beginning in the factories, in the towns, in the countryside, in the cities, and spreading out of control over the entire continent.

This is the definitive awakening of our peoples which has brought millions upon millions of workers to their feet and set them inexorably on the road toward the second independence, toward the definitive elimination of the unjust capitalist system, and the establishment of revolutionary socialism.

The struggle for the leadership of the mass movement. But the revolutionary road is neither simple nor harmless. We do not face only the barbarous military and economic force of imperialism. More subtle enemies and dangers lie in wait at each moment for the revolutionary forces, to prevent them from carrying out the anti-imperialist and anti-capitalist struggle effectively and victoriously.

Today, with respect to the particular situation of the continental revolutionary process, we must refer to two currents of thought and action which conspire powerfully against the revolutionary efforts of the Latin Americans. These are an enemy, bourgeois nationalism, and an erroneous conception in the people's camp, reformism.

The two—at times closely united—are trying to ride the revolutionary wave of our peoples, taking over its direction and imposing their own mistaken and selfish conceptions which unfailingly end in stopping and crushing the revolutionary impulse. Therefore there is a strategic dimension to the intransigent political and ideological struggle we revolutionaries must wage against these currents to win back the leadership of the broad masses, in order to give our peoples a consistent revolutionary leadership that will guide us with perseverance, intelligence, and effectiveness to the final victory.

Bourgeois nationalism is a current approved by imperialism which supports it as a demagogic variant to distract and divert the struggle of the peoples when counterrevolutionary violence loses its effectiveness. Its social nucleus is the pro-imperialist bourgeoisie or an embryo of it that seeks to enrich itself without limit by competing with the oligarchy and the traditional bourgeoisie for the favors of imperialism by presenting itself as the fireman to put out the revolutionary conflagration by means of its popular influence and capacity for negotiation with the mass movement. In their policy of deception they express a verbal anti-imperialism but seek to confuse the masses with their favorite nationalist thesis—the third position. In reality they are not anti-imperialists but smooth the way for new and more subtle forms of foreign economic penetration.

Reformism, on the other hand, is a current that nests in the very womb of the working people, reflecting the fear of a confrontation with the petit-bourgeois sectors and the labor aristocracy. It is characterized by its total rejection in practice of the just and necessary revolutionary violence as the fundamental method in the struggle for power, thus abandoning the Marxist concept of class struggle. Reformism spreads noxious pacifist and liberal ideas among the masses, beautifying the national bourgeoisie and the counterrevolutionary armies with whom they always seek alliances, exaggerating the importance of legality and parliamentarianism. One of their favorite arguments, that it is necessary to reject violence and link up with the bourgeoisie and "patriotic military" in search for a peaceful way that will spare the shedding of blood by the masses on the road to socialism, is circular and painfully refuted by the facts. Where reformism has been able to impose its conciliatory and pacifist policies, the class enemies and their armies have carried out the worst massacres against the people. The nearness of the Chilean experience with more than 20,000 men and women workers assassinated makes further commentary unnecessary.

Against bourgeois nationalism, reformism, and other less important currents, in constant ideological and political struggle against them, the armed people have risen up, a revolutionary pole that day by day consolidates its position among the masses, increasing its influence, improving its political and military capacity, converting itself more and more into a real option for national independence and socialism.

Precisely in order to contribute to the strengthening of this revolutionary pole on a continental scale, the four organizations that signed this document decided to form the present Committee for Revolutionary Coordination. We call upon all the revolutionary vanguard of people and workers in Latin America to organize themselves and fight together.

Naturally this means that the doors of this Committee of Coordination are open to the revolutionary organizations in the different Latin American countries.

The experience of our organizations. In the course of their patriotic and revolutionary struggles, the MLN Tupamaros, the Movement of the Revolutionary Left, the National Liberation Army, and the People's Revolutionary Army have come to understand the need for unity, to affirm by their own experience their internationalist concepts, understanding that the united and organized imperialism and capitalist enemy must be confronted by the most hardened and tightly knit unity of our peoples.

Based on the similarities of our struggles and our lines, the four organizations first established fraternal bonds and an exchange of experiences, then increased active mutual collaboration to the point that today this decisive step which accelerates the coordination and collaboration that undoubtedly will result in greater practical effectiveness in the cruel struggle our people are waging against a fierce common enemy.

The greater development of our organizations, the strengthening of our internationalist concepts and practice, will permit the greater utilization of our people's potentialities in order to build a powerful revolutionary force that can definitively defeat capitalist imperialist reaction, annihilate the counterrevolutionary armies, expel Yankee and European imperialism country by country from Latin American soil, and begin the construction of socialism in each of our countries to achieve the most complete Latin American unity.

Achieving that sacred objective will not be easy. The cruelty and power of imperialism will make necessary—as Comandante Guevara foresaw—the development of a bloody and prolonged revolutionary war that will make the Latin American continent the second or third Vietnam of the world. However, following the glorious example of the heroic Vietnamese people, the Latin American workers will be able to fight without dismay, with increasing effectiveness, unfolding in all their intensity the irresistible energies of the masses and crushing Yankee imperialism and its agents; it will win our happiness and contribute mightily to the definitive destruction of the principal enemy of the international working class, of socialism, and of all the peoples of the world.

Our program. We have united with the understanding that there is no other viable strategy in Latin America than the strategy of revolutionary war. This revolutionary war is a complex process of mass struggle—armed and unarmed, peaceful and violent—in which all forms of struggle develop harmoniously, converging around the axis of armed struggle. In order for this whole process of revolutionary war to unfold victoriously, it is necessary to mobilize the entire people under the leadership of the revolutionary proletariat. The proletarian leadership of the war must be exercised by a Marxist-Leninist combat party of a proletarian character, which is capable of centralizing and directing the popular struggle, guaranteeing a proper strategic leadership, and uniting all aspects in a single and powerful matrix. Under the leadership of the party it is necessary to build a powerful popular army, the iron core of the revolutionary forces. This army, closely united with the masses and nurtured by them, will grow from small to large, erect an impenetrable wall against which the military designs of the reactionaries will be smashed, and have the material quality to assure the total annihilation of the counterrevolutionary armies. At the same time, it is necessary

214

to build a broad mass front of workers and the people that can mobilize all the progressive and revolutionary people, the separate people's parties, the unions, and other similar organizations—in short, the broadest masses whose own struggle parallels and continually converges with the military activities of the people's army and the clandestine political activities of the party of the proletariat.

The response must be clear and none other than armed struggle as the main factor in the polarization, agitation, and, finally, the defeat of the enemy: this is the only possibility for victory. This is not to say that we do not use all forms of organization and struggle possible—legal and clandestine, peaceful and violent, economic and political—all converging with the greatest effectiveness in the armed struggle according to the peculiarities of each region and country.

The character of the struggle is marked fundamentally by the presence of a common enemy. North American imperialism is carrying out an international strategy to stop the Socialist Revolution in Latin America. It is not by chance that fascist regimes have been imposed in countries where the rising mass movement threatens the stability of oligarchical power. The continental strategy of the revolutionaries is in response to the international strategy of the imperialists.

The road to travel in this struggle is not short. The international bourgeoisie is determined to impede the revolution, by whatever method, even if it arises in a single country. It has all the means to employ against the people—official and bureaucratic, military and propagandistic. For this reason, in its first phase, our revolutionary war is one of wearing down the enemy until we can form a people's army that is more powerful than the armies of the enemy. This process is a slow one but, paradoxically, the shortest and least costly road to achieve the strategic objectives of the disadvantaged classes.

Latin American People, to arms! We are living through decisive moments in our history. With this awareness, the MLN Tupamaros, the Movement of the Revolutionary Left, the National Liberation Army, and the People's Revolutionary Army call upon the exploited toilers of Latin America, on the working class, on the poor peasants, on the poor in the cities, on the students and intellectuals, on the revolutionary Christians and all those emerging elements of the exploited classes who are prepared to support the people's just cause, to take up arms with determination and to join actively the revolutionary struggle against imperialism and for socialism, that is already under way on our continent under the banner and example of Comandante Guevara.

Liberty or Death (MLN, Tupamaros)
Win or Die for Argentina (ERP)
Fatherland or Death, We Will Win (MIR)
Victory or Death (ELN)

215

Appendix D

CONFERENCE OF COMMUNIST PARTIES OF LATIN AMERICA AND THE CARIBBEAN, JUNE 1975

The largest meeting of communist parties from Latin America and the Caribbean ever held in the hemisphere took place from 9 to 13 June 1975 in Havana. The twenty-four voting delegations represented the communist parties from all the Latin American countries as well as those from Puerto Rico, Martinique, and Guadeloupe. They were:

Communist Party of Argentina
Communist Party of Bolivia
Brazilian Communist Party
Communist Party of Chile
Communist Party of Colombia
People's Vanguard Party of Costa Rica
Communist Party of Cuba
Dominican Communist Party
Communist Party of Ecuador
Communist Party of El Salvador
Guadeloupean Communist Party
Guatemalan Party of Labor
People's Progressive Party of Guyana
Unified Party of Haitian Communists
Communist Party of Honduras
Martiniquian Communist Party
Mexican Communist Party
Socialist Party of Nicaragua

217

People's Party of Panama
Paraguayan Communist Party
Peruvian Communist Party
Communist Party of Puerto Rico
Communist Party of Uruguay
Communist Party of Venezuela

Delegations from the Communist Party of Canada and the Communist Party of the United States (three persons, headed by national chairman Henry Winston) also attended as observers. Conspicuously (and predictably) absent were representatives of competing Marxist-Leninist organizations, namely, the pro-Chinese and Trotskyist parties and their armed branches (such as the Colombian EPL), castroite organizations (such as the Bolivian ELN, the Uruguayan Tupamaros, and the Chilean MIR), other chiefly guerrilla-oriented organizations (such as the Argentine Montoneros) and Venezuela's independent communist parties, the Movement toward Socialism (MAS) and the Communist Vanguard (VC).

The first public call for this conference came in May 1974 from the 9th Conference of Communist and Workers' Parties of Central America and Mexico. The conference declaration, signed by parties from Mexico, Guatemala, El Salvador, Nicaragua, Costa Rica, and Panama, appealed for a preparatory meeting of all communist and workers' parties in Latin America to discuss organization, agenda, and related matters for a regional conference, concluding: "We believe that the revolutionary movement in Latin America would benefit from such a conference, held in the spirit of unity and aimed at clearing up common viewpoints on such questions as the present state of the revolutionary process, its successes and setbacks, the present alignment of forces, diverse forms and specific features of the revolutionary process, and at making a scientific analysis of possibilities for coordinated action of all our parties and all anti-imperialist forces." [1] According to a press release in the Cuban Communist Party organ, *Granma* (14 June 1975), "the meeting was carefully prepared through a series of activities by the representatives of the Communist Parties of Latin America and the Caribbean, working as a committee to draft the document that served as the basis for discussion in the meeting." The press release continued that the meeting had demonstrated the "firm unity" of the parties and their "fundamental identity of opinion in appraising the international and Latin-American

[1] *Information Bulletin* (Prague), no. 14 (1974), pp. 32-33.

situations and the strategic bases and tactical concepts that serve the Communists and all the revolutionaries and patriots in Latin America and the Caribbean in their struggle against the main enemy, defined by the meeting as Yankee imperialism." [2]

The 20,000-word declaration signed on 13 June was solidly pro-Soviet in orientation though it relied in some instances on generalized formulas that are open to varying interpretations. The nine sections of the statement analyzed the socioeconomic history of Latin America, the impact and importance of the Cuban Revolution, revolutionary developments in Latin America since the fall of Batista in 1959, the international aspects of this "epoch of revolutionary transition from capitalism to socialism," and communist strategies and tactics for the years ahead in Latin America. The document praised the governments in Ecuador, Panama, Venezuela, Mexico, and Peru (then under Juan Velasco), particularly the last, and stressed the need for united anti-imperialist action with other leftists and certain "bourgeois sectors" in the "struggle for economic independence and national sovereignty." Nationalist tendencies can be transformed into anti-imperialist and revolutionary positions with sufficient decisive participation by the "people's forces." The Christian-Marxist dialogue strengthens cooperation between revolutionaries and the "reformist" and "advanced" sectors of the church. The Chilean experience of the early 1970s showed that "revolutionary movements cannot discard any way of democratic access to power" but also that they must be "fully prepared and ready to defend, with the force of weapons, the democratic achievements." The document called for a world conference of communist parties, as sought by the Soviet Union, and "energetically condemned" the "treasonous" foreign policy of the Communist Party of China. The extended passage on China was typical of those issued by most pro-Soviet parties for more than a decade, but was much more forceful than any endorsed by Cuba since 1966. The meeting marked the full return of the Communist Party of Cuba to the company of pro-Soviet communist parties in Latin America.[3]

The pro-Soviet communist positions on reform and revolution in Latin America in the mid-1970s are reflected in sections VI–VIII of the June 1975 conference declaration which follows.[4]

[2] *Granma* (Havana), 22 June 1975.

[3] Portions of this summary are based on my contribution to *Latin American Report* (San Francisco), June 1975.

[4] Document quoted from *Granma* (Havana), 22 June 1975.

VI

The present historic circumstances in Latin America determine that the great battle that lies ahead of its peoples will become the second and final struggle for independence.

But the independence of Latin America must not be conceived now as a simple continuation of the objectives that inspired the heroes and the peoples at the beginning of the nineteenth century, and which were evidently frustrated. We are at a historic moment in which a great part of mankind has already undertaken the road toward the building of socialism and the Soviet Union marches ahead through the final stage which will lead it to a communist society; while capitalism as a system confronts a deep social and economic crisis, in which imperialism, already mortally wounded and encircled, attempts to detain the colonial and dependent world that is escaping from it, introducing neocolonial forms of domination that will contribute to soften or postpone the very crisis of the system.

The workers, peasants, and other workers, of Latin America will not find a complete solution to the problems of unemployment, misery, low wages, ignorance, land hunger and social inequality by only eliminating foreign exploitation from their countries. Those problems would only begin to be definitely solved by the elimination of the exploitation of all big landowners and the bourgeoisie which becomes even more acute when these countries have to compete under disadvantageous conditions with the products of the almost omnipotent imperialist corporations which dominate the capitalist world market.

Whereas the Soviet Union and Cuba—just to mention two different experiences in regard to extension and geographic location—have given the example of progressive economic development, in spite of external aggressions, blockade and the attempt to maintain technological backwardness with which more than half a century ago they attempted to stifle newly-born socialism; means used even today in the attempts to stop revolutionary Cuba. There is not one single case of successful economic and social development in the countries of Asia, Africa or Latin America among those which have tried to accomplish it through the traditional ways of capitalist development.

Economic development cannot attain the accelerated pace necessary for our countries to bring about a solution to their serious problems of backwardness, unemployment, misery, illiteracy, without a decisive participation of the people's forces, of the workers, working peasants, and the urban and rural middle strata. And our peoples, just as Cuba's example indicates, will be mobilized to that extraordinary degree only through profound transformations which—in practice—prove to the workers of the countryside and the cities, to the intellectuals and professionals, that the revolution is theirs.

We communists consider that socialism is the only system capable of truly guaranteeing the development of Latin America at the accelerated pace which our countries demand. Cuba has proved to the brother peoples that in our time, it is possible to undertake the building of socialism under existing conditions in the American continent and is able to show its victorious accomplishments. Socialism is our unforsakeable objective. Nevertheless, we communists understand that socialism will become an immediate program for all the countries of Latin America only through a period of intense struggles and radical transformations, of direct experiences of the workers and of consistent and tenacious ideological struggle of all those who aspire to socialism, in order to overcome ideological deformations and confusion introduced by imperialism and the oligarchies in sectors of the Latin-American people's forces through their control over the mass media and education.

At the same time, it is evident that the Latin-American peoples will not be able to achieve true progress without the political overthrow of the representatives of the classes and sectors allied to imperialism; nor will it be possible for them to introduce substantial socioeconomic changes in our countries—much less pass on to the achievement of socialism—without defeating the oppression of U.S. imperialism over each one of our countries, without eliminating the control of the transnational corporations.

The battle for democracy for the masses, the struggle for urgent structural changes and for the transition to socialism, are indissolubly linked to the struggle against monopolies and imperialism which, aside from maintaining control over our riches, uphold and support the oligarchies and their governments.

Since U.S. imperialism is the main, common enemy, the strategy and the tactics of the revolution in Latin America, for those of us who conceive it as a revolution whose final aim is socialism, go through antiimperialism. Therefore, we communists judge the political positions of the other Latin-American forces fundamentally by their attitude toward that enemy. Without diminishing the importance of the struggle for democratic rights and for the achievement of new structures within our countries, we communists are willing to support and push forward those positions of Latin-American governments which may constitute a defense of our natural resources or the efforts to put an end to the pretensions of transnational corporations to maintain and increasingly extend the control over our economies.

It is true that the measures of defense of the domestic economy are not always accompanied by a genuine anti-imperialist policy. In some cases, it is strictly bourgeois nationalism which does not result in aspirations of transformation of the domestic economy, nor places the government that puts them into practice in progressive positions in view of the principal problems debated today. Nationalism can be transformed into anti-imperialist and revolutionary positions to the extent that the people's forces decisively participate in the struggle, to the extent to which the contradictions between nationalistic governments and imperialism sharpen.

221

There are countries in which the defense of the national resources and the determination to recover the economy from the hands of the transnational enterprises are effectively united to programs of social transformation. Where governments go beyond the nationalization of the riches controlled by imperialism and carry out a people's program for the development of the domestic economy like in Peru, the communists—as the ones in that country do—can grant their most loyal and resolute support to these measures. The fact that communists have a conception of social development different from the one that guides those programs will not weaken their support to the positions of the government, nor will it be an obstacle to jointly face the problems of the future.

The anti-imperialist struggle that will lead Latin America to final independence allows and demands the participation of the broadest social sectors, and the leading role in that struggle corresponds to the working class. The working peasants are their natural allies. These are the social classes that aspire to the most profound transformations.

Although under the domination and dependency of imperialism, the capitalist development of Latin America has generated important modifications in the social composition of the different countries.

The growth of the urban and rural working class stands out. The number of wage-earners today surpasses fifty million and represents more than sixty percent of the economically active population of the continent. Approximately one-half of the wage-earners is made up by agricultural workers. The structure of the working class has also changed and its concentration in the big factories has grown. All these phenomena are reflected in the heightening of the role of the proletariat as the principal productive and sociopolitical force.

At the same time, the working class betters its organization and projects itself as the social force capable of determining the political panorama in the different countries of Latin America. The proletariat also tends to become the principal factor for the unification of the other democratic and anti-imperialist social sectors.

The struggle for achieving full national liberation and economic independence is interrelated with an intense class struggle against capitalist exploitation, fundamentally against foreign and local monopolies and latifundia. Under the yoke of capital, the degree of exploitation of the working class grows. Sheer hunger wages prevail in many places of Latin America. The part of the National Income received by the working class diminishes progressively and the real wage decreases due to inflation and the ever higher cost of living.

The experience of the revolutionary movement in Latin America, rich in heroic and combative actions of the working class, clearly shows that this class also represents the most firm principles of solidarity with the struggle of other peoples against imperialism, for the triumph of the national liberation revolution, for democracy and socialism.

Capitalist development has provoked as well the growth of the social

222

reserve army, made up of millions of unemployed and landless peasants who emigrate from the rural areas and wander about in the large urban centers of the continent.

Agricultural workers, semi-proletarians, landless peasants, small proprietors, sharecroppers and all impoverished sectors of our countryside constitute a powerful human contingent interested in the changing of the system of land ownership and deep changes in the economic and political life of our countries. The exploitation and misery they live in, lead them to multiple class confrontations, which form part of the emancipating struggle.

The incapacity of agricultural economy and the limitations of industrial development prevent the absorption of new labor coming from the massive displacement of the rural population to the urban zones. This determines the growth of social sectors without stable jobs, homeless and with no means of living, who vegetate in the slums of the great cities whose number grows beyond control in many countries.

The social drama of these people, those who live in the favelas, ranchos, tugurios, callampes, villas miserias, constitutes one of the most blatant manifestations of the unjust, exploiting and oppressive character of capitalism.

Under the guidance of the working class, important sectors of these masses can be taken away from the demagogic influence of petty-bourgeois bosses and reactionary elements, and organized with the aim not only of demanding solutions for their urgent problems, but also of contributing to the anti-imperialist and revolutionary struggle.

The structure of Latin-American economies has originated a broad middle strata made up of not only craftsmen and small businessmen but also elements coming from the service sector that have a growing importance in the economies of the continent. Social instability is a factor which drives this strata to engage in political activities in the same way as the students, intellectuals, technicians, etc. In some cases they join the communist vanguards and the democratic and anti-imperialist movements and in others they form groupings in which the typical petty-bourgeois radicalism becomes manifest. Likewise, they also form reactionary groups which are penetrated by the CIA and used by the oligarchies as shock forces. In Chile they played an important role at the service of the fascist coup. All these facts stress the need for a tenacious struggle to win the middle strata over to the positions of the proletariat, considering the dynamic role they are called to play in the whole of Latin America.

The example of the governments which in Latin America today resist imperialism and attempt to implement programs of true national recovery, shows that the struggle for Latin-American anti-imperialist liberation can count on other social forces and elements which constitute, due to their contradictions with imperialism, allies to which the progressive forces cannot but grant attention.

223

The economic process of the countries of Latin America created a situation in which the highest levels of their local bourgeoisies became so greatly linked to and dependent on imperialism for its own growth and invigoration that in fact they have become part of the mechanism of imperialist domination in their own countries. That is the way it happened in Cuba with the sugar and importing bourgeoisie; that is the way it happens today with a great part of the bourgeoisies which in Mexico, Argentina, Colombia, Brazil share monopolistic positions linked to the domination of these economies by imperialist corporations. Those denationalized bourgeoisies defend the dependence and oppose the anti-imperialist process. Even in the cases where differences or clashes come up between those monopoly bourgeoisies and their imperialist partners, the class interest of the former will lead them to try to solve them through a conciliatory way. At the same time they oppose the attempts made by governments which try to break the ties of foreign domination which suffocate their countries. Some of these bourgeois sectors join the big landowners to whom they are related economically in order to constitute a pro-imperialist local oligarchy opposed to the interests of the working class, of the peasants and middle classes and of other bourgeois sectors interested in the development of an internal market and in national progress.

This historic reality does not mean that there are not sectors of the Latin-American bourgeoisie which, in view of the contradiction of their interests with those of imperialism, adopt positions that coincide with those of the proletariat, the peasants and other noncapitalist strata of the population in their anti-imperialist struggle and for the conquest of economic independence and full national sovereignty. These bourgeois sectors, consequently, can take part in the democratic and anti-imperialist united action together with the people's forces. The communist parties and all other fighters against imperialism and for social progress in Latin America give great importance to that possibility, taking into account that it represents an element found with varying degrees of strength and importance in the different countries, which nevertheless constitutes an indispensable ingredient in that complex, multifarious and difficult struggle.

At the same time, it would be erroneous to ignore the limitations and hesitations of those sectors of the bourgeoisie in regard to its participation in the anti-imperialist process. In Latin America, the bourgeoisie lost a long time ago the possibility of playing the leading role which belongs to the proletariat. It cannot carry on the new battle for independence to the end. The incorporation of forces and organizations representative of such sectors of the bourgeoisie to the wide front of anti-imperialist and anti-oligarchic struggle is highly important; but it will never take place at the expense of the essential alliance of workers, peasants and the middle strata, nor of the class independence of the proletariat for the benefit of junctural compromises.

In recent years deep ideological, political and social changes have taken place among important forces which in the past were instruments at the service of the oligarchy and imperialism and that today become elements of progress and even of revolutionary potentiality.

Those changes are perceptible within some Latin-American armed forces. The movement of revolutionary origin and content, which, under the leadership of important nuclei of the highest-ranking officers of the armed forces is under way in Peru and the movement initiated by leaders of the National Guard which deepens today in Panama are a clear evidence of the deepening of the general crisis of the system of imperialist oppression and of the firm evolution of the patriotic consciousness.

It is now more difficult for imperialism to convince people that internal repression has any relation with the safeguard of national sovereignty and territorial integrity and not with the maintaining of small minorities of privileged natives and foreigners. It will not be easy for the United States and its OAS to deploy Latin-American troops the way it did hardly ten years ago during the interventionist aggression of U.S. imperialism against the Dominican Republic, an aggression which was heroically rejected by the constitutionalist sector of the Dominican army.

The process that takes place within the armed forces is complex. Imperialism increases by every possible means its work within the armed forces, with the aim of using reactionary elements and creating the illusion among the officers of a popular origin that they can quickly become bourgeois, thus trying to corrupt them. In the face of the development of the people's struggles, imperialism encourages military coups to establish reactionary or fascist dictatorships. But in taking the armed forces away from the garrisons and transforming them into arbitrators of social life, in making many soldiers stain their hands with the blood of their brothers, workers and peasants, in transforming those who were trained to handle weapons to defend their homeland into torturers, they increase the ideological struggle within the armed forces. Those officers, who feel that the oligarchies that hold political power betray the patriotic ideals in which many were educated, are understanding that reason and right are not on the side of those whose privileges they have defended.

Having received the anti-communist poison through the training in the garrisons, under the influence of imperialism and reaction, the reality of life makes ever-increasing sectors of the Latin-American military realize the lies that had surrounded them, the bankruptcy of the ideology and practice of anti-communism.

Christians, especially Catholics, the lower clergy and even some representatives of their highest hierarchies, have an increasingly active participation in the people's struggles for their demands and for national and social progress. They are encouraged by the idea of a church on the side of the people, as in Brazil and other countries, a church which also rejects commitments with reaction and imperialism. Representative spokesmen of the church speak against fascist terror and for democratic rights and social progress.

Movements of laymen and priests sensitive to the problems of the workers and of the country, make their significant contribution and learn through their personal experience the need for unity in action against the common enemies. They sometimes materialize like the admirable and heroic example of Camilo Torres who fell in guerrilla action, and was an open enemy of anti-communism and tireless preacher for the people's unity.

The growth of the people's struggle has conditioned the existence, generally speaking of three currents within the Latin-American Christians, conservative, reformist and vanguard. The reformist and vanguard currents represent the immense majority and in all countries it is both possible and necessary to work with them. The dialogue between believers and Marxists is facilitating the advance of unity of action in the struggle for deep transformations against imperialism and the fascist threat and lays the foundations for a lasting alliance which will lead to the building of a new society.

In the context of the battles waged by the Latin-American peoples, the defense of the democratic institutions and of the rights of the people acquire a special significance. Full national liberation, which implies the defeat and elimination of the oligarchies in power, is unavoidably linked to the effort to achieve an authentic democracy.

Progressive forces, communists among them, have always defended the democratic and representative possibilities and have been able to maintain, in some countries, long periods of people's access to parliament in spite of fraud and reactionary violence, which has allowed the use of this rostrum, combined with extraparliamentary actions. The Chilean experience which took the Unidad Popular parties to the government through elections shows that the democratic forms can be developed by the working class and the people, and confirms at the same time, the complete lack of respect of imperialism and oligarchy for the democratic will of the peoples.

The abolition of the democratic rights of the working class and of the peoples, the use of troops against the workers' movement, the establishment of brutal tyrannies, have been ingredients indispensable to the tactics followed by imperialism and the Latin-American oligarchies in their struggle to maintain their domination over the continent.

In the last few years, the growth of the awareness of workers and peasants, the radicalization of the middle strata, the incorporation to the forces of the left of ever-broader Christian sectors, and the growing refusal of military elements in some countries to continue serving the repression against their own brothers, deepens the crisis of imperialist domination in Latin America, a crisis which started with the Cuban Revolution. In the context of that crisis, people's struggles in all their forms increase, and therefore imperialism, its ideologists and Latin-

American servants—without discarding the covert methods of domination where they can still be used—seek to utilize increasingly ruthless ways and means of government as brutal as those imposed in Chile. U.S. imperialism, promoter of those regimes, offers its own repressive bodies as trainers in charge of performing the worst atrocities.

The criminal blow against Chile confirms the urgency of closing ranks for the defense of the democracy and against fascist threats in Latin America and its inseparable unity with anti-imperialist struggle.

The relation of the fight for socialism and for democratic demands has been clearly present since the initial days in which Marx and Engels elaborated the thesis of the participation of the incipient European communist movement in the 1848 and 1851 revolutions for the democratization and liberation of Europe. Lenin brilliantly developed the thesis of this close relation, stressed later on at the Seventh Congress of the Communist International.

We Latin-American communists desire true democracy for our peoples, a democracy based on the power of the working class and of the people, on full freedom for the elimination of private property over the basic means of production, that is, a socialist democracy. However, we are not and cannot be indifferent to the destinies of relatively democratic situations which, although they may not correspond to the true and deepest democracy we wish to achieve.

We communists will always join our efforts with all the democrats, with all those who are against the fascist brutality of the likes of Pinochet, Banzer, Somoza, Stroessner, Laugerud, the Brazilian gorillas, Duvalier or Bordaberry. At the same time we are opposed to accept that the defense of bourgeois democracy against the fascist threat should lead to giving up social progress and to accepting an unjust state of things.

The unity in the struggle for democracy is dialectically linked to the broader framework of the anti-imperialist revolutionary unity. The road toward revolutionary transformations in Latin America presupposes a joint, constant struggle, one in which the fight against fascism, the defense of democracy and the struggle against imperialism and the oligarchies, and the effective participation of the people in defining their political life, develops as a part of the same process.

VII

The immediate and constant struggles for economic, political and social aspirations of the masses are indissolubly linked to the efforts for national and social liberation.

Communists continue being related to the masses in the trade union movement, understand their immediate needs and contribute to formulating their demands and giving their struggles a true class content.

Trade union unity, conceived and performed as a broadening of the struggles which comprise all forces of the trade union movement, as proved by many experiences, helps to incorporate legions of new combatants both workers and others from different social strata, to this great struggle for social progress.

The trade union movement is a vital part of the forces that struggle for the national and social liberation of our countries. There can be no democracy without respect for the rights of the working class. Trade union freedom, the right to strike, trade union democracy and independence, are part of the common interest of all the democratic and anti-imperialist forces. The building of a powerful, organized and unified trade union force, from the factories to the highest possible levels, is fundamental.

Unity of action is a necessary condition to consolidate trade union unity; it is achieved through the common effort of all those concerned for the working class historic role. To overcome division is of vital importance not only for the working class, but also for the whole democratic and advanced movement, and implies the defeat of anti-communism.

The struggle for the democratic agrarian reform, which in the majority of our countries is closely linked to the struggles for national and social liberation, is the task of the whole democratic and revolutionary movement and one of the essential elements of the worker-peasant alliance.

The democratic agrarian reform has basically as its objectives; doing away with large private landholdings and semifeudal forms of exploitation, giving land free to those who work it, and achieving advanced forms of production which, as they incorporate huge masses of peasants to the economy, also allow the development of an indispensable domestic market for the industrialization process which may contribute to an independent economic development. It has been proved, in practice, that the bourgeois government programs for changing landholding structures by means of selling land to the peasants on credit, or by plans to "colonize" wild and barren areas, do not solve the agrarian problem, but on the contrary, turn it into a profitable business for the landholding bourgeoisie and imperialist monopolies, and into maneuvers for frustrating the struggles for a true agrarian reform.

The defense of the national cultural traditions, attacked and deformed by the ideological pressures of imperialism, interrelates with the general struggle for liberation.

The officialized culture is subjected to the interests of the reactionary minorities, closely linked to models set by U.S. imperialism. This is worsened under fascist regimes such as the one in Chile, where all manifestations of the people's and progressive culture are intended to be wiped out.

The democratic demands in the field of culture call for a broadening of the possibilities of teaching, access to and democratization of education, as well as the aspirations of the cultural, scientific, educational and artistic workers.

The interests of the majority of the intellectuals are linked to profound democratic and revolutionary transformations in order to open the path to a new society in which education and culture cease to be the monopoly of a minority and become the patrimony of all the people.

It is indispensable that the workers in the field of culture, guided by the awareness of their duty toward the peoples, carry forward their united and organized participation in the great mainstream of the struggle of Latin America for complete emancipation. This is the only road toward spiritual independence and the cultural flourishing of our peoples and nations.

An essential chapter of the common anti-imperialist struggle and for social progress of the peoples on the continent is constituted by the movements which express and organize reciprocal solidarity against the common enemy, promote political and practical aid to all those who confront imperialism throughout the world.

VIII

The revolutionary struggle of Latin America is characterized as a difficult and complex battle in which all forces that oppose U.S. imperialism have their place, and in which the most varied forms and methods of struggle should be used by the Latin-American revolutionary movement, adequately adapting its location and moment of use to the diversity of conditions in each country. The utilization of all legal possibilities is an indispensable obligation of the anti-imperialist forces, and the defense of the right of the peoples to decide, through democratic means, the transformations they demand, is a constant principle of our struggle.

Revolutionaries are not the first to resort to violence. But, it is the right and duty of all people's and revolutionary forces to be ready to answer counter-revolutionary violence with revolutionary violence and open the way, through various means, to the peoples' actions, including armed struggle to the sovereign decision of majorities.

Communist parties which deepen their roots in the cardinal interests of the working class, play a decisive historical role and have an exceptional responsibility in the struggle. As political forces that are guided by the Marxist-Leninist doctrine, the only one capable of setting an adequate course in the complex contemporary conditions, they have the possibility of playing that role within the alliance of the revolutionary forces. But that role is not guaranteed only by virtue of the social forces they represent and the exact theory that guides them. They will fulfill it to the extent that they become the most firm combatants for national and social liberation, taking authentic vanguard positions in the struggle, through practice, showing the peoples their programs of action, their strategic and tactical positions directed to unite all anti-imperialist forces and to orient the processes for ultimate revolutionary transformations.

We communists have the right to expect from those who act jointly with us in the national struggles of each of our countries, in spite of the immediate programmatic differences and the varied final aspirations, reciprocal respect for our political stands and our ideology.

The leaders of the various movements who from within governments of Latin America or from without, have today as their purpose the liberty of their peoples, have every right to categorically define their socioeconomic aims as noncommunist. History will decide who has been right in the selection of the options for Latin-American development. We communists have no doubt about that verdict.

There is a difference between being noncommunist and being anti-communist. To be anti-communist means a historical blindness that places those who suffer from it on the road of identifying themselves with the worst, backward forces and inevitably leads them to failure. Anti-communism is a reactionary position and the center of the counter-revolutionary ideologies of our epoch. We can respect those who are not communists, but we can never silence our criticism of those who, by mistake, define themselves, as anti-communists, nor can we avoid the combat to death against those who consciously take on anti-communist positions.

If anti-imperialist unity is indispensable, the unity of the forces of the left within it is even more essential.

The influence of socialist ideas in the world, resulting from the irreversible victories of the Soviet Union and the other socialist countries of Europe and Asia, and from the example of an unbreakable confidence in Cuba's economic, political and social progress, the advance of Marxist-Leninist theory as the only one capable of giving a solution to the problems contemporary society faces and the active presence of the communist parties permit in Latin America today—outside the framework of these parties and of the old socialist organizations—the existence of a left of various shades, some of whose organizations call themselves Marxist-Leninist and proclaim socialism as their objective of struggle.

The communist parties when pointing out what they disagree with in regard to the strategic conceptions or tactical approaches of those forces, will take into account that some of these movements are guided by the purpose of defeating imperialist oppression and advancing toward genuine socialist positions.

The communist parties do not silence their discrepancies with these trends, but they distinguish between erroneous positions and the adventurist attitudes they condemn. The anti-communist or anti-Soviet left is inconceivable and, with this criterion, the communists endeavour to isolate those who adopt such attitudes.

Controversy between the forces of the left must always start from positions of unity and serve unity on the basis of shared principles and purpose, and tactics appropriate to the circumstances and conditions in which the common struggle is waged.

We communists, sure of our positions, are willing to lead that necessary discussion through channels of mutual respect, in order to allow the working masses to discern the true nature of the problems. This is not incompatible with the open and full analysis of each of the positions under debate. We must work for the strengthening of unity of action of the left. On making this call for reflection and analysis, we communists of Latin America proclaim our willingness to overcome misunderstandings so as to advance toward unity of action.

Although proud of considering themselves genuine representatives of socialism in Latin America, communist parties are willing to participate in the struggle with all those who seriously fight for similar objectives at present. The possibilities opening for the Latin American revolutionaries in this period of our struggle, the proximity of great decisive confrontations with the imperialist enemy and the oligarchs which support them, demand the greatest efforts for unity and mutual understanding among all of those who are part of the anti-imperialist forces.

In their decision to contribute with all their efforts to the development of the revolutionary process in Latin America, the communist parties consider it indispensable to extend their political influence and that of Marxist-Leninist ideas to the masses, especially the working class and its trade union organizations, the working peasants' leagues, agrarian associations and other groups; increase the ideological work with the middle strata of the city and the countryside, strengthen the advancement of Marxism-Leninism among students, professionals, intellectuals, technicians, and thus become a mass force capable of attaining a decisive influence on the policy of each of our countries.

The tenacious struggle for the ideological strengthening of their militants, for the theoretical and practical Marxist-Leninist education, for the purging of all reformist or so-called leftist tendencies, is an essential element for the strengthening of communist ranks. The increasingly complete ideological enrichment and constant criticism of dogmatic sectarianism and liberal laxity, will allow the communist parties to guide the ideological struggle against imperialism and the oligarchies more successfully.

At different moments of the development of anti-imperialist struggle, various social sectors might fall into attitudes or be influenced by conciliating reformist conceptions or narrowly sectarian ones. The permanent struggle against both noxious influences will allow the consolidation of unity of action on a truly solid basis, affirming more and more the independent and class role of the revolutionary proletariat.

On this occasion of reckoning, the communist parties of Latin America pay homage with our banners to the thousands of communist combatants who have fallen during the last decades in every corner of Latin America for the cause of the independence of their countries and for the achievement of socialism. We greet all communist militants who are imprisoned, who are being tortured and persecuted, among whom we specially recall comrades Luis Corvalán, Antonio Maidana, Jaime Pérez, whose freedom we demand. We greet the revolutionaries and patriots—nonmembers of our parties—who suffer imprisonment and torture and we renew our homage to those who have fallen in the common struggle for national liberation.

The fierce repression unleashed against the patriots and progressive forces and very especially against the Brazilian Communist Party and its leadership, due to its firm opposition to the fascist regime, and against all progressive forces, affirms the need to continue and broaden the solidarity of Latin America with the democratic and anti-imperialist struggle of the Brazilian people.

We likewise express our solidarity with the vigorous resistance of the workers and the people of Bolivia against the affliction suffered under Banzer's dictatorship; with the patriots who suffer persecution and imprisonment in Paraguay; with the people of Haiti, oppressed by a terrible dictatorship; with the progressive forces of Argentina, subjected to barbarous provocations by the groups of fascist murderers organized into the so-called "Triple A"; with those who suffer from the fascist persecution of Bordaberry in Uruguay; with the Puerto Rican patriots, persecuted and imprisoned by the colonial regime, and with all those who suffer imprisonment and tortures at the hands of dictatorial and anti-democratic governments in other places of our America. We ratify our support to the people of Guatemala and the Guatemalan Labor Party, stressing the courage and the decision with which they wage battles for national and social emancipation in Guatemala in the face of an usurping and bloody regime; with the revolutionaries and democrats of Nicaragua who suffer from all types of persecution on the part of the Somoza dynasty, which together with the reactionary government of Guatemala, perpetrates an abusive interference in the internal affairs of the countries of the area.

We express our special solidarity with Lolita Lebrón, Puerto Rican patriot who is the oldest political prisoner of the continent and who is a symbol of all those who suffer imprisonment because of their ideas.

In proclaiming close unity and solidarity for the common struggle against imperialism, which has working class internationalism as its firm basis, we communists of Latin America reaffirm that each of our parties, following the principles of Marxism-Leninism and taking into consideration concrete national conditions, elaborates its own policy.

Index

Confederation of Latin American Workers (CTAL): 5, 69
Confederation of Workers of Colombia (CSTC): 61
Confederation of Workers of Peru (CTP): 60
Conference of Latin American Communist Parties (1964): 96, 195-98
Conference of Latin American Communist Parties (1975): 38, 47, 217-32
Congo (Brazzaville): 42
Conservative Party, Colombia: 68
Continental Organization of Latin American Students (OCLAE): 201
Continental revolution: 34, 116, 147, 188
COPEI, Venezuela. *See* Social Christian Party–COPEI
Corvalán, Luis: 54, 57, 78-80, 157, 158, 160-64, 166, 180, 231
Costa Rica: 9, 59, 61, 63, 69, 77, 129, 199, 200, 204, 208
Council for Mutual Economic Assistance (COMECON): 14
Creydt, Oscar: 55
Cruz, Luciano: 172
Cuba: 3, 5-6, 9-14, 18-25, 27-51, 53, 63, 64, 74, 82, 85, 99, 100, 101, 108, 111, 113, 117, 118, 123, 124, 129, 130, 132, 136, 139, 141, 147, 152, 157, 159, 162, 176, 192-208, 211, 217-32
Czechoslovakia: 14, 45, 54, 55, 63, 82, 201

Dalton, Roque: 62, 75, 76, 201
Debray, Régis: 20, 27, 30-32, 35-36, 71, 79, 81, 95, 100, 102-4, 107-9, 113, 147, 151-52, 154, 186, 188, 201
Democratic Action (AD), Venezuela: 68, 77, 100, 105, 107, 109
Díaz, José: 200
Díaz, Víctor: 158
Díaz Rangel, Eleazar: 56
Dominican Communist Party (PCD): 54, 58
Dominican Republic: 9, 18, 34, 40, 54, 87, 88, 147, 199, 200, 204, 217, 225
Donaldson, Robert H.: 11
Dorticós, Osvaldo: 33, 204, 205

Ecuador: 2, 5, 9, 11, 59, 61, 87, 88, 199, 200, 204, 219
El Salvador: 9, 59, 75, 199, 200, 208

Elections: 5, 65-70, 94, 158-60, 172-73, 182
Engels, Friedrich: 227
Enríquez, Edgardo: 176
Enríquez, Miguel: 171, 172, 173, 187
Epaminondas: 147
Equatorial Guinea: 42
Escalante, Aníbal: 13, 43

Faría, Jesús: 55, 196
Fatherland and Freedom: 165
Federation of University Students of Uruguay (FEUU): 63
Feng Piao: 21
Fernández C., Manuel: 169
Ferreira, Joaquim Camara: 139, 141
Feuer, Lewis: 32
Figueroa, Luis: 75, 76, 158, 159, 199
First International: 4
Fly, Claude: 134
Fonseca Amador, Carlos: 128-30
Fortuny, José Manuel: 70, 71, 75
Frei, Eduardo: 156, 159, 160, 162, 167, 169
French Guiana: 199, 200
Frondizi, Arturo: 67

Gadea, Ricardo: 103, 121, 122
Galeano, Eduardo: 113
Garaudy, Roger: 55
General Confederation of Costa Rican Workers (CGTC): 61
General Confederation of Labor (CGT), Argentina: 60
General Confederation of Workers (CGTP), Peru: 60
General Directorate of Intelligence (DGI), Cuba: 41, 42
Gerassi, John: 118
German Democratic Republic: 201
Germany, Federal Republic of: 116
Ghioldi, Rodolfo: 81
Godoy, Jorge: 158
Gomide, Aloysio Dias: 134
Goulart, João: 8, 141
Gouré, Leon: 14, 16
Great Britain: 66
Great Leap Forward, China: 23
Great Proletarian Cultural Revolution, China: 23
Guadeloupe: 199, 200
Guadeloupean Communist Party (PCG): 217

Pajetta, Giuliano: 54
Palma, Oscar: 113, 200
Panama: 9, 11, 22, 38, 63, 196, 199, 200, 219, 225
Paraguay: 3, 9, 18, 39, 55, 79, 88, 196, 199, 200, 232
Paraguayan Communist Party (PCP): 55, 57, 58, 73, 74, 218
Paris Commune: 4
Pascal Allende, Andrés: 171
Pastorino, Enrique: 60
People's Communes, China: 23
People's Liberation Army (EPL), Colombia: 88, 218
People's National Congress (PNC), Guyana: 65
People's Party of Panama (PDP): 58, 218
People's Progressive Party (PPP), Guyana: 61, 217
People's Revolutionary Army (ERP), Argentina: 78, 97, 133, 138, 143-46, 153, 209-15
People's Socialist Party (PSP), Cuba: 18, 48, 49
People's Vanguard Party (PVP), Costa Rica: 217, 218
Pepe, Comandante: 171
Peredo, Antonio: 123, 128
Peredo, Guido "Inti": 96, 103, 123, 126-28
Peredo, Osvaldo "Chato": 103, 123
Peredo, Roberto "Coco": 103, 123
Pereira, Astrogildo: 197
Pérez, Jaime: 237
Pérez Jiménez, Marcos: 5, 67, 71
Permanent Congress of Trade Union Unity of Latin America: 200
Perón, Isabel: 145, 146
Perón, Juan: 67, 145
Peronism: 133, 143, 144-45
Peru: 2, 3, 9, 11, 22, 24, 38, 55, 59, 60, 69-70, 77, 87, 88, 121-23, 133, 199, 200, 204, 219, 222, 225
Peruvian Communist Party (PCP), pro-Chinese: 91, 92, 94
Peruvian Communist Party (PCP), pro-Soviet: 57, 58, 60, 69-70, 74, 78, 79, 83, 123, 218
Petkoff, Luben: 103, 106, 107
Petkoff, Teodoro: 55, 72, 107
Piñeiro, Manuel: 42
Pinochet, Augusto: 24, 39, 227
Ponomarev, Boris: 14, 16
Poppino, Rollie: 4, 54

Popular Action Front (FRAP), Chile: 83, 158, 161
Popular Movement for the Liberation of Angola (MPLA): 24, 41
Popular Unity (UP), Chile: 14-15, 66, 84, 99, 155-56, 158-90, 226
Popular Vanguard Party (PVP), Costa Rica: 57, 58, 61, 69
Posadas, Juan: 117
Prada, Francisco: 103, 104, 106, 107, 200, 201, 204
Premo, Daniel: 61
Prensa Latina: 200
Progressive Youth Organization (PYO), Guyana: 63
Puente Uceda, Luis de la: 100, 103, 121-22
Puerto Rico: 51, 196, 199, 200, 210, 232

Quadros, Janio: 8

Radical Party (PR), Chile: 156
Ramona Parra Brigades (BRP), Chile: 160, 190
Rangel, Domingo Alberto: 109
Rashidov, Sharaf R.: 9
Ratliff, William E.: 18, 24, 56, 98, 134
Ravines, Eudocio: 86
Rebel Armed Forces (FAR), Guatemala: 71, 112-17, 133
Revolutionary Armed Forces (FAR), Argentina: 144-45
Revolutionary Armed Forces (FAR), Cuba: 42, 100
Revolutionary Armed Forces (FAR), Guatemala: 115
Revolutionary Armed Forces of Colombia (FARC): 73
Revolutionary Communist Party of Chile (PCRCh): 78, 89, 90, 92, 93, 94, 95, 97
Revolutionary Coordinating Committee (JCR): 128, 138, 153, 209-15
Revolutionary Movement 8 (MR-8), Brazil: 139
Revolutionary Peasant Movement (MCR), Chile: 170, 171, 183
Revolutionary People's Vanguard (VPR), Brazil: 139
Revolutionary Socialist League (LSR), Peru: 122
Revolutionary Students' Front (FER), Chile: 170
Revolutionary Workers' Front (FTR), Chile: 170, 174

238

Reyes, Eliseo ("Rolando"): 124
Reyes, Israel ("Braulio"): 124
Ribeiro, Iván: 197
Rodríguez, Carlos Rafael: 5, 39, 41, 46, 48
Rothenberg, Morris: 14, 16
Rowan, Carl T.: 42
Ruiz Paz, Jorge: 123
Rumania: 201
Rumyantsev, A. M.: 74
Russell, Charles A.: 133

Saad, Pedro: 197
Salazar, Gabriel: 114
San Martin: 205, 211
Sánchez, Camilo: 114
Sánchez, Gerardo: 201
Sánchez Sancho, Efraín: 129
Sandinist Front of National Liberation (FSLN), Nicaragua: 128-30
Sandino, Augusto César: 128, 211
Santamaria, Haydée: 200
Santucho, Mario Roberto: 143, 144-45, 146
Schenkel, James F.: 133
Sendic, Raúl: 134, 135, 136
Shlyapnikov, Rodolf: 55-56
Shragin, Viktor: 168
Sierra Leone: 42
Sigmund, Paul: 179
Single Center of Chilean Workers (CUTCh): 76, 159, 160, 170
Sino-Soviet dispute: 11, 19, 44, 45, 53, 78, 87, 93, 98, 107, 116, 195
Sivolobov, A. M.: 8
Sobolev, A.: 15, 16
Social Christian Party-COPEI, Venezuela: 106, 107
Socialist Action Party (PASO), Costa Rica: 69
Socialist Party of Chile (PSCh): 21, 99, 155-57, 159, 165, 166, 167, 169, 170, 171, 175, 177-79, 181, 184
Socialist Party of Nicaragua (PSN): 58, 128, 217, 218
Socialist Party of Uruguay (PSU): 134
Socialist People's Party (PPS), Mexico: 69
Somalia: 42
Somoza, Anastasio: 130, 227, 232
Soviet Union: see Union of Soviet Socialist Republics
Spirin, V. G.: 14
Spreti, Count Karl von: 116
Stalinism: 12, 55

Stroessner, Alfredo: 3, 227
Sun Tzu: 147
Surinam: 200
Sweezy, Paul: 32, 35, 36
Syria: 205

Tanzania: 42
Teitelboim, Volodia: 157, 158, 164, 180, 200, 204
Terrorism: 81-82, 97, 104, 116, 129-30, 134-36, 141-43, 145-46, 151, 179-80
Texier, Jorge: 180
Thant, U: 9
Theberge, James D.: 11
Theisen, Gerald: 118
Thomas, Hugh: 146
Tomic, Radomiro: 24, 182
Toro, Víctor: 170, 176
Torres, Camilo: 118, 226
Torres, Juan José: 11, 127
Torres, Simón: 35
Tricontinental: 9, 10, 19, 124, 147, 203
Trinidad-Tobago: 199, 200
Trotskyism: 4, 63, 77, 78, 93, 112, 116, 117, 143, 147
Trotskyist Revolutionary Party (PRT), Argentina: 143
Tupac Amaru: 133
Tupamaros: see National Liberation Movement
Turcios Lima, Luis Augusto: 103, 112, 199
Turner, Jorge: 199

Union for Advancement (UPA), Venezuela: 68
Union of Communist Youth (UJC), Uruguay: 63
Union of Soviet Socialist Republics: 4, 7-16, 19, 20, 22, 23, 25, 27, 34, 43-48, 49, 53-56, 63, 64, 66, 76-77, 82, 85, 86, 87, 88, 98, 99, 107, 117, 118, 149, 190, 192, 193, 201, 202, 205, 208, 219, 220, 230
Unitary Popular Action Movement (MAPU), Chile: 100, 156, 166, 171, 174, 175
United Nations: 9, 41
United Party of Haitian Communists (PUCH): 57, 58, 73, 217
United States: 1, 3, 7, 8, 10, 11, 21, 22, 24, 40, 43, 51, 70, 84, 116, 128, 129, 130, 131, 134, 137, 144, 146, 147, 148, 169, 178-79, 187, 189, 200, 204, 205, 207, 227, 228, 229

6127